Mapping Academic Values in the Disciplines

Linguistic Insights

Studies in Language and Communication

Edited by Maurizio Gotti,
University of Bergamo

Volume 124

PETER LANG
Bern · Berlin · Bruxelles · Frankfurt am Main · New York · Oxford · Wien

Davide Simone Giannoni

Mapping Academic Values in the Disciplines

A Corpus-Based Approach

PETER LANG
Bern · Berlin · Bruxelles · Frankfurt am Main · New York · Oxford · Wien

Bibliographic information published by Die Deutsche Nationalbibliothek
Die Deutsche Nationalbibliothek lists this publication in the Deutsche National-bibliografie; detailed bibliographic data is available on the Internet at ‹http://dnb.d-nb.de›.

British Library and Library of Congress Cataloguing-in-Publication Data:
A catalogue record for this book is available from *The British Library*, Great Britain.

Library of Congress Cataloging-in-Publication Data

Giannoni, Davide S.
Mapping academic values in the disciplines : a corpus-based approach / Davide Simone Giannoni.
p. cm. – (Linguistic insights : Studies in language and communication; v. 124)
Includes bibliographical references and index.
ISBN 978-3-0343-0488-7
1. Linguistic analysis (Linguistics) 2. Computational linguistics. I. Title.
P126.G53 2010
001.201'4–dc22

2010022945

This volume is linked to a national research project on *Tension and Change in English Domain-Specific Genres* (COFIN Grant No. 2007JCY9Y9) and is published under the auspices of the University of Bergamo – Dipartimento di Lingue, Letterature e Culture Comparate.

ISSN 1424-8689
ISBN 978-3-0343-0488-7

Hochfeldstrasse 32, CH-3012 Bern, Switzerland
info@peterlang.com, www.peterlang.com, www.peterlang.net

Printed in Switzerland

To my parents

Contents

Acknowledgements

Any academic achievement is built on the shoulders of others. In my case gratitude is due first of all to Paul Thompson (now Director of the Centre for Corpus Research, University of Birmingham) for guidance during the doctoral stage of the research. Among those who variously contributed to this project, I am indebted to Clare Furneaux and to the series editor Maurizio Gotti for their comments. A word of thanks goes to librarians at the universities of Reading, Lancaster and London. Finally, on a more personal level, I am grateful to my wife for making me see the wood beyond the trees and to my Maker who allowed the trees to bear fruit.

1. Introduction

The notion of *value* is central to the development of Western thought. For the OED (2009) 'value' is "The relative status of a thing, or the estimate in which it is held, according to its real or supposed worth, usefulness, or importance [...] the personal or societal judgment of what is valuable and important in life" – a definition that reflects the relativity of value and its dependence upon social interaction. Human transactions rely heavily on this notion and a whole strand of economic research is devoted to the investigation of value theory. The concept is equally prominent in the social sciences, psychology and theology. In philosophy it is the domain of axiology, which targets the investigation of what is both ethically and aesthetically appropriate in human experience.

As discourse reflects and reinforces the values prized by a given community, its investigation is likely to provide textual evidence of which qualities or aspects of reality are regarded as desirable or undesirable by its members. Whatever the field of enquiry, knowledge claims are being constantly challenged and (re)negotiated through language. This area of linguistic research has particularly attracted scholars concerned with the wording of scientific writing, which "illustrates one way in which the values of academic communities are articulated in discourse meanings" (Hyland 1997: 20). Some of the most often-quoted values that guide the academic community are collegiality, competitiveness and empiricism.

The aim of the present study is to extend our understanding of what values are most prominent in English disciplinary discourse and what linguistic resources are most likely to be used to signal such values. The analysis is evidence-based, as it investigates a corpus of authentic texts drawn from leading scholarly journals in ten different disciplinary areas. Its methodology includes the use of corpus-analysis tools (wordlist builders, concordancers, collocate calculators, etc.) as well as manual investigation of the object of value judgements in academic writing. Apart from Thetela's (1997) small-scale study of 'parameters of value' in academic discourse, this is to my knowledge the first systematic attempt to explore the value system that underlies scholarship published in English-medium journals. A sample of texts was analysed lexically, semantically and contextually in order to identify the main values encoded by relevant occurrences in each of the disciplines represented in the corpus.

It is hoped that this volume will provide further evidence not only of the evaluative dimension of domain-specific communication, which has extensively been dealt with in the literature on evaluation and stance, but also of the epistemological priorities upheld by academics in their search for knowledge and recognition. In addition, it may shed light on any overt reference to the institutional constraints placed on scientific enquiry (cf. Ali *et al.* 1996; van Damme 2002), whose educational and political implications have so far been more researched than their linguistic dimension.

1.1. Mapping discipline-specific values

The main purpose of this volume is therefore to describe the specific values signalled by research article authors belonging to different disciplinary communities through realisations that employ explicit lexical types. The classification of such variables will be made inductively rather than deductively: in other words, I will attempt to interpret the emerging corpus data (as in Channell 2000) rather than apply it to an existing framework. To date there have been few attempts to seek out this kind of evidence, though several authors have speculated as to what aspects of science are normally regarded as desirable or undesirable. The values encoded by scholars are expected to share a common concern for the quality, reliability and impact of research in their field. While for some of these a negative counterpart is likely to occur in the corpus (e.g. *useful/useless, interesting/dull*), for others it may not be lexically signalled or available.

One aspect that deserves special attention is how values are distributed across the different domains represented in the corpus, in terms of number and choice of lexis, and whether there are common patterns within the corpus sections. Such variables can either be encoded by highly vague markers (e.g. *well, nice, interesting*) or single out specific facets of value (*systematic, clear, expert, innovative*) that deserve to be carefully investigated and classified. At the same time, the proportion of directly positive vs. negative lexis and the polarisation of lexicalisations may vary according to the degree of agonism present in each discipline (cf. Salager-Meyer 2001a; Tannen 2002, 2002).

A further dimension worth investigating in order to account for variation across domains is represented by the entities being evaluated through such judgements. Each claim identified in the corpus establishes a link between a given quality and an entity endowed (or not endowed) with such a quality. Within this dyad it is therefore essential to explore what is being evaluated if we are to understand how academic values operate in context. The corpus was scanned manually to map the referent linked to each value claim and a list of the options prevalent in each domain was drawn up for insights into how different disciplinary cultures attribute certain qualities to specific aspects of research or even to entities that lie outside the immediate realm of their enquiry. This type of analysis is useful for pedagogic as well as descriptive purposes, since undergraduates and novice writers do not necessarily appreciate what aspects of research deserve to be prized or stigmatised through appropriate evaluative acts (cf. Mei 2006a, 2006b).

The lines of enquiry described above seek to address three research questions whose combined insights can shed further light on an important part of the complex web of evaluative meanings embedded in published English-medium scholarship:

- What academic values are signalled in the discourse of research articles belonging to different disciplines?
- What lexical resources are employed to signal academic values and to what degree are such lexicalisations transparent?
- With what evaluated entities do academic values tend to correlate, both within and across disciplines?

1.2. Outline of contents

The theoretical background to this volume is presented in Chapter 2, which reviews the main approaches to the study of academic discourse relevant to the notion of value in context. After an overview of the historical development of academia from its medieval origins to contemporary debates on the role of tertiary education, the chapter looks at the evolving status of academic disciplines, whose recognition is reflected in the taxonomy and nomenclature used by the central libraries that disseminate/archive their published output. Disciplines are at the same time organisms formed by experts with similar interests and institutions with a life of their own: these two dimensions define the norms that regulate communication among peers and mark the 'territorial boundaries' within which they are allowed to operate. Central to academic discourse is the notion of genre, especially in its most standardised published form (i.e. the research article). When dealing with values, the main references are to be found in the extensive literature on evaluative speech acts, and particularly on the linguistic resources involved in the expression of academic criticisms. Far less is known of the *parameters* on which such claims are based, though much work in the social sciences recognises the fundamental importance of axiological variables in human interaction.

Chapter 3 describes the various sources of textual material selected for analysis. The decision to opt for ten disciplinary fields is explained and accounted for as representative of a suitably broad spectrum of academic domains. The method employed in the selection of appropriate journals from which to extract a suitable number of recent texts is explained in detail, in line with standard practices for the construction of specialised corpora. This is followed by a description of the procedure adopted to convert the 100 texts in the corpus into a format compatible with concordancing software.

Chapter 4 presents the methodology used to analyse the texts in hand. After a quantitative outline of the corpus, it explains how potential value-marking items were identified and investigated through a combination of automated processing tools and manual inspection. The relevant lexical items are listed with reference to the semantics of the four values chosen for further investigation. In order to answer the three research questions listed in this Introduction, the corpus will be examined for evidence of how such values are distributed across disciplines but also of the linguistic resources that mark them out and of the entities they evaluate. The analysis will include collocational aspects of the target items, as well as recurring lexico-grammatical patterns within and across disciplines. Finally the procedure used to interpret the findings is accounted for, where possible, in the light of other corpus-based studies of evaluative phenomena in academic discourse.

The results are illustrated and discussed in Chapters 5-8, devoted respectively to the values of goodness, size, novelty and relevance. The textual evidence extracted from the corpus as outlined in Chapter 4, is described both quantitatively and through a number of salient examples. Difficult cases and analytical problems emerging from the data will also be considered, suggesting if possible an alternative approach. When results show significant divergences between domains, the discussion of each variable is contextualised within the epistemology and concerns of its parent disciplinary culture, bearing in mind Becher/Trowler's (2001) mapping of academia into 'tribes' and 'territories'.

Chapter 9 offers a comparative assessment of the main results of this study, with a general discussion of their bearing on the initial research questions and on the literature. Finally Chapter 10 critically highlights the strengths and inevitable weaknesses of the approach adopted and identifies avenues for further research. Despite its imperfections, this volume provides a detailed account of the theoretical and empirical challenges faced by the analyst when reconstructing semantic variables rooted in the values and beliefs of a community of practice. It is hoped that its findings may be of interest not only to the applied linguistics community but also to EAP practitioners and novice researchers engaged in English-medium scholarship across the world.

2. Theoretical background

2.1. Academia and the disciplines

Academic institutions are entrusted with the production and dissemination of knowledge in virtually every field of study amenable to systematic investigation. Many of the intellectual revolutions that have shaped Western civilization, from humanism to the Protestant reformation, from Cartesian science to rationalism, were a result of academic debates spilling over into society, often beyond the original intention of their proponents. The century-old history of academia reaches back to the late Middle Ages, when the *Universitas magistrorum* (literally, 'corporation of teachers') gained control of educational functions previously reserved to monks and clerics. For this reason, universities are among the oldest surviving European institutions, with Bologna, Cambridge, Coimbra, Naples, Oxford, Padua, Paris and Siena established as early as the 12th-13th centuries (cf. Feingold 2000). But age alone is not a fair predictor of future success: in a recent list of world universities ranked chiefly by peer-review score, scholarly impact and student/faculty ratio, only four European universities – all British – appeared among the top twenty institutions (THES 2007).

Since the 1870s, European universities have been deeply influenced by the German model advocated by Wilhelm von Humboldt (cf. Anderson 2004), which pursues an integration of educational and research activities to serve the converging interests of faculty and students. However, a recent assessment (Pritchard 2004) of Humboldtian values in German universities exposes the distance between reality and the ideal: unsolved issues in the faculty-student relationship are today complicated by the 'corporate university' model, driven by such market-oriented values as employability, consumer satisfaction and brand management (Faber 2003). Because of the increasingly competitive environment in which they operate, many academic bodies "have moved away from their traditional role to one more closely aligned to the business sector [...], students are now viewed as 'clients', deans are regarded as 'managers' and knowledge is marketed as a commodity, to be bought and sold" (Morris 2005: 387). The linguistic impact of this shift is especially noticeable in the language of university prospectuses and course descriptions, to the point that Fairclough (1993, 1995) complains of a gradual *marketisation* of academic discourse. Several authors have pointed to the implications of such practices, which

> first destabilise and subsequently transform students' and indeed the public's perceptions and expectations of what university education is about and restructure not only the identity and function of universities but also the relations between academic staff and students. (Teo 2007: 106)

With the proliferation of new universities observed in most developed countries since the 1960s – partly in response to a wider demand for tertiary education – academia has strengthened its presence especially in urban areas, forging close links with local government, businesses, the media and various interest groups. At the same time, universities have shed much of the 'ivory tower' legacy of earlier days, when access to tertiary education was a privilege of the aristocracy or of wealthier middle-class families. The rate of change experienced by academia in recent decades is remarkable by any standard and accounts for much of the uncertainty experienced by its main actors (faculty, students and management) in the performance of their respective duties. At the same time, scientific and technological progress in the industrialised world has hugely extended the body of published knowledge available to scholars and produced new fields of enquiry at an unprecedented rate. One consequence of this is the fast obsolescence of theoretical models and analytical tools in many fields, as they are superseded by more advanced acquisitions. The factual knowledge that counts as scientific truth (cf. Latour 1987) is thus in a state of constant flux, leading to a more fluid notion of the distinctions between separate areas of academic enquiry.

The world view or *ideology* (cf. Ventola 1998b) embedded in the body of knowledge accumulated by scholars shapes not only the policies of academia but also the way different fields of enquiry are constructed and perceived over time. Because of the influence they exert over human society, academic disciplines have in fact been equated to ideological systems whose discourses are "used to justify power relations and conflate a particular view of knowledge as *truth*" (Hyland 2000: 159). Universities have always been key actors in the endless struggle between tradition and innovation, change and continuity that allows advancement in disciplinary knowledge. Sometimes the new assumptions propounded by innovators are so disruptive that they lead to a scientific revolution or 'paradigm shift' (Kuhn 1970). Medieval academics (cf. Wagner 1983) generally upheld the Scholastic tradition, which emphasised the study of seven liberal arts: three language sciences (grammar, rhetoric and logic) and four mathematico-physical sciences (arithmetic, geometry, astronomy and music). These were considered superior to the more utilitarian disciplines – known as *artes illiberales* – whose concern was primarily vocational. Although this division no longer holds, it clearly involves a value judgement whose impact on the relative status of different disciplines can be felt to this day.

It is no easy matter to distinguish between various realms of research because of the dualism built into the very notion of 'discipline'. On the one hand this embodies a categorisation of scientific knowledge shaped by the object of investigation (whether the human mind, the natural world or man-made devices); on the other hand it reflects the way scholars socialise and validate knowledge within peer-based networks. Relations between the content-based and the community-based perspective are especially blurred when interdisciplinary research is pursued or when an emerging new (sub)discipline displaces well-established practices. Compounded with this is the presence of alternative and occasionally conflicting approaches or schools of thought within the same discipline: e.g. neoliberal economics, neoclassic economics and Keynesian economics. Hyland aptly defines disciplines as "human institutions [...], sites where differences in worldview or language usage intersect as a result of the myriad backgrounds and overlapping memberships of participants" (2006b: 20). By defining disciplines as *institutions*, he offers an implicit recognition that they have a life of their own, which is partly independent both of their content and their originators. This aspect will be covered by the working definition adopted at the end of the present section.

One field where the systematic mapping of academic disciplines plays a crucial role is of course library science. The need to catalogue and archive library holdings in a way that reflects their content has produced several classification systems, two of which are particularly common and worth mentioning as an illustration of the challenges inherent in such efforts. The first system, known as Dewey Decimal Classification, was created in the 1880s and is now into its 22nd edition (cf. DDC 2003). It allows for ten classes of disciplines, each of which has 100 possible sections grouped into ten divisions. Figure 1 below shows how it maps publications in Linguistics, which belongs to class 400 (Language) and embraces nine sections, from 'Writing systems' to 'Verbal language not spoken or written'.

It is important to stress that the DDC system classifies holdings by discipline rather than subject, so that the same subject may be assigned different codes, depending on the disciplinary angle from which it is approached. Most of the labels applied to the ten main classes at the top of the diagram are self-explanatory, though some are much broader than others: class 300 (Social sciences), for example, covers sociology, anthropology, statistics, political science, economics, law, public administration, social problems and services, education, commerce, communications, transportation and customs. The DDC classification of disciplines and specialisms inevitably reflects the concerns of academic research at the end of the nineteenth century and is still clearly Eurocentric, as illustrated by the grouping of languages within Linguistics.

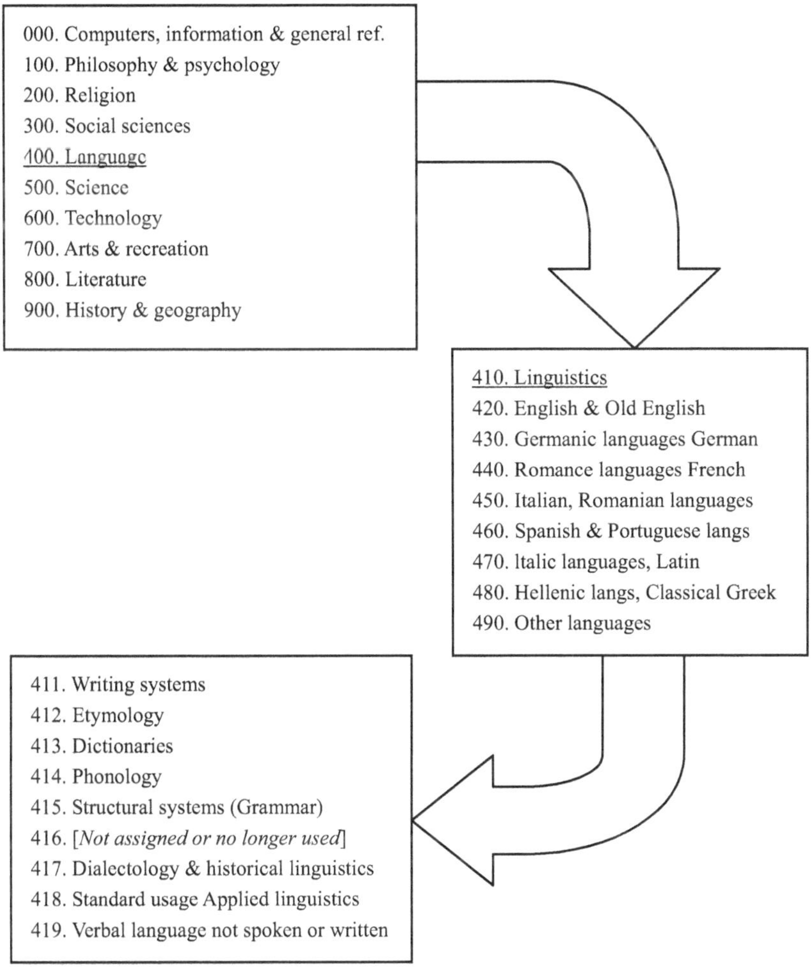

Figure 1. Dewey Decimal Classification of disciplines (based on DDC 2003).

Another highly influential system used for cataloguing research is the Library of Congress Classification of knowledge (LCC 2003), which also dates from the late nineteenth century and is today a standard feature in the copyright page of most academic monographs (Figure 2).

A. General Works
B. Philosophy. Psychology. Religion
C. Auxiliary sciences of history
D. World history and history of Europe, Asia, Africa, Australia, New Zealand, etc.
E. History of the Americas
F. History of the Americas
G. Geography. Anthropology. Recreation
H. Social sciences
J. Political science
K. Law
L. Education
M. Music and books on music
N. Fine arts
P. Language and literature
Q. Science
R. Medicine
S. Agriculture
T. Technology
U. Military science
V. Naval Science
Z. Bibliography. Library Science. Information Resources

PA. Greek lang. lit. Latin lang. lit.
PB. Modern languages. Celtic langs
PC. Romanic languages
PD. Germanic langs. Scandin. langs
PE. English language
PF. West Germanic languages
PG. Slavic languages. Baltic languages. Albanian language
PH. Uralic languages. Basque lang.
PJ. Oriental langs and literatures
PK. Indo-Iranian langs and lit.
PL. Languages and literatures of Eastern Asia, Africa, Oceania
PM. Hyperborean, Indian, and artificial languages
PN. Literature (General)
PP. Philology. Linguistics
PQ. French lit. - Italian lit. - Spanish lit. - Portuguese lit.
PR. English literature
PS. American literature
PT German lit., Dutch lit., Flemish lit., Afrik. lit., Scan. lit., O Nor. lit., O Icelandic and Old Norwegian, Modern Icelandic lit., Faroese lit., Danish lit., Norw. lit., Swedish lit.
PZ. Fiction & juvenile belles lettres

P1-85. General
P87-96. Communication. Mass media
P94.7. Interpersonal communication
P95-95.6. Oral communication. Speech
P98-98.5. Computational ling. Nat. lang. proc.
P99-99.4. Semiotics. Signs and symbols
P99.5-99.6. Nonverbal communication
P101-410. Language. Ling. theory. Com. gram.
P118-118.75. Language acquisition
P121-149. Science of language (Linguistics)
P201-299. Comparative grammar
P301-301.5. Style. Composition. Rhetoric
P302-302.87. Discourse analysis
P306-310. Translating and interpreting
P321-324.5. Etymology
P325-325.5. Semantics
P326-326.5. Lexicology
P327-327.5. Lexicography
P375-381. Linguistic geography
P501-769. Indo-European (Indo-Germ.) phil.
P901-1091. Extinct ancient or medieval langs

Figure 2. Library of Congress Classification of knowledge (based on LCC 2003).

The LCC comprises 21 main classes, identified by letters of the alphabet. These incorporate a potentially equal number of subclasses, whose topics are organised into divisions identified by a number or range of numbers. It differs from the DDC system in many ways, with a strong emphasis on the Americas in its main classes (two of which are devoted to the continents' history) and separate entries for disciplines that in the DDC would appear under the 'Social sciences' (law, political science, education), as well as for military and naval science. Figure 2 above offers an illustration of its approach to Linguistics, which occurs alongside Philology as a subclass of Language and literature.

Although these bibliographic taxonomies were not created as abstract constructs but serve an eminently practical purpose, their divergences and contradictions highlight an important aspect of any approach to the classification of academic knowledge: its inevitable dependence upon the developmental stage reached by various fields of enquiry at a given stage in history. In order to be recognised as a discipline, rather than a specialism (or mere topic) among other disciplines, any area of research needs a critical mass of research and researchers; this point underlies Kuhn's admission that people "tend to see as a science any field in which progress is marked" (1962: 162). In other words, the quantitative element is crucial not only when classifying library holdings but also academic knowledge itself, especially since established disciplines are often unwilling to surrender ownership of emerging areas of research within their midst. Applied linguistics is a case in point of this tension, as shown by the number of articles attempting to define the contour of a relatively young discipline that makes a virtue of its strong interdisciplinary connections (cf. Brumfit 1995, 1997; Crystal 2003; Roberts 2003).

Another important element to consider when classifying an emerging discipline is its degree of institutionalisation across the world, as signalled by the naming of academic positions and departments – a factor recalled not long ago in an insider's discussion of the international status and prospects of research in LSP (Languages for Specific Purposes):

> LSP has a highly variable status as both a discipline and a profession in different parts of the world [...] The ESL/FL field as a whole, and as seen

> internationally, is known for having 'a long tail'. In other words, there are very few senior (professorial) positions but many lecturers, adjuncts, and part-timers. This situation is also largely true of ESP/LSP where traditional forces in language, literature, and linguistics departments have operated to preserve senior posts for established areas of scholarship, and where many LSP practitioners have unstable careers as independent consultants. [...] ESP/LSP has yet to establish itself as either a full profession or as clear sub-discipline in the language sciences [...] the lack of institutional structure will probably be seen as more of a deficit than will its more optimistic interpretation – entrepreneurial flexibility – be believed to be an asset. (Swales 2000: 61-62)

Yet even the institutionalisation of a disciplinary area is not, ultimately, a yardstick for recognition when it runs counter to entrenched modes of scientific enquiry and communication. An example of this is the reorganisation of academic subjects and tenures introduced by the Italian government a decade ago (cf. Ministero dell'Università 2000), listing a total of 350 'scientific-disciplinary sectors'. This forced many academics whose sector had been abolished to reposition themselves: those belonging to 'English language and literature' (L18A), for example, had to opt either for 'English literature' (L-LIN/10) or for 'Language and translation – English' (L-LIN/12), based on their interests and research record. The present government is planning a further reorganisation that would streamline the whole system down to fewer than 100 sectors, thus marking another seismic transition for the country's academic community.

The progress of modern scientific knowledge remains to a large extent unpredictable. Disciplines usually achieve distinction and recognition on their own merit rather than by a premeditated plan. Thus the development of scholarship follows a largely utilitarian course, with disciplinary status awarded when strictly necessary rather than theoretically desirable. There have been attempts, however, to elaborate a general framework capable of classifying disciplines according to a common set of criteria. One such proposal (Evensen 1997) identifies three key dimensions:

- epistemology (the kind of knowledge gained and how it is gained);
- history of science (where we came from and how we got here);
- sociology of knowledge (who does what with whom and how).

Although the use of this framework is anything but straightforward and remains largely subjective, it does signal the search for a multidimensional approach to knowledge systems, capable of combining information on the communities engaged in research, the reasoning models appropriate to that research and the diachronic development of the two.

For the discourse analyst interested in academic communication, taxonomies are less of a concern that one might imagine. Two of the best-known contrastive studies of variation in disciplinary texts adopt a relatively straightforward classification of their material in this respect. Hyland, for example, divides the eight disciplines covered by his corpus, representing "a deliberately broad cross-section of academic practice" (2000: xi), into:

- pure sciences (molecular biology, magnetic physics);
- applied sciences (mechanical engineering, electronic engineering);
- humanities or social sciences (philosophy, sociology);
- applied social sciences (marketing, applied linguistics).

A second classification, suggested in research on the University of Bergen's KIAP Corpus, assigns disciplines to only three categories: the natural sciences, the social sciences and the humanities. Of these, the natural sciences "may be said to have a relatively homogeneous and objective knowledge base", whereas the social sciences "occupy a middle position between natural science and the humanities, with some of the knowledge base rooted in more objective natural science matters, e.g. mathematics, while other parts represent more subjective, interpretive aspects"; the third group (the humanities) "is in many contexts considered to be hermeneutical, with subjective interpretation as a prominent feature" (Fløttum *et al.* 2006a: 20-21).

The way these two models intersect and partly contradict each other is indicative of the analyst's efforts to force the complexities of modern science into simple inventories whose validity is more of a subjective statement than a demonstrable fact. When one group is regarded as being in an intermediate position with respect to others the distinction becomes blurred and it is no longer clear whether a new criterion is needed. Using a visual metaphor, it is like placing black at one end of the spectrum and white at the other, with anything in between identifiable as black + white or as grey.

An attempt to solve such difficulties is found in Becher and Trowler's (2001) work – first published in Becher (1981) – which remains the most authoritative study on the nature of academic disciplines, equated to 'territories' appropriated by scientific communities acting as 'tribes'. The authors put forward a model based on two cognitive dyads, namely hard vs. soft and pure vs. applied, whose combinations constitute four disciplinary groups:

Disciplinary groupings	*Nature of knowledge*
Pure sciences (e.g. physics) 'hard-pure'	Cumulative; atomistic (crystalline/tree-like); concerned with universals, quantities, simplification; impersonal, value-free; clear criteria for knowledge verification and obsolescence; consensus over significant questions to address, now and in the future; results in discovery/explanation.
Humanities (e.g. history) and pure social sciences (e.g. anthropology) 'soft-pure'	Reiterative; holistic (organic/river-like); concerned with particulars, qualities, complication; personal, value-laden; dispute over criteria for knowledge verification and obsolescence; lack of consensus over significant questions to address; results in understanding/interpretation.
Technologies (e.g. mechanical engineering, clinical medicine) 'hard-applied'	Purposive; pragmatic (know-how via hard knowledge); concerned with mastery of physical environment; applied heuristic approaches; uses both qualitative and quantitative approaches; criteria for judgement are purposive, functional; results in products/techniques.
Applied social science (e.g. education, law, social administration) 'soft-applied'	Functional; utilitarian (know-how via soft knowledge); concerned with enhancement of [semi-] professional practice; uses case studies and case law to a large extent; results in protocols/procedures.

Table 1. Disciplinary groupings of knowledge (from Becher/Trowler 2001: 36).

The hard/soft dyad was first proposed in Biglan's (1973) multi-dimensional survey of academics' perceptions of different disciplinary fields. It is frequently used in the literature (cf. Hyland 1999; Kertész 2001; Stotesbury 2003) to distinguish between the more science-based disciplines, on the one hand, and the social sciences and humanities on the other hand. Becher and Trowler's framework uses a range of qualifiers – e.g. *cumulative, reiterative, purposive, functional* and *atomistic, holistic, pragmatic, utilitarian* – to define the nature of knowledge production in each grouping. There is an explicit recognition, however, that such features are indicative of general trends and do not constitute neat pigeonholes. The cognitive categories listed in Table 1 interact with two others (urban vs. rural and convergent vs. divergent) that define the scientific community associated with each discipline. The former dyad refers to "the number of researchers engaged at any one time on a particular problem or constellation of problems", whereas the latter indicates "the maintenance of reasonably uniform standards and procedures" (Becher/Trowler 2001: 185). In other words, disciplines are defined by their reliance upon variably dense, closely-focused communities and, at the same time, by a set of common practices whose sociolinguistic implications will be discussed at greater length in the next section.

Taking into account these converging insights, I shall adopt a working definition that views a discipline as any relatively well-established subdivision of academic research with specific norms of scientific enquiry and communication but also a certain degree of recognition from academic institutions and other disciplines. The presence of a discipline is signalled, among other things, by (standardising) terminologies and nomenclatures.

2.2. Discourse communities

The linguistic dimension of academic communication cannot be properly understood without taking account of the scholars who collectively form what are conventionally referred to as 'scientific communities'. An in-depth understanding of their discourse is possible only if the analytical standpoint is broadened by looking at texts as a site of engagement with peers rather than a mere product of linguistic craftsmanship. This type of approach is important because:

> Essentially, the idea of community draws together a number of key aspects of context that are crucial to the production and interpretation of spoken and written discourse: knowledge of a cultural and interpersonal situation, knowledge of interlocutors, knowledge of the world, and knowledge of texts and conventions for saying things. (Hyland 2006b: 19)

Albeit useful, however, the community metaphor may apparently imply a static, unproblematic view of how disciplinary knowledge is socialised, thus overshadowing the tensions inherent in academic environments between cohesion and competition, collegiality and individualism (cf. Tannen 2000, 2002). Communities are indeed subject to "considerable variations in the extent to which members identify with their myriad goals, methods and beliefs, participate in their diverse activities, and identify themselves with their conventions, histories or values" (Hyland 2000: 9). As in other professional groups, the allegiance of individual scholars to the disciplinary 'social network' (cf. Milroy 1984; Brodkey 1987) is variably strong depending on their level of commitment, power and enculturation.

Thus while authors generally agree that academic discourse cannot be investigated without recognition of the people it serves, the definition of its community has been a matter of extensive debate. The term *scientific community*, used almost universally when referring to peers in academic settings, is too narrow because it appears to single out areas of inquiry recognised as 'scientific', thus raising the question of whether speculative knowledge can be classified as science in the same way as experimental knowledge. Similarly, this term may convey the impression that researchers in the hard sciences form a single community regardless of their disciplinary affiliation, as suggested in early analyses targeting the common traits of academic discourse across languages and disciplines. Widdowson, for instance, famously argued that "scientific exposition is structured according to certain patterns of rhetorical organization which, with some tolerance for individual stylistic variation, imposes a conformity on members of the scientific community no matter what language they happen to use" (1979: 61).

Following Overington's (1977) description of science as a 'rhetorical construct', the understanding of academic communication has been deeply influenced for at least three decades by the ethnographically-inspired social constructivist view of discourse, which stresses the circular relationship between social and linguistic practices (Latour/Woolgar 1979; Knorr-Cetina 1981, 1983; Knorr-Cetina/Cicourel 1981; Latour 1987). Texts are not only the outcome of scholarly enquiry but also a process whereby social networks are constructed and reaffirmed within domains. Academic communities may be viewed accordingly both as the originators and outcome of their discourse (based on the reiteration of disciplinary norms and boundaries). This perspective borrows from the so-called Sapir-Whorf hypothesis (Whorf 1956), with its claim that our understanding of the world is heavily influenced by the semantic structure of language. Taken together, these two approaches point to the bi-univocal relationship between human communication, cognition and social action, which come together in the notion of *discourse community*.

Any specific interest group – whether of an academic, professional, humanitarian or recreational nature – may be seen as a discourse community, provided that verbal communication is central to its existence and activities and that its members "communicate through approved channels" (Porter 1986: 38). The defining characteristics suggested by Swales (1990) are a set of common public goals; mechanisms of intercommunication among its members; ways of providing information and feedback; one or more genres suited to its aims; some specific lexis; and a threshold number of members with suitable content and discursive expertise. These sociorhetorical networks are subject to the centripetal force of common goals and communicative norms, making such considerations as class, culture and language background (which regulate access to other types of community) relatively unimportant. The appeal of this concept, when applied to communities operating in different academic fields, lies in its relative simplicity and universalism: mastering the genres of a discipline becomes the ultimate demonstration of membership, available to young and old, native and non-native speakers alike in the 'invisible college' of international scholarly exchange. Importantly, discourse communities are not limited to a specific physical setting and their presence can be "inferred from the discourse that members of a disciplinary subspecialty use to communicate with each other" (Berkenkotter *et al.* 1991: 191-192).

Though valuable for pedagogic purposes, the notion of discourse community has occasionally been criticised for its somewhat oversimplified, deterministic outlook, which fails to account for different levels of specialisation and localisation within academia. For some authors it remains useful as an umbrella term that incorporates "speech community, interpretive community, argument field, and the like" (Herndl *et al.* 1991: 304) or should be used loosely for "a group of individuals who share ways of understanding and communicating" (Lauer 2005: 151). The reassessment of this concept has been influenced both by Lave and Wenger's (1991) conceptualisation of academic networks as 'communities of knowledge and practice' – that is networks regulated by learning processes that introduce novice members to the community's activities, identities and artefacts – and by Killingsworth and Gilbertson's (1992) distinction between local/global discourse communities. To account for such elements, Swales later introduced the term *place discourse community*, defined as a group of people who work together and "have a settled (if evolving) sense of their aggregation's roles and purposes", including "a range of spoken, spoken-written, and written genres to channel, develop, and monitor those roles and purposes" (1998a: 204). This new term highlights the fact that scholars are not isolated individuals addressing global audiences in an apparent vacuum, but actors whose behaviour is influenced by collaborative teamwork and institutional affiliation.

It is a fact of life that most people belong to several discourse communities (Porter 1986), whether of a vocational or private nature, and that their degree of membership varies according to how far they identify with a given group (Bex 1996). Overlapping allegiances are the norm rather than the exception also in academia, where individuals "act in multiple, interacting systems of activity" and "the writing that mediates human activities is as full of contradictions as the activities themselves" (Ketter/Hunter 2003: 359). Whether localised or globalised, such communities intersect each other within discursive systems reaching beyond the realm of scholarship, into that of personal, institutional and sociocultural needs:

> The ‘scientific community’ is not a monolithic, stable and wholly autonomous entity but rather comprises a number of variously organised social structures, whose internal relationships change and whose connections with non-scientific groups are also varied and changeable. Furthermore, what constitutes knowledge has changed and depends upon particular social relationships and collective judgements. ‘Facts’ are socially constructed cognitive objects, liable to reinterpretation and change, which become established through negotiations and extensive communication among scientists. (Whitley 1985: 11)

It is also important to recognise that the democratic rhetoric of science, with its emphasis on fairness and equal consideration of all contributions in the field, originates from a setting where knowledge is “distributed in a differentiated pattern within the community-of-practice according to the particular professional roles of individual members” (Smart 2003: 34). Such considerations as seniority, status and experience inevitably constrain the textual practices available to individual scholars. As observed by Hyland (2000), there is also variation in the degree of commitment shown by scholars to their fellow researchers in terms of goals, methods and beliefs: this depends partly on the position they hold (e.g. neophyte laboratory assistant, professional theorist, industrial applied scientist) and partly on the disciplinary conflicts that arise between competing models and research centres.

Bearing in mind all of these factors, I shall hereafter employ the relatively broad term *disciplinary community* when referring to academics that are linked to a given branch of scholarship. As a concept it is more manageable than other, less transparent categorisations of the collaborative dimension of science, because it does not directly refer to the linguistic practices or prerogatives of its members. It is admittedly a simplification of reality – especially when different disciplines merge or cross-fertilise – but has the advantage of clearly expressing the collaborative, compartmentalised dimension of modern scholarship. Even in the most individualistic disciplines (e.g. literary criticism, history, law, linguistics), scholars remain accountable to their peers through a dialogue with other authors; and even the broadest cross-disciplinary research implies some recognition of which disciplinary boundaries are being crossed and why.

Unlike academic communities and discourse communities, the disciplinary community only comprises those who exert a minimum degree of power or 'ownership' over knowledge, whether as researchers, teachers, reviewers or popularisers. It therefore excludes undergraduate students, publishers, managers and policy-makers, whose relationship with the discipline depends on the mediation of the disciplinary community. Like all social groupings, disciplinary communities are heterogeneous and can be defined more or less narrowly: for example, in terms of size (large/small), position on the economic map (central/peripheral) or age (old/new/emerging), depending on how firmly a discipline is established. My contention here is that this theoretically-neutral term is sufficiently inclusive and yet capable of accounting for the complications mentioned earlier and for further questions that may emerge in the course of this study.

2.3. Academic English and ELF

The issues outlined so far are particularly cogent in the case of English, which has become the medium of choice for scholarly communication across national and linguistic boundaries (cf. Swales 1998b; Flowerdew 2000; Swales/Feak 2000, 2004; Canagarajah 2002a). While the availability of a single widely-accessible language, combined with such momentous technological tools as online communication and digital publishing (which have made the exchange of scientific findings faster, simpler and often cheaper) is a clear advantage, the use of English should be seen as culturally or economically neutral. In this respect, Anglophone countries enjoy what may be seen as an undue advantage (cf. van Parijs 2007), because of the relatively minor effort made by native speakers to achieve high levels of linguistic proficiency. In a recent survey of Korean scientists, for example, half of respondents complained that improving their English absorbs a considerable amount of time that could otherwise be devoted to research (Hwang 2005).

Apart from the eminently descriptive work on microtextual proclivities linked to the cultural and/or L1 background of participants, the literature dealing with variation in non-native academic English tends to fall into two fields: contributions challenging the discursive colonisation inherent in Anglo-American textual models; and studies describing the features of emerging international varieties of English whose ownership is no longer dominated by Anglophone countries or academics. Faced with a publishing system that tends to under-represent the research of non-Anglophone academics, especially those affiliated to universities in developing nations, Swales (1985, 1998b) urges EAP practitioners to better equip scholars from disadvantaged academic backgrounds for this global struggle for recognition.

The phenomenon has far-reaching implications also for other languages, whose specialised registers (whether in academic domains or professional settings) may be eroded or lost as a consequence of the dominance of English. Even in highly-developed nations, smaller academic languages are under threat and should be treated as endangered ecosystems that deserve protection on a par with 'cultural rainforests' (Mauranen 1993a, 1993b). One of the most frequent recommendations made to academic gatekeepers – e.g. editors, reviewers and supervisors – is to accept greater deviation from native-speaker norms (cf. Duszak 1997b; Swales 1997; Flowerdew 2000, 2001), allowing the incorporation into English of some of the textual and rhetorical features of other academic cultures, so as to reflect the increasing diversity of its changing constituency. A similar solution is advocated by Canagarajah (1999, 2002a, 2002b), who stigmatises the unhealthy link between 'linguistic imperialism' and global inequality in access to educational/academic resources.

The internationalisation of academic English may be a slow process but there are unmistakable signs that the dominance of Anglo-American gatekeepers is slowly easing. There is increasing diversity in journals' editorial boards and faculty membership, coupled with greater postgraduate student mobility within and across continents. Albeit an abstraction, the most obvious outcome of this trend would be a mutually beneficial, global variety of English, free of national or culture-specific connotations. Mauranen argues that the proportion of non-native speakers in academia is so prevalent that English is in fact already a *lingua franca* or ELF – "a new variety that emerges in situations where interlocutors do not share an L1" (2003: 514) – in private as well as public settings (see also Mauranen 2006a). The belief that a global discourse community will inevitably develop a variety of English that embodies its diversity is an appealing one for reasons of equality and discoursal democracy though, as in the World English argument, it remains largely an objective to pursue rather than a reality (cf. McArthur 2001; Seidlhofer 2001). Viewing academic English as ELF rather than EFL implies a shift of focus from the inner circle to the expanding circle of English-speaking nations (Jenkins 2001).

Academic discourse is evolving not only in response to changes in scientific communication but also in the student population. The number of overseas students studying in the US and UK alone approaches one million and projections suggest that for the UK most of these will soon be 'transnational students' from Asia studying in a British campus established abroad by (or in a partnership with) their home university (Graddol 2006: 79). What some authors refer to as the *massification* of higher education (cf. Becher/Trowler 2001) goes hand in hand with globalisation and its easing of financial and national barriers; the success of distance-learning courses, pioneered by the Open University in the 1960s, has further contributed to this trend.

The role of English is particularly important in graduate education, which generally marks a student's initiation to the world of research. A recent survey (Tardy 2004) shows that international students are aware of their linguistic disadvantage but seldom know how to respond and, on the other hand, that EAP practitioners feel torn between a need to teach the unmarked features validated by academic gatekeepers and a desire to encourage more open, ELF-oriented textualisations. One solution to this dilemma is of course to make graduates understand the power relations embedded in language, emphasising the positive implications of multilingualism rather than its threats. A more extreme way to overcome the cognitive-linguistic gap between experts and neophytes – first suggested by Nida (1992) – would be to 'semipopularise' some of the genres appearing in academic journals and in certain fields there are indications that this is already the case (Blakeslee 1994; Giannoni 2008).

Although the L1 background of an academic is only one factor among others in his/her progress from obscurity to visibility, the linguistic hurdles confronted by non-native speakers should not let us underestimate the unifying force exerted by disciplinary cultures. Contrastive evidence based on a large corpus of research articles in different languages – English, French and Norwegian – indicates that disciplines may in fact be more important than languages when accounting for textual variation (Fløttum 2006; Fløttum *et al.* 2006a). This means that disciplinary cultures exert a centripetal force across as well as within languages capable of displacing national and language-based proclivities in scholarly communication (cf. Yakhontova 2006).

2.4. Research genres

Central to the study of academic discourse is the notion of *genre*, first introduced by Hymes (1974) to conceptualise the fact that communicative events follow predictable regularities in the realisation of specific purposes and activities. The term was later used to account for the way texts unfold in a staged sequence following their 'generic structural potential' (Hasan 1978, 1989) and has become closely associated with the context of culture, which constrains the plane of register and its linguistic realisations (cf. Ventola 1987). Since the late 1980s, countless authors have applied the notion of genre to the analysis of academic communication, on the assumption that the recurring features in a certain kind of text (e.g. a conference abstract, a book review or a research article introduction) are constitutive of the genre they embody.

Genre usefully links the individual and social dimensions of language: as explained in an early paper on the subject, "a genre is a rhetorical means for mediating private intentions and social exigence" (Miller 1984: 163). The same view is adopted in Bazerman's often-quoted work on scientific rhetoric, where genre is defined as "a sociopsychological category which we use to recognize and construct typified actions within typified situations. It is a way of creating order in the ever-fluid symbolic world" (1988: 319). Like other cultural artefacts, genres have a life of their own, they tend to evolve over time and can be grouped into 'families' (Fishelov 1993).

In disciplinary communication, genres provide textual evidence of the epistemology, ideology and social ontology of the parent discourse community. For this reason, they can be understood as forms of situated cognition, affecting a text's content qualitatively as well as quantitatively. Berkenkotter and Huckin explain that the choice of genre implies "a sense of what content is appropriate to a particular purpose in a particular situation at a particular time" (1995: 13), based on norms that reflect the discourse community's values and ideology. In order to master a given genre, users must be aware of these underlying factors and weaker members of the academic community can be empowered to do so through suitable pedagogic activities (cf. Christie 1989; Martin 1989).

Most of the literature on the subject is indebted to the work of Swales, whose famous definition of genre is "a class of communicative events, the members of which share some set of communicative purposes" (1990: 58). Genres embody the teleological dimension of communication, i.e. the purpose-driven nature of discourse embedded in the sociorhetorical functions deployed (sometimes unknowingly) by interactants to achieve their goals. This aspect is stressed also by Martin, who states that "the notion of *telos* is a useful one for glossing systemic relations between combinations of field, mode and tenor choices at the level of genre" (1992: 503). In line with the fact that rhetorical communities operate "by instantiation and by engagement" (Swales 1993: 696) rather than through mere affiliation, genres can therefore be defined as the institutional site where scholars publicly engage with each other and their discipline in ways that approximate the norms and expectations enforced by academic gatekeepers.

Since genres are an expression of shared cultural norms, an understanding of their interrelations can reveal how culture and language interface within each disciplinary community. In a recent reassessment of the concept, Swales (2004a) advocates a systematic investigation of *genre constellations*, which incorporate the notion of genre hierarchies (the functions of different genres in the same disciplinary area), chains (sequences of genres used for a given objective) and sets (repertoires of genres employed by an individual at a given stage in his/her career). The whole generic array available to a community forms a network which, despite attempts to achieve permanence, remains unstable and time-dependent, as new genres are introduced and existing ones reshaped or phased out.

A fundamental distinction is made in academic discourse between texts intended for peer-to-peer communication ('primary genres'), texts produced for educational purposes ('secondary genres') and institutional forms of communication ('occluded genres') which stand apart as a form of semi-private discourse involving academic gatekeepers. Table 2 below provides an overview of this taxonomy.

	Primary genres	*Secondary genres*	*Occluded genres*
WRITTEN	Research article	Textbook	External evaluation
	Journal abstract	Introductory text	Evaluation letter for tenure
	Monograph	Post-introductory text	and promotion
	Conference abstract	Course description	Book or grant proposal review
	Dissertation	Lecture notes	Review of articles submitted
	Thesis	Handout	to refereed journals
	Chapter in edited book		Research grant proposal
	Case report		Initiating or responsive e-mail
	Book review		Application, invitation, request,
	Review article		submission and editorial-
	Editorial		response letters
SPOKEN	Conference presentation	Lecture	Discussion between examiners
	Plenary lecture	Tutorial	Initiating or responsive
	Thesis defence	Seminar	phone call

Table 2. Taxonomy of academic genres (cf. Swales 1990, 1996, 2004a).

The difficulty with this classification, as in most nomenclatorial systems, is the appropriate level of delicacy to be used when selecting entries that qualify for inclusion. Apart from the impermanence of certain genres (hastened by the introduction of online publishing) generic norms are subject to a natural evolution that tends to blur traditional textual definitions. A clear example of this difficulty is the classification of research articles, which constitute the most important type of publication in many disciplines. Also the subdivision of research articles into sections has attracted different interpretations: Dudley-Evans (1995) and Swales (2004a), for example, refer to them as 'part-genres' subservient to the communicative purposes of the host text, whereas Hyland and Tse (2004b) prefer to see them as separate genres independent of their co-text.

2.4.1. The research article

As the corpus analysed in this volume consists entirely of research articles, a clarification of the term is essential. Such texts form the most prestigious part of a scholarly journal, which in turn provides an accredited channel for international disciplinary communication. Journal articles are vital to the advancement of knowledge as "significant issues are raised, defined, and debated within these forums. In this sense, to publish and to be cited is to enter the community's discourse" (Berkenkotter *et al.* 1991: 192). Publication is not only a means of communication – rather it co-constructs the disciplines by enforcing the criteria for membership and for acceptance or rejection of knowledge claims. Research articles are "a window on the practices and beliefs of the communities for whom they have meaning" and their language "has evolved as a means of funding, constructing, evaluating, displaying and negotiating knowledge" (Hyland 2000: 5). Academic discourse is far more than a tool used by authors to exchange findings. It has gained a life of its own over time by serving the communicative needs of a relatively small group of intellectuals:

> As an enormous library of individual tongues that have adopted a single style of truth telling, 'the common language of science' (as Einstein called it) has evolved to a level where it seems as fully absolute, independent, self-justifying, and unassailable as the facts it claims to transmit. Indeed, it would be hard – perhaps impossible – to deny the impression that here lies the grand

> master narrative of modernism, ideally suited to its content. What sort of faith, then, might we say seems to beat at the heart of this discourse? Simply this: that language can be made a form of technology, a device able to contain and transfer *knowledge without touching it*. (Montgomery 1996: 2)

Although its rhetoric and structure may vary from discipline to discipline, in most of the experimental sciences a research article tends to meet four types of requirement:

> It must demonstrate (or at least claim) that it contributes knowledge to the field, it must demonstrate familiarity with the work of previous researchers in the field, it must use a scientific method in analyzing its results (showing acceptance of the truth-value of statistical demonstration), it must meet standards for the test design and analysis of results, it must adhere to standards determining degree of accuracy. (Porter 1986: 39-40)

Article-length publications have been investigated mainly in the natural and social sciences, which make the most of the experimental article format, while in other fields (most notably mathematics and the humanities) the speculative nature of intellectual enquiry does not follow the traditional Introduction-Methods-Results-Discussion structure of evidence-based research. Among the first authors to address this aspect, Bazerman (1988: 327-328) introduced a helpful distinction between the experimental and the theoretical research article, observing that the former has been particularly successful because it "has found ways of bringing to bear on any particular argument the literature of the field, the currently accepted theory, deductive reasoning, representations of method, and representation of empirical experience" and it "requires a certain amount of explicit representation of selected parts of the process that goes into its creation, such as the after-the-fact reconstruction of the intellectual genealogy in the review of the literature, the focused procedural account of methods, and the selective narrative of results".

In *The research article revisited*, Swales (2004a: 217) argues that the label has in fact been used for three distinct genres: the experimental article, the theoretical article and the review article, which may be referred to collectively as 'serially published research communications'. The experimental article is regarded as the standard research article because of its quantitative prevalence in scholarly serials, though a clear-cut distinction between experimental and theoretical articles is far from straightforward and most papers are positioned on a continuum between the two. Gross *et al.* (2002: 187-188) suggest detailed generic labels to account for such intermediate options (i.e. experimental, theoretical, methodological, observational, observational/theoretical, experimental/theoretical, mathematical and reviews) but conclude that "the typical scientific article in the 20th century is experimental and includes some engagement with theory".

Taking into account these considerations and the fact that not all fields of learning exploit the genre's meaning potential in the same manner, the working definition of *research article* adopted here extends to any published contribution providing new experimental evidence (where envisaged by the discipline) coupled with an element of theoretical speculation.

2.5. The values of academia

The focus of this study is on the value system encoded in academic discourse, that is in the language used by researchers to disseminate their findings and engage in scholarly debate. Virtually all scholars, however, are affiliated to a research body – whether private or state-run – which is usually part of the academic system insofar as it provides not only research facilities but also educational courses at undergraduate and/or postgraduate level. The word *academia* is particularly useful here, as an inclusive term embracing the system's social (academic community), cultural (academic culture) and institutional (academic governance) dimension. A similar distinction underlies Brodkey's (1987) reference to the 'academic community' (the university as a body of scholars) as opposed to the 'academy' (the university as an institution).

Academic values may therefore be defined as variables pertaining especially to the social and cultural dimension of academia across a range of disciplines and specialisms. The close link between such variables and the texts that encode them has been aptly described as follows:

> Getting the words right depends not just on an individual's choice. The words are shaped by the discipline – in its communally developed linguistic resources and expectations; in its stylized identification and structuring of realities to be discussed; in its literature; in its active procedures of reading, evaluating, and using texts; in its structured interactions between writer and reader. The words arise out of the activity, procedures, and relationships within the community. (Bazerman 1988: 47)

But what is meant exactly by academic values and how can they be measured? In answering this question it is useful to draw on the insights of various disciplinary viewpoints – an early attempt of this may be found in Lepley (1957). Cultural psychologists approach values as regulatory mechanisms that mediate between the self and its social environment, reflecting both an individual's stage of socialisation and his/her level of personal growth (Reed 1996). This is an important aspect because it recognises the fact that we experience values both as recipients of their authority and, more actively, as agents of their perpetuation or transformation. Schwartz (1992, 1994) claims that it is possible to draw up an inventory of the values at work in any cultural setting by focusing on phenomena that guide our selection and evaluation of events beyond specific situations; these consist of 'concepts and beliefs' about desirable behaviours and outcomes that can generally be ranked by relative importance. The argument is that values operate when individuals engage with the world and interpret experience through criteria that are interrelated and can be ranked hierarchically. This model has been used, among other things, to measure the altruistic proclivities of environmental activists (Stern *et al.* 1998).

Value is also a key concept in economics. Marketing and trade rely on the (real or perceived) well-balanced exchange of commodities, but non-monetary values also have a role to play. There is evidence that consumer behaviour is influenced by human values associated with certain goods (Allen/Ng 1999) and that consumers act according to timeframes reflecting their personal value systems

(Valette-Florence *et al.* 1999). Corporations are particularly interested in such data, as they seek to predict the evolution of global values to adjust their products and marketing strategies accordingly. Social trends are subject to similar influences. Graddol's (1997) analysis of international phenomena affecting the English language, for example, has a diagram of past and future changes in the attitude of influential social groups or 'trend-setters' predicting, somewhat optimistically, a global shift in values from economic efficiency to social justice by the year 2000.

Not many authors, however, have turned their attention to academic settings. Among these, Gordon (1984) offers some insights into the values that guide biochemists in their choice of where to submit a paper – the most frequent being the audience associated with a journal rather than other types of reward. Student values were targeted by a survey of undergraduates in Japan and the US (Oishi *et al.* 2006), which concluded that Japanese students ranked higher for hedonism, stimulation, universalism, benevolence, tradition and security, while Americans favoured power, achievement, self-direction and conformity. This type of variation seems to confirm the view that values are strong markers of cultural identity, since "the idea of aligning oneself with particular values, beliefs and interests through social practices, including literary practices, concerns the interface between 'culture' and 'identity'" (Ivanič 1997: 66).

More central to our concerns here is Roy and Dhawan's investigation of the 'value space' of Indian scientists, where value indicates "a broad general belief about some way of behaving or some end state that is preferable to the individual" (2004: 2). Its results show that the importance assigned to ethical values (i.e. those related to right/wrong) increased with seniority, while pragmatic values (related to success/failure) were less prominent and decreased with seniority; affective values (pleasant/unpleasant) were relatively unimportant. The authors conclude that the special cultural environment of Indian scientists, steeped in deeply-held religious beliefs, also reverberates in the workplace. While certainly useful, these studies generally employ psychometric methods to process self-reported data, whose reliability depends on introspection. To what extent, however, are respondents aware of the relative importance they assign to values in their workplace and, what is more, do such values exist only 'in the mind' or do they translate into actual behaviour?

One way to answer these questions is to search for evidence of the values held by a given community of practice in the texts they use for peer-to-peer communication. This approach has been seldom adopted in the social sciences because it requires discourse analytical skills that belong to applied linguistics, while on the other hand no linguist has yet engaged in a systematic study of disciplinary values in academic texts. One of the few studies to move in this direction (Blakeslee 1994) deals with the construction of 'newsworthiness' in readers' letters to the *Physical Review*; by foregrounding such elements as novelty, usefulness and juxtaposition to existing claims, authors emphasise the importance of their letters, to the point that "in keeping with their function of announcing innovations, letters have come to resemble journalistic accounts of scientific findings" (Blakeslee 1994: 91). Another paper that deserves mention, albeit devoted to business discourse, is Felices Lago and Hewitt's (2004) analysis of the personal qualities of job applicants listed by employers advertising in the Spanish press. The lexical items marking such qualities, in decreasing order of importance, were assigned to four categories:

- group-related values (collectivism/affiliation; communication skills; negotiation; leadership; multicultural diversity; flexibility; customer orientation; persuasion);
- individual values (vitality; individualism/independence; innovation; vitality/individualism; business sense; adventure);
- work-related values (work-related skills/attitude; achievement; prospect/future; presentation skills);
- intellectual values (general; specific).

The results of this approach shed light both on the desirable 'axiologically-loaded' qualities of candidates applying for specific jobs and on the type of employer advertising those positions. What remains unclear, however, is the method adopted to quantify such lexis in texts that are presumably diverse in terms of length and structure. A similar attempt to classify values in the press is Bednarek's (2006a) study of expressions of writer opinion in British newspaper reports. These are ascribed to ten 'evaluative parameters' (emotivity, importance, expectedness, comprehensibility, seriousness, possibility/necessity, reliability, style, mental state, evidentiality and importance) whose negative markers are more explicit in tabloids than in broadsheets.

There is a close relationship between certain values and the interactional plane of discourse, as pragmatic norms reflect the interlocutor's needs and concerns in a given context. The literature on linguistic politeness (cf. Brown/Levinson 1987; Myers 1989; Watts *et al.* 1992; Gea Valor 2000) offers a wealth of insights into the textualisation of urbane behaviour across groups and cultures. Albeit wary of linguistic prescriptivism, Leech explicitly acknowledges that pragmatic principles (and the maxims they subsume) are an expression of social values:

> In saying that people normally follow the CP [Cooperative Principle], then, one is by no means taking a moral stance. But one thing that cannot be denied is that [conversational] principles introduce communicative values, such as truthfulness, into the study of language. Traditionally, linguists have avoided referring to such values, feeling that they undermine one's claim for objectivity. But so long as the values we consider are ones we suppose, on empirical grounds, to be operative in society, rather than ones we impose on society, then there is no reason to exclude them from our inquiry. (Leech 1983: 9-10)

Besides the values (whether individual or collective) held by a community of practice and its members, it is important to consider the role of textual values. These measure the quality of discourse as a textual artefact and contribute significantly to the impact of publications but are seldom made explicit outside such evaluative genres as book reviews, review articles and journal editorials. One of such values is 'clarity', which can be defined as the level of comprehensibility inherent in a given text. It has been investigated mainly by educationalists and rhetoricians: Hartley *et al.* (2004), for example, measured clarity in terms of mean sentence-length, percentage of passive sentences and readability in the sciences, social sciences and arts/humanities. While in journal articles the sciences had the least clear texts in academic journals, they were the most clear in university textbooks and popular magazines – the implication being that despite their complexity in peer-to-peer communication, the hard sciences show a greater regard for their readership, compared to other disciplines, in asymmetric contexts.

Related to clarity is a broader distinction between writer-responsible and reader-responsible cultures (cf. Hinds 1987; McCagg 1996), built on the 'contrastive rhetoric' approach spearheaded by Kaplan (1966, 1988). By looking at the linguistic features (word order, terminology, metatextual organisers) and cognitive features (organisation of thought, knowledge assumptions) that facilitate or hinder comprehension, such studies argue that certain academic cultures place the onus of bridging the gap between text and meaning mainly on the reader/listener while for others (notably in the Anglo-American world) the writer/speaker is ultimately responsible for communicating meaning explicitly and unambiguously. Even clarity, therefore, is not as universal a value as one might assume, since it conflicts with other values (e.g. writer authority and in-group marking) that are given precedence in certain settings. The mere fact that these guiding principles/beliefs of communicative behaviour tend to operate hierarchically means that where two or more values apply, interactants are likely to prefer the least marked option (unless they are willing to justify their departure from the norm). The picture is complicated in many cases by the rhetorical displacement caused by the shift to English (cf. Duszak 2005), which inevitably alters the criteria contributing to textual value.

The sociology of science takes a special interest in the principles guiding the behaviour of academics. Most of its work stems from Merton's (1942) claim that scientific enquiry is governed by four universal norms: *communalism*, in that the results of research are made public and generally available; *universalism*, because scientific claims are measured against widely accepted criteria; *disinterestedness*, that is the pursuit of knowledge for its own sake rather than personal interest; and *organised scepticism*, which means a critical approach to the evidence supporting new knowledge claims. Later theories have challenged or amended the Mertonian model, claiming that it embodies only an ideal state of affairs, often contradicted by the actual behaviour of scientists.

Mulkay argues that such norms are an expression of ideology, as they are followed out of personal conviction rather than for utilitarian purposes (even the academic reward system does not allow for their presence): when scientists adopt these norms they act as "an interest group with a dominating elite, and a justificatory ideology" (Mulkay 1976: 78). Instead of looking for an abstract moral code constitutive of what counts as 'science', the attention shifts to language itself – an approach followed up in later studies of scientific rhetoric by the same author (Mulkay *et al.* 1983; Gilbert/Mulkay 1984). Like any other ideological system, therefore, science evolves in time and is subject to outside pressures that may undermine its practices and institutional arrangements (cf. Smokler 1983). This aspect is confirmed by Hyland's remark that "the discourses of the academy are not merely credible systems of making meaning within sealed disciplines. Rather they are extremely valued and influential ideological systems in the wider community" (2000: 159).

The beliefs held by individual scholars tend to vary, however, according to their affiliation. Braxton (1989) claims that the norms of communalism and universalism function as 'compensatory integrating mechanisms', while conversely disinterestedness and scepticism produce fragmentation within the academic community. This reminds us of the potentially conflictual nature of academic values, which seek to reconcile the advancement of knowledge with scientists' collective/individual needs but neglect the potentially dysfunctional influence of the setting in which researchers live and work. In a major overhaul of the Mertonian model, Ziman (2000) argues that over the last forty years academia has moved to a 'post-academic ethos', driven by increasingly commercial/managerial standards that stress the exclusive ownership of knowledge, its subservience to local interests, the hierarchical accountability of researchers and the desirability of projects carried out on commission – with the researcher acting as a paid problem-solver rather than a creative free agent. On a similar note, Mautner (2005) is highly suspicious of the 'business buzzwords' that have colonised governance in higher education institutions. It is also wrong – as claimed by critics of Goffman's 'monolithic view' of values (Ivanič 1997) – to assume that academic values command unconditioned compliance. Their occasionally controversial status, combined with the multiple allegiances of academics, means they may be opposed if not openly challenged.

This section would not be complete without mention of three values which, though less linguistically evident in academic texts, are often cited in the literature. The most basic is "an underlying belief in the value of science" (Mukerji 1996: 261) as a reliable source of knowledge. It is a well-known fact that scientists struggled for centuries, sometimes at their own peril, to achieve this goal (cf. Kuhn 1962; Atkinson 1999; Gross *et al.* 2002). Without that belief – and a 'willing suspension of disbelief' among readers – the knowledge claims made in print would be nothing but words on paper. Despite its incongruences and internal tensions, science is an ideological system that commands both respect and compliance from its constituency.

Another value entrenched in academic communication is a belief in figures of authority or 'great minds' guiding the work of scientists, whether as mentors, pioneering scholars or Nobel laureates. The social and bibliographic networks established with such figures are similar to intellectual genealogies or "ways of claiming credentials and acquiring status by association" (Mukerji 1996: 263). In other words, value is not distributed evenly within science but tends to cluster around certain thinkers and their followers, producing a state of affairs that is not devoid of controversy, as new authorities emerge and challenge earlier arrangements in the allocation of recognition. Clear indication of these tensions may be found in a statement issued by the American Association of University Professors, which rejects collegiality as a criterion for faculty evaluation, on the grounds that "the very real potential for a distinct criterion of 'collegiality' to cast a pall of stale uniformity places it in direct tension with the value of faculty diversity in all its contemporary manifestations" (AAUP 1999: 40).

The third value is the use of English, rather than other languages, as a medium for publication. Although largely of a utilitarian nature – driven by the need to reach as wide an audience as possible through well-known journals and publishers – this variable has far-reaching implications. Swales (1997), for instance, blames EAP practitioners of an 'accomodationist' and 'technocratic' stance, fostering a passive attitude to English as the default language of science. Whether or not the use of English inevitably implies acceptance of the cultural baggage associated with Anglo-American rhetoric remains, however, a highly controversial matter (cf.

Mauranen 1993a; Canagarajah 1999; Tardy 2004; Duszak 2005). Some economists have developed statistical tools to measure the relative value of a language through such parameters as 'Estimated economic strength' and 'Gross Language Product' in billions of dollars (Graddol 1997). An interesting distinction suggested by Coulmas (1992) is that between 'utility value' and 'exchange value', which means that a language is valued according to the communicative range of its linguistic resources (linked to the number of L1 and SL users) and its use in economic transactions (linked to the number of FL users and the strength of the economies involved).

It is clear from this overview of the literature that academic values (whatever their nature) lie at the heart of scientific enquiry but shape disciplinary epistemologies and beliefs differently across domains. There is an unavoidable relationship between such values and their object, insofar as science follows priorities whose 'narrative' is shaped by the author's interpretation of the world (Myers 1990). While it is arduous to infer academic values from the way research is conducted or from the quality of its findings (a point confirmed by the reliance of most sociological analyses on introspective data), explicit reference to such values is provided in the textual outcome of research – whether as an article, case report, conference presentation or other forms of expert communication. A hermeneutic distinction should finally be made between literary and non-literary texts, in keeping with Halliday and Martin's (1993: 93) observation that if research genres were approached as works of literature, the analyst would have to employ "two value systems which intersect in a series of complementarities".

The notion of value assumed in this study will thus embrace any aspect of academic research (whether in the experimental process, theoretical argumentation, or written presentation) to which the parent disciplinary community assigns an interpretation whose polarity reflects its current standards, beliefs and practices. A bottom-up approach will be adopted for the identification of academic values, using textual data to isolate the most quantitatively significant positive/negative lexicalisations and subsequently to investigate the collocates associated with such items. The analysis will not exclude metaphoric lexis, whose contribution to the signalling of academic value is the object of two small-scale studies conducted at the University of Bergamo (Giannoni 2009a, 2010). By transferring the positive/negative associations of source words to a given target, metaphors encode a range of affective values, along a scale of goodness or badness, linked to the attitudes, beliefs and emotions of participants (Charteris-Black 2005; Cameron/Deignan 2006). Although relatively familiar in conversational exchanges (cf. Morgan 1993; Martin 2000), metaphors are prominent also in academic communication, where they "structure how we perceive, how we think, and what we do" (Lakoff/Johnson 1980: 4). This is confirmed by the high proportion of scientific terminology whose status is inherently metaphorical (cf. Salager-Meyer 1990).

The most frequent lexicalisations found in research articles from four disciplinary fields (applied linguistics, economics, law and medicine) signalled, in order of occurrence, significance, consistency, clarity, strength and manageability (Giannoni 2010). Of these, significance appears to be the most important, quantitatively speaking, throughout the corpus. Consistency is emphasised especially in medicine and economics, when discussing data or experimental results. Clarity is mentioned above all in the law and applied linguistics, where it may represent a reaction to the more speculative and potentially controversial orientation of both disciplines. Strength, though less prominent, is invoked either as a quality of data and its interpretation (in economics and applied linguistics) or of legal motives and actions (in law); interestingly, *strong/weak* are also among the most common evaluative metaphors used in academic speech, as shown by a recent investigation of business studies lectures (Crawford Camiciottoli 2004). Finally, manageability is signalled almost exclusively by legal scholars when presenting cases, claims or practices as more or less 'judicially manageable', whereas in medicine it is likely to refer to patients or laboratory data. By signalling the value (or non-value) of knowledge claims in the field, academics assert their authority and construct a credible authorial voice. Evaluators such as *clear*, *strong* and *significant* are part and parcel of the rhetoric of academia and retain metaphorical connotations which, albeit unnoticed, influence the reader's understanding of scientific facts, ideas and observations and reflect the presence of underlying disciplinary cultures based on shared "codes of conduct, sets of values and distinctive intellectual tasks" (Becher 1981: 109).

The second study of metaphorical value markers (Giannoni 2009a) is based on normalised data from four research genres – i.e. journal editorials, article abstracts, research articles and book reviews. Its results show a common axiological base shared by all the disciplines considered, though some were more prone to signal certain academic values. Clarity, strength and inclusiveness were on average equally represented in the corpus, but applied linguists tended to stress clarity (along the *clear* → *unclear* continuum) as a quality of research, whereas legal scholars placed greater emphasis on inclusiveness (*broad/wide* → *narrow*). The other disciplines marked value less frequently, with centrality (*central* → *marginal*) expressed least often by economists and strength (*strong* → *weak*) by medical researchers. The distribution of such variables is summarised in the graph below, which plots the normalised number of relevant tokens in each domain.

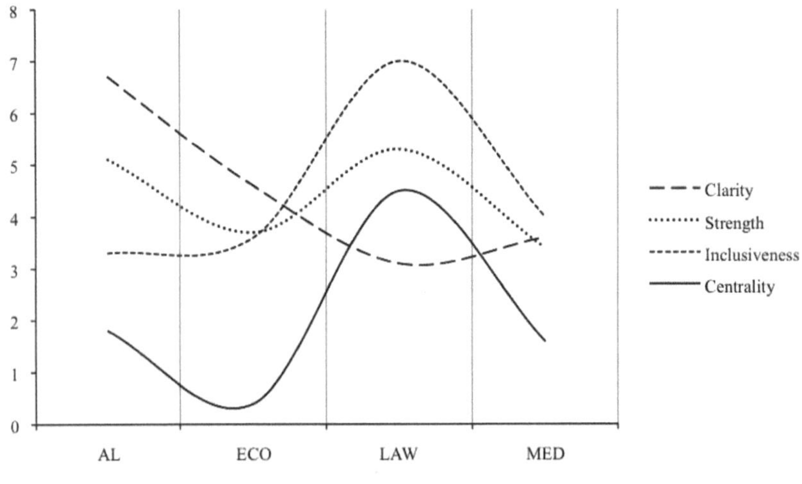

Figure 3. Metaphorical values across academic domains (Giannoni 2009a: 177).

As indicated by these preliminary findings, a value can be expressed through positive and/or negative markers. In some cases – namely clarity, inclusiveness and manageability – negative forms were extremely rare, probably for interpersonal reasons. On the other hand, disciplines focusing on issues whose lexical repertoire is rich in problematic terms with no positive counterpart (e.g. *polluting* in engineering, *sexism* in law and *infectious* in medicine) tend to exhibit the opposite behaviour. This means there is a semantic gap between such textualisations and the value itself which needs to be dealt with methodologically. In the above-mentioned cases that may mean deciding whether to include only non-prefixed forms as their antonyms or also more inclusive items (e.g. *safe, environmentally-friendly; fairness, gender-neutrality*). When selecting the analytical tools for the present study I decided therefore to focus on a limited range of high-occurrence, explicit items rather than embark on the impossible task of accounting for each and every possible marker of a given value throughout the corpus.

2.6. Evaluation and stance

The interface between academic values and the evaluative function of discourse has attracted a wealth of theoretical and textual studies over the last two decades. The earliest contribution of this kind is Thompson and Ye's pedagogically-oriented paper on reporting verbs in English research articles, where evaluation is defined as "the conveying of the writer's view of the status of the information in her text" (1991: 367). Like modality, evaluation constitutes a layer of the text's meaning potential, realised not only by discrete elements but also cumulatively and contextually. A distinction is made between evaluative reporting verbs that convey stance and those expressing interpretation: stance signals the 'truth/correctness or otherwise' of the reported proposition, either positively (e.g. *demonstrate, throw light on*), negatively (*disregard, dismiss*) or neutrally (*examine, focus on*). Interpretation, on the other hand, signals the specific argumentative function of the proposition (e.g. *add, comment, confirm, insist*). Apart from its taxonomical value, whose rationale appears today rather elusive, Thompson and Ye's paper is important for adding the term 'stance' to our metalinguistic repertoire and for encouraging other authors to look at how evaluation is realised in academic genres. It also highlights the analytical challenge of separating overtly judgmental textual items, classified as stance-markers, from those merely contributing to the ideational construction of discourse – a conundrum that seems to accompany most of the literature dealing with evaluation. The distinction is particularly relevant here because evaluation is conceptualised more broadly by authors interested in the mental process of interpreting experience (with the ultimate result that almost any linguistic feature can be interpreted evaluatively), whereas other authors take a narrower view, limited to the interpersonal significance of items that encode speaker/writer opinion.

Apart from a few studies dealing with the wording of conflict and disagreement in academic/professional discourse (cf. Hunston 1993a; Salager-Meyer 1999a), the analysis of evaluative speech acts is particularly indebted to the contributions published in *Evaluation in Text. Authorial Stance and the Construction of Discourse* (Hunston/ Thompson 2000). In its Introduction, the editors explain that "for us evaluation is the broad cover term for the expression of the speaker's attitude or stance towards, viewpoint on, or feelings about the entities or propositions that he or she is talking about. This attitude may relate to certainty or obligation or desirability or any of a number of other sets of values" (Thompson/Hunston 2000: 5). As the volume makes clear, the relative novelty of this area of research has produced considerable divergences in the choice of terminology and conceptual frameworks employed by different authors. The term 'stance', for example, is used by Conrad and Biber (2000) to identify three kinds of meaning: *epistemic stance* (the degree of certainty of a proposition); *attitudinal stance* (feelings or judgements about a proposition); and *style stance* (indication of how a proposition is expressed). Hyland later applies 'stance' only to the attitudinal dimension of academic discourse – where "writers intrude into the discourse to stamp their personal authority onto their arguments or step back from their discourse and disguise their involvement" (2004: 15) through boosters, hedges, attitude markers and self-mention.

Other authors (cf. Tucker 2003) stress the emotional element of attitudinal markers, so that stance identifies primarily the 'affective judgements' embedded in discourse. Commenting on the variety of approaches presented at a conference on evaluation in academic discourse, Mauranen (2004: 204) admits that "a number of terminological problems still remain, several with more than terminological implications, that is, they point to lack of clarity in the conceptualisation of the object of research". A well-known attempt to construct a single theoretical framework is that propounded by linguists dealing with appraisal systems, that is with "the semantic resources used to negotiate emotions, judgements, and valuations, alongside resources for amplifying and engaging with these evaluations" (Martin 2000: 145). Their model consists of four interlocking systems: *affect* (the expression of emotional responses); *judgement* (moral evaluations of behaviour); *appreciation* (concerned with the aesthetic quality of texts or phenomena); and *engagement* (the speaker's commitment to what he/she is saying). A further distinction is made between collective compliance to institutional rules, conveyed by judgement, and individual feelings or values, conveyed by appreciation. Despite the detailed modelling built into appraisal theory (especially since Martin/White 2005), its empirical value remains debatable and somewhat hard to prove – a point also made by Swales (2004b: 34-35) when commenting on a conference paper on the subject.

Whatever the coverage of the analysis, evaluation constitutes a central aspect of communication for it conveys not only factual information (ideational meanings) but also judgements that intersect the interpersonal plane of discourse (illocutionary meanings). For this reason it can be arduous to trace a dividing line between evaluative and non-evaluative speech acts – an issue tackled by Shaw's (2004: 123) scale of 'evaluative explicitness', where the most explicit items are either lexemes that are invariably positive or negative in polarity or expressions that appeal to widely-held values. Like modality, the notion of evaluation is therefore extremely elastic and has been applied to a surprising range of textual features in academic writing:

- academic value and relevance (Hunston 1994, 2000);
- reporting verbs (Hyland 1999);
- embedded/unsupported evaluation (Hoey 2000);

- the wording of direct/indirect conflicts (Salager-Meyer; 2001a; Salager-Meyer/Zambrano 2001a, 2001b; Breivega *et al.* 2002; Badger 2004);
- the construction of evaluative evidence (Dressen 2003);
- epistemic stance adverbials (Silver 2003);
- evaluation vs. stance markers (Tucker 2003);
- expressions of stance and engagement (Hyland 2004);
- the use of references (Koskela 2004);
- negation (Webber 2004);
- self-promotional first-person pronouns (Harwood 2005).

Spoken academic genres have also attracted a fair amount of attention (cf. Swales/Burke 2003; Anderson/Bamford 2004; Swales 2004b).

The focus, however, has generally been on the grammar of evaluation rather than the type of value conveyed, so that very little is yet known about academic values *per se*. In other words, what counts as good/indifferent/bad on a scale expressing the writer's stance (whether attitudinal or affective) has been largely overlooked. Contributions dealing with the rhetoric of academic conflicts tend to account for the wording of evaluative acts in terms of power relations within the academic community or of rhetorical conventions appropriate to a given genre or setting. A rare exception is Thetela's (1997) paper on the parameters of value signalled in research articles across disciplines, which uses semantically-related lexis to identify common research values; unfortunately, it is mostly centred on epistemic evaluation and provides little detail beyond such general labels as 'significance' or 'worthiness'.

The fact that evaluation can be performed along several parameters is also recognised by Thompson and Hunston (2000), who add certainty, expectedness and importance to the more obvious positive/negative dyad. Whether speculatively or empirically reconstructed, there is a fundamental difference between 'values' that approximate cognitive universals (often linked to modality) and values that belong to the ethos of a given discourse community. In addition, it is reasonable to assume that certain elements of the latter group may be specific to academia and/or to a certain discipline.

A useful piece of research targeting the evaluation-value interface in academic texts is Swales and Burke's (2003) study of adjectivation in the MICASE (cf. Swales 2003) and Hyland corpora. It compares the quantitative distribution of polarised vs. centralised adjectives by assigning relevant lexical items to seven categories: 'deviance' for distance from expectations (e.g. *typical, strange, crazy*); 'relevance' for distance from the topic or field of discussion (e.g. *important, irrelevant, fundamental*); 'assessment' for general evaluation of something (e.g. *excellent, terrible, incredible*); 'acuity' for the intellectual quality of something (e.g. *smart, stupid*); 'aesthetic appeal' (e.g. *beautiful, elegant*); 'size' (e.g. *small, huge*); 'strength' (e.g. *weak, strong*). The results show a considerable prevalence of size, relevance and assessment over the other categories in both MICASE (lectures and other speech events) and the Hyland research-article corpus. The main difference between the two corpora is that research articles are far more likely to stress relevance and far less likely to stress size and assessment.

Unfortunately, there is no indication as to how such data may be interpreted, apart from the evidence that academics tend to employ more adjectives, intensifiers and polarised forms in speech than in writing. The use of evaluative adjectives may, of course, be influenced by the language adopted and by a writer's L1 background, as suggested in Shaw's (2003) analysis of English research article introductions written by Danish authors, as compared to those by native speakers. A similar methodology will be adopted in this volume, using concordancing tools to investigate the distribution of related words (adjectives but also other parts of speech) within semantic-conceptual categories.

It has often been remarked the evaluative meanings are not easy to quantify because of the multitude of linguistic (and pragmatic) resources involved in their construction. As mentioned earlier, the difficulty depends largely on the indeterminacy of the phenomena that qualify for attention: the wider the definition of 'evaluation', the harder any attempt to locate it in a large sample of discourse. For this reason, studies of evaluative language are often based on a very small number of texts (cf. Hunston 1993a, 1994; Anderson 2004; Fortanet-Gómez 2004). To overcome this risk, it is generally desirable to narrow down the research focus and concentrate specifically on the first of the three functions of evaluation (i.e. expressing opinion, rather than maintaining relations or organising the discourse), which Thompson and Hunston describe in the following terms:

> Identifying 'what the writer thinks' tells us about more than just one person's ideas [...] Every act of evaluation expresses a communal value-system, and every act of evaluation goes towards building up that value-system. This value-system in turn is a component of the ideology which lies behind every text. Thus, identifying what the writer thinks reveals the ideology of the society that has produced that text. (Thompson/Hunston 2000: 6)

Expressing writer opinion (i.e. stance) is the most prominent type of evaluative act observed in research articles, where it is usually interpretable as an affirmation of allegiance to – rather than divergence from – the values held by a disciplinary community. Since it is impossible to account for the whole range of variably explicit linguistic resources 'expressing opinion', this function will be investigated by looking at "the lexis of judgement and subjectivity" (Thompson/Hunston 2000: 16) encoded by evaluative adjectives (e.g. *splendid, terrible, obvious*), adverbs (*happily, unfortunately, plainly*), nouns (*success, failure, triumph*) and verbs (*succeed, win, lose*). Using morphological and semantic criteria, the relevant lexical items can be grouped into conceptually homogeneous categories (cf. in particular Giannoni 2009a, 2010) that signal the values embedded in discourse. This procedure would be impossible without the use of corpus analysis and concordancing tools, whose role in this study is discussed in the next section.

2.7. Working with corpora

The idea of using large collections of written or spoken texts for linguistic analysis is not a new one. Since the pioneering efforts of computational linguists almost four decades ago, corpus linguistics has slowly gained recognition as part of mainstream research. A key contribution to this new branch of scholarship came from the so-called ‘language processing movement’, which remained at the forefront of corpus studies for about a decade, demonstrating that corpora are a treasure-trove of information when probed with suitable tools and procedures. Moving away from the early word-frequency lists and raw quantitative data, corpus linguistics has extended its reach to lexicology and lexicography, grammar and discourse analysis, historical linguistics and even pragmatics (cf. Thomas/Short 1996; Biber *et al.* 1998; Partington 2004).

The first English dictionary based on corpus data was edited by Sinclair (1987) using the Collins/Birmingham University International Language Database (COBUILD). A similar approach produced the first corpus-oriented grammar of the English language which, as explained eloquently in the editor’s Introduction, marked a turning point in the field:

> The information in this book is taken from a long and careful study of present-day English. Many millions of words from speech and writing have been gathered together in a computer and analyzed, partly by the computer and partly by a team of expert compilers. It is the first grammar of its kind, and it is different in many respects from other kinds of grammar.
> This grammar attempts to make accurate statements about English, as seen in the huge Birmingham Collection of English Texts. The main patterns of English are picked out and described, and the typical phrases found in each pattern are listed.
> This is what a grammar ought to do, but only very recently has it been possible. For a long time there has been a credibility gap between a grammar and the language it is supposed to describe. (Sinclair 1990: v)

Whether extracted for descriptive or pedagogical purposes, corpus data allows the analyst to gauge features of language in use that were inaccessible before the age of computers and digital archival. Any text can be used as part of a corpus to provide real-world data rather than claims based on mere introspection or intuition. The change undergone by applied linguistics as a result of this development has been equated to a shift from palaeontology, with its relative dearth of data and abundant speculation, to particle physics, with a mass of data that is manageable only through computer ‘crunching’ (Sinclair 2006). As a result, the way corpora are designed, assembled, processed and probed for information is essential to the validity of results based on such material. A badly-constructed corpus is as representative of language use as an arbitrary assortment of webpages or TV broadcasts.

A division arose in the 1990s between *corpus-based* and *corpus-driven* methodologies. The former rely holistically on the text as the sole source of knowledge, to avoid any bias due to the analyst's assumptions or expectations. Their approach is similar to that propounded by the 'etic' principle in anthropological research (cf. Headland/Pike 1990), whereby knowledge is collected by an external observer liberated of all preconceptions. Corpus-driven studies, on the other hand, allow researchers to employ textual data also to prove/disprove their assumptions and intuitions. Scientific enquiry is conducted in a dialogic relationship with the text rather than monologically, thus inevitably allowing a certain degree of subjectivity (cf. Francis 1993; Tognini Bonelli 2001).

While this distinction is essential for lexicographers and formal grammarians, it tends to be less clear-cut in text linguistics, where corpora are extremely valuable but do not constitute the sole source of information and can be integrated with non-textual insights from other disciplines. The fact that corpus linguistics could not exist without some kind of assumption about the target language is stressed also by Knowles (1996), who observes that annotation (i.e. tagging and parsing) cannot be added to a corpus unless the researcher has a theoretical framework in his/her mind. The methodology employed in this volume will therefore combine elements of both approaches, taking on board Sinclair's advice that

> We should trust the text. We should be open to what it may tell us. We should not impose our ideas on it, except perhaps just to get started. We should only apply loose and flexible frameworks until we see what the preliminary results are in order to accommodate the new information that will come from the text.
> (Sinclair 1994: 25)

Parallel to the growth of this subdiscipline has been a shift to increasingly large corpora (cf. Burnard 2007 on the 100 million word BNC) which aspire to be more representative of specific text types and speaker profiles. At the same time, the use of corpus analysis beyond its early applications has inspired a whole range of specialised corpora serving the interests of projects covering diachronic, diatopic or diastratic variation. Such developments were envisaged over ten years ago by Svartvik (1996), who predicted that corpora would become larger, better (i.e. tagged and specialised) and more easily available. Among specialised corpora, there are also major collections representative of different types of academic discourse (cf. Swales 2006); an overview of the best-known, listed by size, is given in Table 3 below with mention of the genre(s) and language(s) they include.

Corpus	*Language*	*Words*	*Types of text*	*Reference*
BAWE British Academic Written English Corpus	English (NS)	6.5 m	student assignments	Ebeling/Heuboeck (2007)
AWL Academic Word List Corpus	English	3.5 m	journal articles book chapters workbooks laboratory manuals course notes	Coxhead (2000)
KIAP Cultural Identity in Academic Prose	English (NS) French Norwegian	3.1 m	research articles	Fløttum *et al.* (2006a)
T2K-SWAL TOEFL 2000 Spoken and Written Academic Language	English (NNS)	2.7 m	class sessions and labs office hours study groups service encounters textbooks course packs assignments	Biber *et al.* (2004a)
CADIS Corpus of Academic Discourse	English (NS, NNS) Italian	2.0 m	research articles book reviews article abstracts editorials	Gotti/D'Angelo (2008)
MICASE Michigan Corpus of Academic Spoken English	English (NS, NNS)	1.8 m	lectures colloquia office hours lab sessions discussion sections study groups seminars, etc.	Sampson *et al.* (2007)

BASE British Academic Spoken English Corpus	English (NS)	1.6 m	lectures seminars	Nesi/Thompson (2006)
ELFA English as a Lingua Franca in Academic Settings	English (NNS)	0.7 m	lectures seminar sessions	Mauranen (2006b)

Table 3. Corpora of English academic discourse.

These corpora were assembled either for the investigation of textual features (e.g. BASE and ELFA below), the development of more adequate pedagogic materials (AWL, T2K-SWAL), or both purposes (MICASE). Two of these (KIAP and CADIS) are *homothematic*, insofar as they seek to cover the same content across different languages. Interestingly, most of the texts are either transcriptions of spoken events or genres produced for/by students. This is partly due to legal requirements that make it impossible to share material taken from commercial publications without explicit permission from the copyright holders. Cambridge University Press, for example, claim to hold a 25-million word corpus of academic English (presumably drawn from their books and journals) used for developing their IELTS tests and textbooks, but are unwilling to make it available to linguists. Academic corpora can be easily assembled for individual research purposes, however, from e-journals and other digital publications. Widespread access to online content in recent years has encouraged the use of corpus linguistics not only for descriptive purposes but also as a pedagogic tool. Swales stresses the link between these two applications by noting that "a personal investment in becoming, on occasion, a corpus linguist can lead [...] to considerable linguistic and rhetorical consciousness raising" (2004c: 20).

Corpus evidence of value-related realisations will be collected in this study bearing in mind Hunston's (2004a) experience of searching for evaluative lexis in the Bank of English. Because of their inherent polysemy, certain words were found to change their evaluative strength according to the context, so that *dramatic* may mean 'aesthetically pleasing', 'unreliably exaggerate' or 'with important negative effects'; even the polarity of certain items is not univocal but linked to their collocates. What is more, evaluation may be conveyed by indirect realisations (including specific grammatical features) that are not amenable to measurement. Her conclusion is that "reliable automatic identification and quantification can be carried out on only a limited set of realizations of evaluation" (2004a: 186). In other words, it is pointless to aim for total coverage of such a complex and pervasive phenomenon. Instead, the analyst should settle for a limited range of markers (cf. Diani 2004) covering the more explicit, lexically transparent lexis used by academics to signal what standard qualities should (or should not) qualify the research process and the activities of scholars within their community of practice.

3. Materials and data

3.1. Disciplinary fields

A total of ten academic domains, representing a broad spectrum of scientific enquiry in international English-medium scholarship, were included in the corpus assembled for this study. As argued in the previous chapter, the subdivision of scholarship into separate fields is in many ways an approximation because of the increasing specialisation and interdisciplinarity of contemporary research, with branches of knowledge that did not even exist until a short time ago (e.g. nanotechnology) now at the forefront of research. Even the basic distinction between sciences and humanities, or theoretical and applied disciplines, is not as clear-cut as might be thought. In biological parlance, disciplines are more akin to *genera* than *species*, insofar as they imply a conflation of subdisciplines that may eventually aspire to recognition as separate domains, with considerable implications in terms of status, visibility and allocation of resources and facilities.

Bearing in mind these limitations, I selected for the corpus a range of disciplines representative of five scientific groupings, whose nature can be briefly described as follows:

- The *natural sciences* deal primarily with the detailed description of phenomena occurring in the natural world that may also be relevant also to the applied sciences and technologies. The two domains from this category are BIOLOGY and PHYSICS, which in Becher and Trowler's (2001) classification (cf. Chapter 2, Table 1) would belong to the 'pure sciences' group, where they are defined as hard-pure disciplines.
- The *applied sciences* deal primarily with the manipulation of reality, based on procedural knowledge and man-made tools. MEDICINE and ENGINEERING were chosen from this category, which is found in Hyland (2000). Becher and Trowler

(2001) prefer the term 'technologies', which count as hard-applied disciplines.

- The *human sciences* deal with the human species in terms of individual evolution and material culture. The two representatives of this group are ANTHROPOLOGY and HISTORY, which Becher and Trowler (2001) also place in the same category, as 'soft-pure' disciplines, albeit with a distinction between the former (a 'pure social science') and the latter (a 'humanity').
- The *social sciences* deal with the interactional plane of human society in its various instantiations. ECONOMICS and SOCIOLOGY were chosen from this category, which is 'applied social sciences' by both Hyland (2000) and Becher and Trowler (2001).
- Finally, the *mathematical sciences* deal with theoretical and applied knowledge based on mathematical models. The two disciplines representative of this group, which has been generally neglected in earlier corpus-based studies, are MATHEMATICS and COMPUTER SCIENCE.

The rationale underlying this selection is that each domain reflects a discipline-specific academic culture based on shared "codes of conduct, sets of values and distinctive intellectual tasks" (Becher 1981: 109).

3.2. Source journals

Having chosen what disciplines to include in the corpus, the next step was to select the journals most representative of such fields of knowledge. For this purpose, I turned to the most authoritative bibliometric tool available to the international academic community, namely the *Journal Citation Reports* (JCRs) compiled by the ISI Web of Knowledge – a databank covering no less than 22,000 scholarly journals in the sciences, social sciences, arts and humanities (ISI 2006). JCRs allow users to identify the most influential journals in a range of disciplines, based on impact factor (IF). This parameter indicates the frequency with which articles in a journal are cited in the literature within a given period; it is calculated by dividing the total number of citations to a journal over two years by the number of articles published in that journal during the same period. The IF thus provides a quantitative assessment of a journal's impact on current literature, which is the main reason why it is often quoted by leading journals as a yardstick of their standing and is also used by academic libraries when reviewing subscriptions.

The following procedure was adopted to identify the relevant source journals. Through the ISI Web of Knowledge portal <http://www.isiwebofknowledge.com>, the JCRs for 2005 (the latest available edition when this phase of research was conducted) were accessed online. The *JCR Science Edition* was searched by Subject Category to identify the disciplines of BIOLOGY, MEDICINE, COMPUTER SCIENCE, MATHEMATICS, PHYSICS and ENGINEERING. Within each of these categories, the top-ranking journal was located by listing all journals by decreasing IF. The same steps were repeated using the *JCR Social Sciences Edition* for the disciplines of ANTHROPOLOGY, SOCIOLOGY, ECONOMICS and HISTORY. This method ensures that the choice of journal does not rely on such subjective parameters as availability, place of publication or theoretical orientation but only on the citing behaviour of specialists, which in turn reflects the greater authority wielded by certain journals (due to the quality of their content) as compared to others. Its results are summarised in the table below:

	Subject category	*Journal Title*	*Total Cites*	*IF*
JCR Science	BIOLOGY	PLOS Biology	3,618	14.672
	MEDICINE, General and Internal	The New England Journal of Medicine	167,894	44.016
	COMPUTER SCIENCE Cybernetics	Human-Computer Interaction	665	4.682
	MATHEMATICS	Journal of the American Mathematical Society	1,230	2.323
	PHYSICS, Particles and Fields	Journal of Cosmology and Astroparticle Physics	1,890	6.739
	ENGINEERING Civil	Journal of Hydrology	8,658	1.745

JCR Social Sc.	ANTHROPOLOGY	Journal of Human Evolution	2,491	3.077
	SOCIOLOGY	American Journal of Sociology	6,189	3.262
	ECONOMICS	The Quarterly Journal of Economics	6,947	4.775
	HISTORY	The American Historical Review	923	1.623

Table 1. Top-ranking journals by discipline (JCR 2005 data).

The JCR search was generally straightforward because the Subject Category was found to coincide with the name of the discipline chosen for inclusion in the corpus. There were four instances, however, where no single subject category was available but only a number of disciplinary options to choose from. For MEDICINE the broadest of these (i.e. General and Internal Medicine) was selected. For COMPUTER SCIENCE the choice fell on Cybernetics, which is one of the options with the highest IF journals. For PHYSICS, I selected one of the major research areas (Particles and Fields Physics). For ENGINEERING the area selected was Civil Engineering, which is arguably the oldest branch of the discipline.

All of these journals are an expression of international cutting-edge scholarship in their field. The fact that they are all published in the US and Europe depends more directly on the geography of academic publishing than on their identification with Anglo-American (or Western) research communities. Their content is therefore representative of how top scientists across the world communicate their findings to peers through the medium of prominent peer-reviewed journals with a wide academic readership and circulation.

3.3. Text selection

As the purpose of this volume is to explore lexicalisations of value parameters in academic research writing, an effort was made to select publications contributing new evidence or insights to their field. In many disciplines this type of text is labelled 'research article' (RA) but not all journals employ the same label to identify such content. Information on the publisher and academic affiliation of each journal is given below, together with the criteria followed when extracting the ten latest texts from their archives.

- *PLOS Biology* is a "peer-reviewed open-access journal" published monthly since 2003 by the Public Library of Science (USA) and available at <http://biology.plosjournals.org>. Only texts labelled 'Research Article' were downloaded (range 2007-2008).
- *The New England Journal of Medicine*, published weekly by the Massachusetts Medical Society, was established in 1751 and is by far the most influential serial in its field. The latest 'Original Articles' were selected (range 2007-2008).
- *Human-Computer Interaction* was established in 1985 and is published quarterly by Taylor & Francis (Philadephia, USA). The RAs chosen from this journal are all labelled 'Article' (range 2006-2007).
- The *Journal of the American Mathematical Society* has been published quarterly since 1996 by the American Mathematical Society in Providence (USA). RA texts, simply identified as 'Article', were selected (all from 2008).
- The *Journal of Cosmology and Astroparticle Physics* is an international monthly serial established in 2002 by the International School for Advanced Studies (Triest, Italy) and published by IOP Journals (Bristol, UK). RA texts, identified as 'Paper', were selected (all from 2008).
- The *Journal of Hydrology* is a quarterly established in 1963 and published by Elsevier (Amsterdam, Netherlands). The texts chosen for analysis (all from 2008) are labelled 'Research Paper'.
- The *Journal of Human Evolution*, first established in 1972, is published bi-monthly by Elsevier imprint Academic Press (Amsterdam, Netherlands). The RA texts from this journal are simply identified as 'Article' (range 2007-2008).
- The *American Journal of Sociology*, a bi-monthly serial established in 1895, is "the first U.S. scholarly journal in its

field", published by the University of Chicago Press. The RAs extracted are all labelled 'Article' (range 2006-2008).

- *The Quarterly Journal of Economics*, published by MIT Press (USA) was established in 1886 at Harvard University and is described in its homepage as "the oldest professional journal of economics in the English language". Its RA texts are all identified as 'Paper' (range 2007-2008).
- *The American Historical Review*, founded in 1884 and published five times a year by the University of Chicago Press, is the official publication of the American Historical Association. All RA texts in this journal were labelled 'Article' (range 2006-2007).

These articles were usually set apart in the Tables of Contents from such genres as editorials, reviews, round tables, letters and other features. Though different in terms of length and structure, they all provide a rhetorical space where new knowledge claims can be made, whether on mainly experimental or speculative grounds. As our focus here is on disciplinary rather than genre-related variation, the fact that the corpus is not totally homogeneous (in generic terms) justifies the presence of such differences.

A total of 100 RAs in ten academic domains were thus assembled for analysis as detailed above. These were all archived in pdf format and coded alphanumerically by discipline. Full details of each article – including author(s), date, title, host journal, volume and pages – are given in Appendix 1. The downloaded files were then converted and 'sanitised' for further processing as follows:

- removal of ancillary information and paratextual elements, i.e. authors' names and contact details, references, footnotes/endnotes, charts/diagrams and appendices;
- removal of page headers and footers, including page numbers:
- removal of the opening summary or abstract (where present);
- removal of the appended Supporting Information section in BIOLOGY articles.

My decision to omit article abstracts reflects the need for consistency across the corpus (because they were found only in some of the texts considered) and the fact that abstracts in the literature are normally treated as a separate genre to RAs in the literature. On the other hand, Acknowledgements were retained if included in the body of the article.

A second set of changes involved the remaining non-integral elements in each text. These were table/figure captions and complex mathematical expressions (e.g. functions, equations, formulae), which were marked up as follows: captions were identified and prefixed by the string *CAPTION* (where present, caption legends and data were omitted); complex mathematical expressions were identified and replaced by the string *EXPRESSION*. Finally, each file was converted to txt format, with the text-encoding option set to UTF-8 so as to minimise character conversion errors. The 100 plain text files thus obtained were coded and grouped into separate folders for investigation. The detailed list of these texts given in Appendix 1 provides interesting information as to the number/origin of RA authors in different disciplines. At the same time, their titles confirm that the breadth of topics addressed by international academic journals extends far beyond concerns directly linked to the country of publication.

4. Methodology

4.1. Corpus data

The files assembled as described in the previous chapter were grouped by domain and uploaded to a well-known concordancing application – WordSmith Tools, hence WST (Scott 2006) – for textual data extraction. After generating a wordlist (WL) for each set of texts it was possible to access a number of quantitative parameters (as listed in the Statistics window) across the corpus, which totals almost one million words. Detailed data for each text are listed in Appendix 2, while the table below shows how such parameters vary across disciplines.

	Tokens	*WL tokens*	*Types*	*TTR*	*STTR*	*Sentence length*
ANTH	85,958	81,547	7,004	8.59	36.42	23.52
BIO	79,891	74,199	6,495	8.75	35.52	26.49
CS	138,038	133,408	8,244	6.18	37.20	23.87
ECO	106,370	103,399	7,220	6.98	36.63	24.28
ENG	69,885	65,706	5,765	8.77	34.28	26.44
HIST	106,393	105,399	11,757	11.15	45.93	25.55
MATH	171,872	155,407	4,925	3.17	24.71	16.21
MED	39,973	36,846	3,837	10.41	33.29	30.18
PHY	63,032	59,325	3,646	6.15	31.77	26.77
SOC	124,773	121,311	9,513	7.84	41.26	27.51
Overall	*986,185*	*936,547*	*33,073*	*3.53*	*36.10*	*23.32*

Table 1. Corpus data by discipline.

The first column gives the total number of tokens found in each 10-text set. This is followed by a smaller figure, showing the number of tokens actually used in the WL to calculate word frequencies. Next is the number of types (i.e. distinct words) in each set of texts. The relationship between these two variables is given by the type/token ratio (TTR), which provides a rough estimate of lexical density; as the TTR tends to decrease in longer texts, it is better however to consider the standardised type-token ratio (STTR) for contrastive purposes. According to the definition provided in the application, this "is computed every n words as Wordlist goes through each text file [...]. The ratio is calculated for the first 1,000 running words, then calculated afresh for the next 1,000, and so on to the end of your text or corpus" (Scott 2006). The last column shows mean sentence length, based on a count that identifies sentences as a "full-stop, question-mark or exclamation-mark [...] immediately followed by one or more word separators and then a capital letter in the current language, a number or a currency symbol".

These figures highlight a considerable discrepancy in terms of word length between different disciplines, with the most concise RAs in MEDICINE (mean 3,997 tokens per text) followed by PHYSICS (6,303), and the longest in MATHEMATICS (17,187) followed by COMPUTER SCIENCE (13,803); overall, the mean length is 9,861 tokens per text. Despite their limited dimensions, MEDICINE and PHYSICS employ the longest sentences, whereas the shortest are in MATHEMATICS. Finally, lexical density – as measured by STTR – is highest in HISTORY (45.93) followed by SOCIOLOGY (41.26), and lowest in MATHEMATICS (24.71).

The parameters in Table 1 provide only a rough estimate of the lexical repertoire employed by each discipline. The STTR is particularly interesting in this respect, as there may arguably be an inverse relationship between lexical density and frequency of value-laden items. The number of such realisations could therefore be lower when the STTR is higher (i.e. in texts with a wider lexical repertoire). This is only a hypothesis but it is worth testing later in the analysis.

As the analysis progresses, figures will have to be normalised (per 10,000 words) using the WL token count for each discipline to make results comparable across the subcorpora. This is in line with the common procedure adopted in other corpus-based studies of academic writing (cf. Hyland 2001, 2002; Salager-Meyer/Alcaraz Ariza 2003).

4.2. Selection of candidate items

The method adopted to identify the most prominent value-signalling lexical items in the corpus combines quantitative and qualitative techniques, with the former relying largely on wordlists/concordances and the latter on manual inspection of occurrences. Rather than impose a prearranged investigative route on the data, it follows a staged approach that adapts the tools to the data as the analysis unfolds. In so doing, it resembles the so-called *corpus-driven* orientation in corpus linguistics, which allows the methodology to be "justified or modified according to the results of the investigations" (Sinclair 2004: 40). The underlying assumption is that an empiricist methodology should not be subservient to the analyst's preconceptions nor to his/her analytical tools. For this purpose, a pilot study conducted on a small sample of texts (one per discipline) in the early stages of the project helped to test a number of procedural options before engaging in the inspection of the entire corpus. In particular it corroborated Römer's (2008: 126) claim that evaluative lexis cannot be identified with quantitative methods alone and her choice to move "from an automatic computer-based to a mainly manual but in part computer-assisted [...] type of analysis".

Investigation of the corpus began with a scan of the global WL of all the types in the corpus, arranged in order of frequency. This was checked manually for *candidate items* (i.e. potentially value-signalling types). The search was limited to words with ≥100 occurrences in the whole corpus, which on average means as little as one occurrence per text. Out of 1,174 types in this range, a total of 83 candidates were thus isolated for further analysis, taking into account the semantic fields observed in the piloting stage and the recent parameter-based descriptions of evaluative lexis outlined in Chapter 2. As may be noticed in the full list given in Appendix 3, most of these explicit high-frequency evaluators are adjectives (e.g. *new, large, right, simple*), though other parts of speech – especially adverbs (*well, already, typically*) and nouns (*problems, importance, success*) – are also represented. Interestingly, they are all semantically centralised, in line with the general tendency of academic writers to avoid polarised forms in English RAs (Swales and Burke 2003).

The potentially value-laden items were then grouped into categories according to their meaning. These include not only the more obvious associations, such as related lemmas and lexical sets (*interest/interests/interesting, good/better/best*), but also words classifiable as synonyms or antonyms of the target item. The approach taken here goes beyond mere lemmatization (cf. Stubbs 1996, 2001), taking on board Knowles and Zuraidah's (2004: 72) argument that "The concept of the lemma is most useful at a general level in highly abstract discussions of a language, but seems to be of doubtful value for detailed studies of real texts". The classification of candidates by meaning rather than form alone serves two purposes: on the one hand it allows the analyst to concentrate on the more prominent likely value-markers (in terms of overall occurrences); on the other hand it simplifies the retrieval of further related items as the analysis progresses. Table 2 below shows the four main semantic categories of candidate items, in order of size, identified through this procedure.

Goodness	*n*
well	754
positive	357
right	291
good	250
negative	237
problem	229
error	206
best	198
better	197
problems	195
poor	127
Total	*3,041*

Size	*n*
large	615
small	539
larger	261
greater	247
little	184
smaller	165
great	160
limited	150
enough	124
largely	103
substantial	102
Total	*2,650*

Novelty	*n*
new	753
modern	346
recent	188
older	128
novel	122
old	118
Total	*1,655*

Relevance	*n*
important	527
significant	268
major	217
key	172
importance	134
relevant	131
significantly	126
Total	*1,575*

Table 2. Top four categories of candidate items in corpus, listed by frequency.

It is useful to take a close look at these categories, as they not only comprise a considerable amount of tokens but are also mentioned as fundamental variables in the linguistic literature on evaluation. Goodness is of course the most inclusive label, because of its moral, aesthetic and utilitarian implications. Thompson and Hunston state explicitly that "evaluations of good and bad are dependent on the value system underlying the text" (2000: 22). Size is another basic parameter whose non-literal uses are inextricable from argumentative discourse; according to Swales and Burke (2003) it is the second most frequent variable encoded by evaluative adjectives in spoken as well as written academic English. Novelty, despite its prominence here, is cited only in passing by Bednarek (2008). And finally, relevance is listed as a parameter by Thompson and Hunston (2000), while for Bednarek – who prefers the term 'Importance' – it is a core variable whereby speakers judge the world according to "their subjective evaluation of its status in terms of importance, relevance and significance" (2008: 11). This is also the top evaluative category identified in RAs by Swales and Burke (2003).

The assumption made here, therefore, is that each group of items signals an axiological variable or *value* relevant to the disciplinary communities that employ it in the RA genre. The fact that such categories may include a range of realisations whose meanings are not entirely superimposable points to a clustering of 'sub-values' (Bednarek 2008) within academic discourse.

The other, less prominent, lexical groupings identified in the WL but not subjected to further investigation were respectively:

- Value (*value, values*) with 1,080 occurrences;
- Timing (*early, late, earlier, already*) with 881 occurrences;
- Impact (*useful, effective, impact, success, appropriate*) with 791 occurrences;
- Complexity (*simple, complex, simply*) with 657 occurrences;
- Generality (*general, specific*) with 579 occurrences;
- Completeness (*full, complete, entire, whole*) with 529 occurrences;
- Centrality (*central, peripheral*) with 449 occurrences;
- Appeal (*interest, interests, interesting*) with 400 occurrences.

As will be seen later, these candidate items only provide a rough estimate of the actual number of value markers present in the corpus for at least two reasons: firstly because a proportion of these items are irrelevant, being used to convey non-evaluative meanings; secondly because the range of possible realisations of each value also includes other explicit items. It is important to add, however, that most of the categories listed above were observed also in the piloting phase.

Since the aim here is to understand how academic values permeate the lexis of different disciplines, any candidate item that could not be assigned to a superordinate semantic category was excluded from the analysis; significantly, none of these exceeded 215 occurrences. For future reference, however, it may be interesting to record the overall weight of the candidate items identified in the corpus (cf. Appendix 3), which account for around 20,000 tokens. That means an average of 200 occurrences every 10,000 words, i.e. one word in 50.

4.3. Additional candidate items

The explicit signalling of value in RAs also relies on types which, albeit less frequent than the 100 token threshold adopted above, are morphologically and/or semantically inextricable from the candidate items included in the four categories listed in Table 2. The subsequent phase of the analysis centred therefore on the creation of simple lexical sets, capable of completing the picture suggested by the initial candidate items. Under Goodness, for example, the item *positive* warrants the addition of *positively*, *good* of *bad*, *better*, *worse* and so forth. The procedure adopted in each case consisted of four steps:

- lemmatisation of single types;
- construction of lexical sets based on such types;
- addition of antonyms, where available;
- addition of synonyms directly related to each type.

As my focus is on the *most frequent* explicit realisations of the four value categories selected for investigation, the number of additional items was limited to the most adjacent instances (whether in semantic or formal terms). This approach generally excludes less common, polarised or marked forms that are scarcely represented in the core value-marking lexis. It is important to add that goodness, size, novelty and relevance are all – at least in principle – gradable qualities, that is attributes that are interpretable "on a scale which implies a comparison with other possibilities between a positive and negative pole with respect to some polarity" (Downes 2000: 112). When mapping their realisations, the range of types to be considered should therefore take into account the comparative nature of each value along a continuum between maximum positivity and maximum negativity.

4.4. Assessing value-marker status

Given the far-reaching implications of value marking in academic discourse, the identification of words that convey meanings directly linked to such variables is central to the analysis attempted here. While on the surface all the candidates are to a certain extent evaluative, their collocations encode a number of uses that are in fact axiologically neutral. The crtieria for exclusion adopted in the pilot study and later confirmed while scanning the whole corpus, are related to occurrences which are so fully lexicalised that they either inevitable or unrelated to evaluation of what is good/bad, desirable/undesirable in the discipline considered. Value-marker status was therefore denied to tokens whose use and/or collocations assigned them to any of the following classes:

- Proper nouns incorporating evaluative types. These are prevalently geographical (e.g. *New* Orleans, *Great* Britain) but also include buildings (*Central* Station, *Big* Ben), institutions (Tate *Modern*), companies (*General* Electric), surnames (George *Best*) and nicknames (*Little* Dorrit).
- Terms consisting of crystallized noun phrases (*general* manager, *limited* company) which are often antonomastic (*New* Deal, *Old* World).
- Various phrases where the item's original meaning has been lost or is no longer salient (as *well* as, two years *old*, *long* suffering).
- Homonyms within parts of speech (*poor*=bad vs. *poor*=moneyless; *certain*=sure vs. *certain*=some) or across them (*well* as adverb vs. noun; *good* as adjective vs. noun).
- Lexicalised forms linked to discipline-specific terminology, as in '*best* practice' (ECO), '*critical* exponent' (MATH) or 'density *contrast*' (PHY).
- Literal uses of types that signal value only if used metaphorically (*central, dark, depth, highlight, positive*).

To make this selection, a concordance was generated for each of the candidates within the four value categories, including both core items and the additional types described in Section 4.3. The concordances were then manually inspected, checking where necessary also the source texts of specific entries to make sure they qualified for inclusion. Finally, non-relevant entries were individually removed from each concordance and the resulting files saved with the name of the value marker they represented.

4.5. Pilot study

While developing the methodology for this study, its viability was tested on a sample of ten texts (one per discipline) drawn from the wider corpus. The four main value categories identified initially were size, goodness, relevance and value, whose overall presence (63.3 occurrences / 10,000 words) was not too dissimilar from that found here for size, goodness, relevance and novelty (see Chapter 10). This means that novelty (instead of value) appeared among the top four variables in the WL when the procedure developed in the pilot study was applied to the entire corpus. While exploring individual realisations in the corpus, the analysis generally concentrated on co-occurrences to the immediate right or left of each marker, which respectively modulate the intensity of the evaluation and signal what is being evaluated. The phraseological aspects of value marking are not specifically investigated here because they have no direct bearing on the type of judgement expressed or on its target.

For various reasons, the approach developed in the piloting stage does not account for the relative position of value-marking items within texts. The most problematic is the lack of comparable subdivisions in the structure of RAs across journals and disciplines, as shown by the considerable disparity in article length (ranging from an average of under 4,000 words in MED to over 17,000 in MATH) and, more significantly, by the lack of consistency in section labelling. MATH texts, for example, have an Introduction followed by a list of Theorems, while HIST texts have no headings at all; only BIO, CS, MED and PHY are organised in a way resembling the IMRD pattern. Such differences may be partly ascribed to the editorial guidelines of each journal but are more likely to reflect variations in the level of structural standardisation appropriate to each discipline and in the amount of metadiscoursal information that readers expect section headings to provide. It would therefore be arduous to force so many different patterns (or the rhetorical freedom they express) into a single coding/tagging inventory applicable to the whole corpus. Analysts interested in value marking within a specific article section may have to limit their analysis to domains whose RAs adopt a similar (i.e. comparable) macrostructure.

Another option explored in the pilot study was the use of a questionnaire to elicit from expert informants information as to what values define good scholarship and a good research article in their field. A 12-item online survey was set up through SurveyGizmo (<http://www.surveygizmo.com>), based on all the explicit variables identified in the corpus sample: (in alphabetic order) centrality, clarity, consistency, goodness, inclusiveness, novelty, relevance, simplicity, strength, success, utility and value. The introductory question was "To the best of your knowledge as a scholar, specify which of the following qualities of research are most desirable in a research article published in a top journal in your discipline", with each item to be ranked as: extremely important / very important / important / scarcely important / not important. As recommended by Sudman and Bradburn (1982), care was taken to avoid responses driven by the language employed rather than by the respondent's ideas and beliefs.

The questionnaire was then tested on a group of colleagues at the University of Bergamo and suitably adjusted. In particular, it appeared advisable to clearly explain the survey's purpose and background in the email invitation to participate, because "the questionnaire designer may intend one interpretation yet find that individuals presented with the question adopt an alternate understanding that, in retrospect, appears quite reasonable" (Willis 2005: 4). The editorial board of each journal represented in the corpus and dozens of individual scholars were contacted for feedback, but this proved to be almost impossible to obtain. Among the few who responded, most declined to participate (despite assurance that the data gathered would remain entirely anonymous) or failed to complete the questionnaire, so it was eventually put aside. As a tool for gauging authorial awareness of textual variables, surveys are perhaps more suited to studies targeting individual scholars (cf. Hyland 2008, 2009) rather than entire disciplinary communities.

4.6. Linguistic analysis

Having selected a suitable range of value markers, the analysis has to reach further down into the corpus to verify how they are distributed across disciplines. The purpose is twofold: on the one hand to assess the tendency of a given discipline to signal certain values rather than others; on the other hand the need to describe the kind of entities associated with such values, whether in their positive or negative instantiations. These two aspects are related more broadly to the fact that evaluation is a phenomenon combining a *qualitative dimension* (i.e. the kind of quality attributed to a referent) and a *referential dimension* (the object of evaluation). These are both instrumental to the genre employed – a point first noted by Thompson and Hunston (2000) – and to the interpersonal plane of communication, as the author asserts his/her role and relationship with readers. The tools employed are consistent with earlier efforts (cf. Biber *et al.* 2004b) to combine corpus-linguistic and discourse-analytic research methodologies when accounting for lexical variation in academic genres.

4.6.1. Distribution of values across disciplines

The purpose at this point is to understand how the lexico-semantic categories singled out for analysis are distributed across the RA corpus. The analysis is based on the criteria listed above, whereby each occurrence of a target item is checked in context (through a concordance list) to confirm its use as a value marker. It is then possible to calculate the total number of occurrences of that item in the ten domains represented in the corpus. In order to make the data comparable across disciplines irrespective of their number of tokens, the figures were then normalised by 10,000 words, which is the standard parameter used in similar studies (cf. Hyland 2000). The reference length of each section of the corpus used for this purpose is that given earlier in Table 1 (WL tokens), namely: 155,407 words for mathematics; 133,408 for computer science; 121,311 for sociology;

105,399 for history; 103,399 for economics; 81,547 for anthropology; 74,199 for biology; 65,706 for engineering; 59,325 for physics; 36,846 for medicine.

The findings of this first level of investigation (and of the further two steps described below) are illustrated in Chapters 5 to 8, which deal separately with the four academic values chosen for in-depth analysis. Besides reporting the most significant quantitative differences between domains, however, an attempt is made to interpret such data and to account for the fact that some of these values appear to correlate with certain disciplines rather than others. Where available, the results of other studies of academic discourse are called upon to assist in the interpretation or further contextualise the results of the present research.

As most of the markers under scrutiny are either adjectives or adverbs, it will help to bear in mind, when reporting their frequency, the subdivision adopted in Biber's (2004) analysis of the TOEFL 2000 Spoken and Written Academic Language Corpus. The semantic categories of adjectives and adverbs are of special importance as they allow us to further qualify target items according to their meaning. Although no research genres were covered in Biber's corpus, it is notable that attitudinal adverbs are particularly prominent – in terms of positive loading – in the 'academic stance' mode associated with the overt expression of persuasion (Biber *et al.* 2004a: 59).

4.6.2. Qualified entities

The second aspect to be dealt with when investigating a target item is the object of evaluation, i.e. the entity to which a given value is assigned or denied. In the piloting stage certain values were found to correlate more directly with the facts/data considered, others with the research based on such phenomena and yet others with the impact of their presentation. The preliminary assumption made when looking at qualified entities was that variation occurred both within values and across them. Early results thus suggested that value may be viewed as a quality assigned to one of three elements in the process of knowledge construction:

Qualified entity	*Prevalent value*
Facts	Inclusiveness
Science	Goodness
Impact	Novelty

Table 3. Possible research-internal correlations.

The values associated with each of these entities may plausibly comprise the personal qualities of the actors involved in their construction or, impersonally, to the various claims and options with which they are confronted (theories, models, mathematical expressions, standard procedures, statistics). The framework is internal to research and its three components follow each other cyclically, with impact prompting the investigation of further facts, in an endless cumulative evolutionary process. However, we cannot rule out the presence of research-external entities as a potential target of value judgements made by scholars. After all, academic values assert their authority beyond their immediate territory, into the spheres of education, policy-making and the economy.

4.6.3. Collocational evidence

In order to explore how the target items are employed within sentences, their co-text was analysed using the Collocate function of WST concordances. This highlights recurring lexico-grammatical patterns formed by a given word with its collocates. The 'collocational horizon' (i.e. the number of tokens to the left/right of the search-word) was set to a maximum of three words. As these computational tools only provide a rough picture of the linguistic phenomena associated with value marking, prominent collocates were also inspected manually for more qualitative evidence whose features may enrich our understanding of how values are textualised by phraseological units as well as single lexemes in published research.

4.7. Interpretation of data

The four values analysed in this study all pertain to aspects of research that are deemed to be worth signalling overtly by academics. They are by no means the only values at play, given the inevitability of 'textual silence' (Huckin 1996) in academic discourse and the wealth of less evident realisations involving various types of indirect speech acts. By concentrating on the most frequent explicit markers as an entry point for analysis, the methodology adopted here seeks to avoid some of the pitfalls associated with purely quantitative approaches to the identification of evaluative meaning (cf. Römer 2008). At the same time, the shift from evaluative language as a whole to value-marking lexemes alone considerably simplifies the identification of target items as it does not extend to epistemic evaluators, speech-act verbs or types whose evaluative meaning is mainly connotational. This makes it possible to assess the relative weight of value-laden lexis without having to search for the hidden meaning of claims whose presence and/or polarity are not accessible without detailed insider knowledge.

The chapters that follow describe the most salient 'value judgements' (interpretable in terms of desirability) encoded by academic texts, also in the light of previous small-scale studies of academic stance – that is of how scholars textualise "personal feelings, attitudes, value judgements, or assessments" (Biber *et al.* 1999: 966). The prestige of the RA genre and of the international journals considered here adds further authority to the value claims found in the corpus. In addition, the various facets of axiological variation will be interpreted bearing in mind evidence from other multi-disciplinary corpora targeting the linguistic behaviour of academic cultures in different domains – most notably, Hyland (1998, 2000) and Fløttum *et al.* (2006a).

The conclusions drawn at the end of this volume will highlight prominent aspects of the *value system* (Thompson/Hunston 2000: 22) that underlies disciplinary discourses. Even though the marking of desirable and/or salient aspects of research may diverge considerably both in terms of frequency and of wording, the relative pervasiveness of the parameters singled out for investigation suggests that (apart from disciplinary differences) there is an axiological core that belongs to academic culture as a whole. The common roots of Western academic thought, combined with the centripetal institutional forces affecting tertiary education in the modern world, may partly account for such similarities.

No methodological approach would be complete, however, without recognition of its potential shortcomings. In our case, the phenomena under scrutiny are accessed through a procedure that takes lexical visibility (i.e. the semantic transparency of lexis) as a valid entry point for analysis. The simple fact that certain values are referred to explicitly in the corpus is considered to be highly indicative of their importance and the following corpus exploration is conducted on such a basis. On the other hand, this volume makes no claim to map out the *entire* value system of academia, with its potentially unlimited spectrum of linguistic realisations. The textual evidence described in the following chapters may be seen as the tip of an iceberg whose dimensions remain unfathomable. Unlike real icebergs, however, its visible portion has been skilfully constructed and formed by expert hands to communicate what lies at the heart of the entire mass: for this reason it deserves scrutiny in its own right, regardless of any inevitable limitations.

5. Goodness markers

For the purposes of this chapter, goodness is defined as a value that points to qualities that are viewed as positive (or, conversely, as negative) without need to further specify their nature. Vagueness is thus co-integral to the construction of a value which, also in academic discourse, allows the writer to commend or condemn a given referent in very general terms, while placing on the reader the onus to locate whatever led to something being judged as *good* or *bad*. As this is the broadest category identified in the corpus, it is perhaps not surprising that it counts the highest number of candidate items among the four values selected for investigation. Whatever the context, successful communication depends on the interlocutors' ability to find a common ground made of shared meanings that include an essential distinction between good and bad. The axiological structure of this dyad embraces different subvalues, since the 'goodness' of something may pertain to such aspects as its source, appearance, rationality or morality. Anything that diminishes or undermines this quality is perceived, by contrast, as 'bad'. At the same time, the underspecification inherent in the concept of goodness means that it allows for a range of lexicalisations well beyond those found at the top of the global wordlist WL.

5.1. Identification of value-marker status

Every occurrence of the candidate items listed in Table 2 of the previous chapter (*well, positive, right, good, negative, problem, error, best, better, problems, poor*) had to be manually inspected to ensure it encoded an evaluative meaning. The procedure adopted takes into account the different functions and meanings taken on by each item in the corpus. The criteria for excluding certain occurrences rather than others are described word by word below.

Well

Only 227 instances of this marker, out of a total of 754, were found to be relevant. The cases qualifying for exclusion were respectively:

- the fully lexicalised forms *well-being, well-known, well off, well-to-do*;
- the phrases *as well* (=also) and *as well as* (=besides);
- the noun *well* (=hole in ground for drawing water);
- emphatic *well* (=much, very) (e.g. *well ahead/before/beyond/within*);
- the verb *well* (=rise to surface);
- the interjection *well* (e.g. *Well, of course*);
- adverbial *well* (=actually) (e.g. *It may well be*);

Positive

As my concern is with the writer's evaluation of a referent as 'good', only instances conveying such a judgement were considered. This yielded a total of 51 relevant occurrences out of 357. The uses excluded from the count comprised:

- *positive* as a mathematical concept (+ on a scale) (e.g. *positive correlation/ number/relationship/slope*);
- positive as the outcome of a laboratory test (e.g. *IgM positive, HIV-positive*);
- the collocations *positive answer* and *positive response* (=yes).

Some of these (especially the phrase *positive relationship*) required further reading of the co-text to distinguish between statistical and evaluative uses.

Right

Only 13 out of 291 occurrences were considered to be relevant. Making the distinction was not particularly difficult, as it involved removing instances of:

- *right*, as opposed to *left*;
- the noun *right* (=entitlement);
- *right* used as an interjection (e.g. *Right, let's go*);
- the phrase *in its/their own right*;
- emphatic *right* (e.g. *right away/after/next to*).

Good

More than half of the occurrences – 155 out of 250 – were relevant. They were all adjectives, with only two exceptions. The items removed from this count were respectively:
- *good* as an object of trade (=merchandise);
- the fully lexicalised form *good faith*;
- the phrase *a good deal (of)*;
- the idiom *cut a good figure*;
- proper nouns (e.g. *Carolina Council for the Common Good*);
- *Good* as a surname;
- the mathematical term *κ-good.*

Negative

The criteria applied here mirror those used for the lemma *positive* and left 74 relevant items out of 237. Those excluded were:
- mathematical meanings (e.g. *negative correlation/regression/ integers*);
- the outcome of laboratory tests (e.g. *HIV-negative*);
- the collocations *negative answer* and *negative response* (=no).

Cases such as *negative relationship* and *negative effect* had to be double checked to ensure that they were not being used in their statistical sense.

Problem

More than half of the occurrences – 149 out of 229 – were judged to be relevant. Those excluded from the count were largely limited to ECO and MATH, when they denoted a deliberate theoretical construct rather than a difficulty encountered by the researcher. A structural cue to this distinction is that between the patterns *the x problem*, and *the problem of x*.

Error

After inspecting all occurrences of this marker, only 30 out of 206 were included in the count. Those removed were respectively:

- references to statistical error (e.g. *random/standard/sampling/measurement error*);
- the phrase *trial and error.*

Since statistical error is inherent in empirical research and is judged negatively only if it exceeds a certain threshold, it cannot be regarded as a desirable/undesirable feature in its own right and was therefore omitted.

Best

Only 11 occurrences out of 198 were omitted, all involving the economic term *best practice(s)* which incorporates a fully lexicalised form of this lexeme.

Better

All the occurrences were relevant, with the exception of a proper noun phrase (*Committee for a Better Louisiana*).

Problems

Albeit proportionally negligible (8 out of 195), a few occurrences had to be excluded from the count after applying the criteria listed above for the lemma *problem*.

Poor

A large number of occurrences of *poor* were not considered as they were found to express a monetary concept (=impecunious) rather than the evaluative meaning (=bad) sought for here, thus leaving only 44 relevant entries out of 127.

5.2. Preliminary results

The total frequency of these lexical items when used to mark value is summarised in Table 1, with the order in which they appear adjusted to reflect the number of relevant occurrences. The most striking result is that less than half of all instances (43%) are classifiable as value markers – which justifies the manual inspection procedure adopted here. Another aspect is the highly varying proportion of value-marking occurrences for each item, ranging from just under 100% for *best* to a minimum of 4% for *right*. These figures are clearly linked to the different degree of polysemy and/or homonymy associated with certain words in the list.

Item	*Value-marking*	*All*
well	227	754
better	194	197
best	187	198
problems	187	195
good	155	250
problem	149	229
negative	74	237
positive	51	357
poor	44	127
error	30	206
right	13	291
Total	*1,311*	*3,041*

Table 1. Goodness-marking items listed by frequency.

While each entry in the table is related to the notion of goodness, it is useful to distinguish between morphological forms of the same word (i.e. *problem/problems*), grammatical variants (*good/better/best/well*), different parts of speech and entries signalling related subvalues, such as correctness (*error*, *right*). These distinctions were made in the subsequent stage of data collection, which extended the search for relevant lemmas beyond the narrow confines of top-ranking occurrences identified in the global WL.

5.3. Additional items

Most of the additional items to be included in the analysis belong to lexical sets containing the markers identified so far which, as explained in Chapter 4, were integrated with antonyms and occasionally with synonyms pertaining to the same semantic field. Again, these had to be manually inspected to confirm their relevance to the value under scrutiny. The five resulting groupings and further criteria adopted for each addition are detailed below.

Group A. *Good, better, best, well, improve* | bad/poor, worse, worst, badly/poorly, worsen**

Items in this group lie at the core of the value and belong to two clearly-distinguishable polarities. In the positive field, existing items were integrated with a verb expressing variation towards goodness (*improve*) in its various conjugations, plus the adjective *improved* and the nominalisation *improvement*. In line with the criteria adopted earlier, the fully lexicalised comparatives *better off* and *worse off* (=richer/poorer) were omitted. The negative field only included the lemma *poor*, so it had to be reconstructed using antonymous dyads based on their positive counterparts. Finally, all the occurrences of *better* and *worse* were inspected to distinguish between adjectival/ adverbial uses. The asterisk indicates that a verb was considered in all its morphological variants.

Group B. *Positive, positively | negative, negatively*

Two adverbial forms had to be added to complete this grouping. The criteria for inclusion are the same as those followed for the adjectives. Moreover, *positively* was excluded wherever it meant 'certainly' (e.g. *to positively identify*) or 'yes' (*participants responded positively*) and in its mathematical sense (*positively charged/correlated*). Among the few occurrences of the noun, only *negative* (one occurrence) was found to be relevant.

Group C. *Right, rightly* | *wrong, wrongly*

Only the first of these items (*right*) was present in the initial list. The others were an adverbial version of the former (*rightly*) and its two related antonyms (*wrong, wrongly*). Because of their different meaning, the plural forms *rights* and *wrongs* were excluded from the count of value-marking instances.

Group D. *Problem, problems, problematic, problematically, unproblematic*

Unlike the previous groups, this and the following do not have a positive counterpart because they only denote deviation from a default condition. Based on the first two lemmas, their adjectival and adverbial equivalents were added; subsequently the negated form *unproblematic*, present only in one instance, was included in the search. Albeit very rare, the verb *problematise** was excluded because of its intentional (constructive) meaning.

Group E. *Error, errors, erroneous, erroneously*

Starting from the existing item *error*, its plural, adjectival and adverbial forms were included in the analysis following the same criteria adopted earlier.

5.4. Overall results

After the inclusion of additional value-markers and the classification of all relevant items into groups, the results become more significant. They are summarised in Table 2, where the figures in brackets indicate the total number of occurrences when greater than those with value-marking status. The most notable point in their distribution is the overall prevalence of Group A items, accounting for no less than 64% of all value markers. In the positive field, the base form *good* is less frequent than its comparative/superlative or adverbial equivalents – a result that indicates a tendency to signal goodness comparatively or as a procedural quality (*well*) rather than an absolute feature.

	Item	*n*	*Subtotal*
Group A	good (adj)	(248) 149	
	good (n)	2	
	better (adj)	(197) 123	
	better (adv)	70	
	best (adj)	(198) 187	
	well (adv)	(754) 227	
	improve* (v)	110	
	improvement/s (n)	49	
	improved (adj)	16	933
	bad (adj)	33	
	poor (adj)	(127) 44	
	worse (adj)	8	
	worse (adv)	7	
	worst (adj)	16	
	badly (adv)	14	
	poorly (adv)	34	
	worsen* (v)	2	
	worsening (adj)	3	161
Group B	positive (adj)	(357) 51	
	positively (adv)	(40) 6	57
	negative (adj)	(237) 73	
	negative/s (n)	1	
	negatively (adv)	(19) 3	77
Group C	right (adj)	(291) 13	
	rightly (adv)	4	17
	wrong (adj)	12	
	wrong (n)	2	
	wrongly (adv)	1	15
Group D	problem/s (n)	(424) 336	
	problematic (adj)	26	
	problematically (adv)	1	
	unproblematic (adj)	1	364
Group E	error/s (n)	(305) 79	
	erroneous (adj)	4	
	erroneously (adv)	1	84
Total			*(3,516) 1,708*

Table 2. Full list of goodness markers (by group).

A second aspect that deserves attention is that items based on a positive/negative dyad (Groups A-C) are considerably more common than those signalling a specific flaw (Groups D-E). Taken together, the former account for almost three quarters (1,265/1,708) of all the markers considered. Since the latter lack a positive counterpart, however, this finding may be related to the overall preference for positive – as opposed to negative – lexicalisations of goodness, with items in the positive polarity of Groups A-C comprising 59% (1,007/1,708) of all goodness markers. Although these do not necessarily belong to positive evaluative acts, it is significant that as a whole the explicit lexicalisations of desirable traits prevail over those of undesirable traits, at least in the case of goodness.

The discrepancy observed in many cases between the number of corpus tokens (total 3,516) and those directly relevant to this study (total 1,708) confirms the value of a procedure based not only on quantitative tools but also on close scrutiny of the co-text associated with each item. This approach is admittedly laborious, though not excessively so for a corpus of almost one million words; furthermore, it allows the analyst to identify the actual range of realisations embedded in a corpus inductively, rather than through a predefined model, and will also be followed later in this chapter.

The same data can also be interpreted according to the part of speech used to mark goodness. When classified as adjectives, adverbs, verbs and nouns (Table 3), the results highlight interesting differences in the distribution of items – the most noticeable being a prevalence of adjectives that in Biber's (2004) taxonomy are ranked as 'evaluative attributive'. On average, 44% of goodness markers are adjectives, followed by nouns and adverbs, with only a fraction of verbs (7%). Turning from the dyads in Groups A-C dyads to those in Groups D-E, there is a marked shift from adverbs to nouns, which suggests a tendency to mention more general qualities as procedural aspects through verb/adjective modifying adverbs, while specific flaws (*problems* and *errors*) are more likely to be nominalised.

Group	A		B		C		D	E	All
	Pos	Neg	Pos	Neg	Pos	Neg			
Adjectives	475 51%	104 65%	51 89%	73 95%	13 76%	12 80%	27 7%	4 5%	759 44%
Adverbs	297 32%	55 34%	6 11%	3 4%	4 24%	2 13%	1 <1%	1 1%	369 22%
Verbs	110 12%	2 1%	-	-	-	-	-	-	112 7%
Nouns	51 5%	-	-	1 1%	-	1 7%	336 92%	79 94%	468 27%
Total	*933*	*161*	*57*	*77*	*17*	*15*	*364*	*84*	*1,708*

Table 3. Parts of speech serving as goodness markers (occurrences).

In terms of absolute frequency, the second most common item after positive Group A adjectives, is the Group D noun *problem*. As will be seen later in this chapter, *problem* deserves special attention as a negative marker because of its semantic fuzziness. ‘Problems’ are in the main undesirable – and to a large extent unpredictable – phenomena, but at the same time they represent challenges that may open up new avenues of enquiry and in this sense signal a (more or less) desirable development in the researcher’s narrative. The overall impression therefore is that RA authors are particularly prone to highlight goodness in their field by referring on the one hand to what is *good*, and on the other hand to aspects identified as *problems*.

5.5. Distribution across disciplines

While the figures in Table 3 are representative of RA writing in general, they provide no evidence of how and to what extent specific disciplinary communities signal goodness in their lexis. In order to shed light on this dimension, the analysis needs to delve further into the corpus, taking into account the number of relevant realisations present in each of the ten subcorpora considered:

Item	*ANTH*	*BIO*	*CS*	*ECO*	*ENG*	*HIST*	*MATH*	*MED*	*PHY*	*SOC*	*All*
Group A positive	11.3	7.1	12.9	14.9	22.5	11.0	2.3	9.5	6.4	7.3	9.96
good (adj)	(16)	(10)	(24)	(36)	(15)	(15)	(4)	(2)	(14)	(13)	(149)
good (n)	-	-	-	-	-	(2)	-	-	-	-	(2)
better (adj)	(12)	(1)	(20)	(35)	(13)	(19)	(3)	(2)	(4)	(14)	(123)
better (adv)	(4)	(4)	(21)	(14)	(8)	(7)	-	(3)	(1)	(8)	(70)
best (adj)	(11)	(5)	(16)	(16)	(68)	(32)	(4)	(5)	(5)	(25)	(187)
well (adv)	(39)	(28)	(42)	(25)	(17)	(23)	(21)	(1)	(8)	(23)	(227)
improve* (v)	(7)	(3)	(30)	(14)	(19)	(15)	(3)	(12)	(4)	(3)	(110)
improvement/s (n)	(3)	(2)	(16)	(11)	(6)	(3)	-	(5)	(1)	(2)	(49)
improved (adj)	-	-	(3)	(3)	(2)	-	(1)	(5)	(1)	(1)	(16)
Group A negative	1.0	1.5	1.7	5.0	0.8	2.9	-	1.3	0.7	1.9	1.7
bad (adj)	-	-	(5)	(11)	-	(11)	-	-	(2)	(4)	(33)
poor (adj)	(1)	(3)	(11)	(11)	(1)	(2)	-	(3)	(2)	(10)	(44)
worse (adj)	-	-	-	(2)	-	(4)	-	(1)	-	(1)	(8)
worse (adv)	-	-	(1)	(5)	-	(1)	-	-	-	-	(7)
worst (adj)	-	-	(2)	(5)	-	(8)	-	-	-	(1)	(16)
badly (adv)	-	-	-	(13)	-	-	-	-	-	(1)	(14)
poorly (adv)	(7)	(7)	(4)	(4)	(4)	(3)	-	(1)	-	(4)	(34)
worsen* (v)	-	(1)	-	-	-	-	-	-	-	(1)	(2)
worsening (adj)	-	-	-	-	-	(2)	-	-	-	(1)	(3)
Group B positive	0.1	-	2.2	1.2	-	0.4	-	-	0.2	0.7	0.6
positive (adj)	(1)	-	(28)	(10)	-	(4)	-	-	(1)	(7)	(51)
positively (adv)	-	-	(2)	(3)	-	-	-	-	-	(1)	(6)
Group B negative	-	-	3.7	0.1	-	0.6	-	-	-	1.7	0.8
negative (adj)	-	-	(49)	-	-	(5)	-	-	-	(19)	(73)
negative/s (n)	-	-	-	-	-	(1)	-	-	-	-	(1)
negatively (adv)	-	-	-	(1)	-	-	-	-	-	(2)	(3)
Group C positive	-	-	0.5	0.3	-	0.6	-	-	-	0.1	0.2
right (adj)	-	-	(6)	(2)	-	(4)	-	-	-	(1)	(13)
rightly (adv)	-	-	(1)	(1)	-	(2)	-	-	-	-	(4)
Group C negative	0.2	-	0.4	-	-	0.4	-	-	0.2	0.2	0.2
wrong (adj)	(1)	-	(5)	-	-	(2)	-	-	(1)	(3)	(12)
wrong (n)	-	-	-	-	-	(2)	-	-	-	-	(2)
wrongly (adv)	(1)	-	-	-	-	-	-	-	-	-	(1)
Group D	2.4	0.5	12.1	2.0	1.7	4.4	1.8	3.0	4.4	2.9	3.9
problem/s (n)	(16)	(3)	(155)	(20)	(10)	(42)	(28)	(9)	(24)	(29)	(336)
problematic (adj)	(4)	(1)	(5)	(1)	(1)	(4)	-	(2)	(2)	(6)	(26)
problematically (adv)	-	-	(1)	-	-	-	-	-	-	-	(1)
unproblematic (adj)	-	-	-	-	-	(1)	-	-	-	-	(1)
Group E	1.2	0.7	1.9	3.2	0.8	0.2	0.1	-	0.2	0.2	9.0
error/s (n)	(9)	(5)	(22)	(33)	(4)	(2)	(1)	-	(1)	(2)	(79)
erroneous (adj)	-	-	(3)	-	(1)	-	-	-	-	-	(4)
erroneously (adv)	(1)	-	-	-	-	-	-	-	-	-	(1)
Total	*16.3*	*9.8*	*35.4*	*26.7*	*25.7*	*20.5*	*4.2*	*13.8*	*12.0*	*15.0*	*18.2*

Table 4. Distribution of goodness markers across disciplines.

To make results comparable across domains, the occurrences shown in Table 4 have been normalised by 10,000 words, with non-normalised counts shown in round brackets. There are of course many possible approaches to such detailed data. The most straightforward is to consider the relative presence of markers in each of the ten domains – a result summarised in the last line of Table 4. The variation covers a considerable range, from a minimum of 4.2 markers in MATH to a maximum of 35.4 in CS. More specifically, four disciplines (CS, ECO, ENG, HIST) occupy the ≥20 bracket, four others (ANTH, SOC, MED, PHY) the ≥10 bracket, and only two (BIO, MATH) fall below this level. The general impression is that goodness or its absence are more lexically marked in the social sciences and humanities than in the natural sciences. But the distinction is by no means clear-cut, with the mathematical sciences (CS, MATH) at opposite extremes of the range. To gain a better understanding of the phenomena underlying these figures, it is necessary to extend the analysis to other aspects of the target realisations, such as the type of entities qualified and their collocational horizon.

The contribution of the different groups is also highly varied, albeit Group A accounts for most occurrences in all but one (i.e. CS) of the disciplines. Their dimensions are graphically illustrated in Figure 1 below, where the various segments of each column represent the (normalised) number of markers in each group, with Group A positioned at the bottom of the columns and E at the top. While Group A items were generally prevalent throughout the corpus, as observed earlier, the presence of the other four groups is very dissimilar from one discipline to another and almost negligible in at least two cases (ENG and BIO).

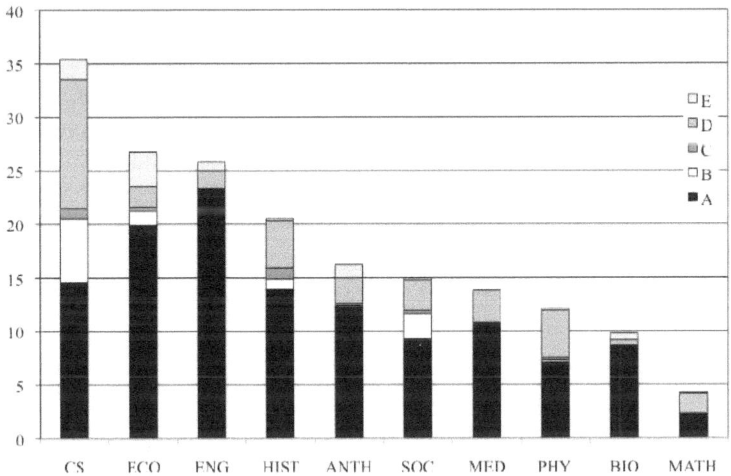

Figure 1. Goodness markers by group and discipline (norm. occurrences).

To do full justice to these results, it is helpful to look also at the proportional contribution of these markers to each domain. Relatively speaking, Group A accounts for over half items in all the disciplines except CS, whereas Group D contributes 30% or more in three domains (MATH, CS, PHY).

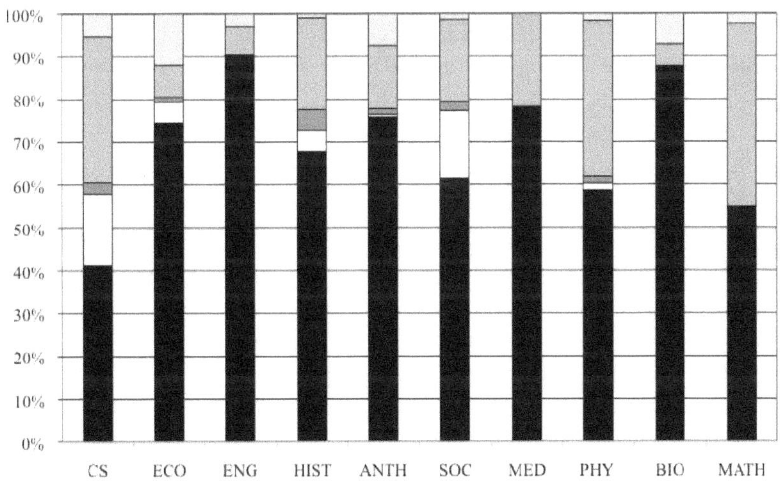

Figure 2. Relative weight of each group by discipline (percentage).

The balancing of lexemes signalling the presence vs. the absence of a given value is also indicative of disciplinary preferences when dealing with goodness. If the (normalised) number of positive markers in Groups A-C is plotted against their negative counterparts in the same groups and all those in Groups D-E, the result across the corpus is as follows:

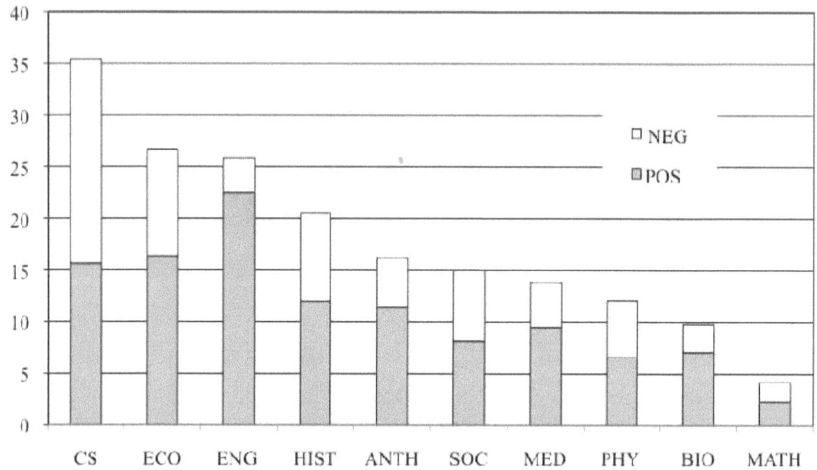

Figure 3. Positive vs. negative goodness markers by discipline (norm. occurrences).

Figure 3 graphically illustrates the fact that, in absolute terms, ENG is the most 'positive' discipline and CS the most 'negative', while in three domains (CS, SOC, MATH) the balance between polarities is approximately even. These results confirm that explicit indication of what is wrong or bad or problematic in research is generally less frequent than mention of what is right or good. CS constitutes the only exception to this trend, with 56% items (19.8/35.4) in the negative field, mostly due to the prominence of *problem/s*. The nature of this discipline and of the specialism considered (human-computer interaction, centred on technical trials and troubleshooting strategies) may help to explain its special position in the corpus.

5.6. Different parts of speech

The saliency given to different parts of speech among these markers by academic authors may vary from one discipline to another. In order to map such variations, the quantitative evidence presented earlier was retabulated to measure the normalised prominence of each part of speech, as well as its weight (as a percentage of all items) in the ten domains considered. The results are shown below:

	ANTH	*BIO*	*CS*	*ECO*	*ENG*	*HIST*	*MATH*	*MED*	*PHY*	*SOC*
Adjectives	5.6	2.7	13.3	12.8	15.4	10.7	0.8	5.4	5.4	8.7
	35%	27%	38%	48%	60%	52%	18%	39%	45%	58%
Adverbs	6.4	5.3	5.4	6.4	4.4	3.4	1.4	1.4	1.5	3.2
	39%	54%	15%	24%	17%	17%	32%	10%	13%	22%
Nouns	3.4	1.3	14.5	6.2	3.0	4.9	1.9	3.8	4.4	2.7
	21%	14%	41%	23%	12%	24%	45%	27%	37%	18%
Verbs	0.8	0.5	2.2	1.3	2.9	1.4	0.2	3.3	0.7	0.3
	5%	5%	6%	5%	11%	7%	5%	24%	5%	2%

Table 5. Use of different parts of speech by discipline, normalised data.

Although part-of-speech frequencies generally reflect the order shown earlier in Figure 1 (i.e. CS, ECO, ENG, HIST, ANTH, SOC, MED, PHY, BIO, MATH), there are several deviations worth noting. The most noticeable are listed below:

- Adjectives are more prominent in ENG (15.4 occurrences) than in CS (13.3), which means that engineers are more likely to adjectivise goodness than would be expected, given the higher level of goodness marking in CS.
- Adverbs are more salient than suggested by the discipline's goodness-marking intensity in ANTH (6.4) and surprisingly in BIO (5.3), while they are under-represented in ENG (4.4) and HIST (3.4).
- Nouns are particularly under-represented in ENG (3.0), which is therefore less prone than expected to signal *problems* and *errors*.
- Finally, verbs peak not in CS or ECO but in MED (3.3), thanks to the saliency given to the verb *improve*.

- If the same results are interpreted in terms of relative discipline-internal percentages rather than normalised frequencies, they provide further evidence of the proclivities of each domain. More specifically, adjectivation is most salient in ENG (60% markers), adverbs in BIO (54%), nouns in MATH (45%) and verbs in MED (24%).

The position of adjectives is another important variable, because it shows how far their meaning is syntactically foregrounded by RA authors. Among the averages for each group shown in Table 6 below, the most noticeable is that only Group D qualifiers (*problematic/ unproblematic*) are prevalently predicative. The criticism embedded in such lexemes seems to reflect a choice that prevails only once in the other groups (in the case of the negative qualifier *worse*).

Adjectives	*Predicative*	*Attributive*	*all*
Group A	13%	87%	579
Group B	4%	96%	124
Group C	24%	76%	25
Group D	78%	22%	27
Group E	-	100%	4
Total	*14%*	*86%*	*759*

Table 6. Syntactic position of goodness-marking adjectives (by group).

5.7. Qualified entities and realisations

We will now move from the overall distribution of goodness markers to their function and actual realisations at a microlinguistic level. For this purpose, their use was assessed contextually, using both WST and manual investigation to identify (i) what type of referents were qualified by such items across the corpus, and (ii) the wording of the target utterances, with special attention paid to the part of speech involved and its collocates. The paragraphs that follow illustrate these features for the five groups of markers considered, with a focus on the most frequent items in each group.

5.7.1. Group A

Most of the words in the first group are 'evaluative attributive adjectives' (Biber 2004) communicating the concept of goodness either in absolute terms or as relative to another entity. The core adjective *good* appears attributively in 66% of cases (98/149), qualifying above all to the procedural value of data, statistical tools or modelling techniques, as shown by its top R1 collocates *example/s* (6), *agreement* (4), *approximation* (4), *fit* (4) and *representation* (3). Most of the collocations in ECO, on the other hand, hinge on the term *management*. Such uses are illustrated for each discipline by the following examples (my emphasis here and subsequently):

(1) Rowlands et al. (2006) have shown that the ratio between crown height and root height is a *good predictor* of gingival emergence times. ANTH

(2) An ME that falls within 61 indicates *good estimation* of a property value by the niche model (see Materials and Methods section Niche model analyses). BIO

(3) Those that had a *good information-sharing practice* have a subsequent decrease in their decision effectiveness. CS

(4) In particular, we hypothesize that firms in a high-skill environment may find *good human-capital management practices* relatively more important than those in a low-skill environment. ECO

(5) Both maps show *good agreement* between the forested, grassland and shrub-covered areas along with the location of water bodies. ENG

(6) That does not mean that public healing is a *good model* for the future of medicine in Africa. Nor does it mean that 'communitarian sentiments' should be promoted as some sort of 'antidote to imperialistic universality'. HIST

(7) We rely on Proposition 4.4 to prove the existence of *good local space-time coordinates* on MI. MATH

(8) The results of this trial indicate that, despite *good biologic plausibility*, acyclovir at a dose of 400 mg twice daily is not a viable public health intervention for preventing infection with HIV. MED

(9) Space-based experiments, such as LISA [2] and BBO [3], will have remarkably *good sensitivity* at frequencies that coincide with the redshifted spectrum of GWs produced during an electroweak phase transition at temperatures T~100 GeV. PHY

(10) Because there is substantial fluctuation in individuals' economic circumstances in the period of early adulthood [...] researchers studying economic mobility typically argue that income or earnings in those years does not provide a *good representation* of adult 'permanent' income or earnings. SOC

There are a small number of cases, however, where *good* denotes an intellectual activity carried out by humans. The link is indirect and by means of nominalised agentive verbs or speech-act nouns implying human engagement:

(11) The economical exchange of kinetic and potential energy during walking in African women [...] may assist carrying, although there is no *good explanation* for the zero energy cost "free ride" phenomenon. ANTH

(12) A *good starting point* is Max Weber's discussion of ethnic group formation as a process of social closure. SOC

(13) However, there are some *good arguments* that the correlation usually obtained between NA and stress or strain indicators does not solely reflect a bias but also a substantial role of dispositional variables in the stress process. CS

Predicative uses, on the other hand, foreground the value claim by placing *good* in rhematic position. Interestingly, none of these occurred in the BIO, ENG or MED texts:

(14) Reliability coefficients (alpha) for all scales *were good* (>.70). CS

(15) Usually it *is considered good* if the number of generators can be reduced or the total length of the relators can be made smaller. MATH

In its moral, non-utilitarian sense, *good* appears only in a few instances (limited to the HIST subcorpus). Such realisations do not signal the RA author's beliefs, however, but only social attitudes rooted in a specific cultural environment:

(16) His goal was to reassure believers that in the midst of fun-loving pursuits, they could still be *good* Muslims as long as they committed no acts that explicitly trampled on Islamic norms and duties. HIST

(17) Yeats concluded that that the Irish must "care for things Gaelic and Irish, not because we hold them better than things Saxon and English, but because they belong to us, and because our lives are to be spent among them, whether they be *good* or evil." HIST

In terms of relative frequency, *good* peaks in ECO (3.5 occurrences/ 10,000 words), where it mostly qualifies *management* or *performance*. Compared to their peers in other disciplines, economists are thus more likely to express goodness through a marker that reflects the need to interpret phenomena as good/bad, whether or not the criteria underlying such judgements are made explicit; this finding is mirrored by the fact that the antonyms *bad* and *poor* also peak in ECO.

Like *good*, the comparative form *better* is prevalently attributive throughout the corpus, when used as an adjective; this occurs in 89% of cases. In normalised terms it is most frequent in ECO (3.4 occurrences). Its main collocates are *understanding* (8 tokens), *performance* (6) and *practice/s* (6), which respectively qualify the intellectual enquiry that drives research, the phenomena it deals with and the methodology employed:

(18) Representing this epistemic uncertainty in transmissivity and storage coefficient values will allow for a *better understanding* of the heterogeneous subsurface. ENG

(19) With regard to the number of returns to the top (right side of Figure 10), the older user group showed 77% *better performance* with the tree aid than with the category aid. CS

(20) We find that *better management practices* are significantly associated with higher productivity, profitability, Tobin's Q, sales growth rates, and firm-survival rates. ECO

The adverbial *better* was most common in CS (1.6 occurrences/10,000 words). It is generally used to premodify the past participle of verbs describing the research (e.g. *endowed, placed, suited*), its performance (e.g. *absorbed, studied, supported*) or interpretation (*understood, documented*). Alternatively it collocates with the infinitive (*characterise, determine, predict*) and at times with the indicative (*explains, capture, performed, matches*). In around one third of cases, it is used to modify an indicative – mainly *perform*, which qualifies the value of a given methodology – or a cognitive verb such as *predict, explain* and *understand*:

(21) It can be seen that the proposed stand-alone wavelet forecasting method is highly accurate for 1 day lead-time flood forecasting, and *performs better* than the MLR, ARIMA, and ANN methods. ENG

(22) Some argue that general external circumstances are determinative whereas others suggest that internal, movement-controlled variables *better explain* movement outcome. SOC

(23) To *better understand* the effects of MCCs, we compared the amount of time participants needed to type the MCC strings letter by letter just before the introduction of MCCs and the time needed to type the new chord. CS

The collocation *better than* was not frequent, with only ten occurrences in the whole corpus. Most of these were observed in HIST, where they convey historically-situated judgements or attitudes, as observed below:

(24) He personally regarded tobacco as deeply repugnant, but after searching legal sources, found insufficient grounds for outlawing it. He consoled himself with the thought that it was at least *better than* opium and hashish. HIST

(25) They argued that while Western accomplishments in the material world were impressive, the spirituality and deeper sensitivity of non-Western people made them potentially *better than* crudely materialistic Westerners. HIST

The superlative *best* is the second most frequent item among Group A markers and peaks in ENG (10.3 occurrences/10,000 words), where it collocates almost exclusively with *model*. Similarly it tends to qualify procedural aspects of research (e.g. *alignments, fit, outcomes, pre-*

dictors) also in other disciplines, with the exception of history. It may also be used adverbially or nominally, as shown by the last two examples below.

(26) A probe set was then assigned to a retrocopy if its *best hit* overlapped with the retrocopy. BIO

(27) The following are the *best* four *models* which were developed from the four methods to forecast the stream flow in the Rideau River for 2 days lead-time. ENG

(28) For the nMSSM our results are *best summarized* by figure 6 which displays the spectrum of GW densities for several parameter sets. PHY

(29) Physicians should *do their best* to estimate and interpret these probabilities in counseling parents. MED

Overall, the most prominent item in this group is the adverb *well*, which collocates in 73% of cases with a past participle in adjectival or verbal position. This means that goodness qualifies a physical or intellectual act, subsequent to its performance. 'Doing things well' appears to be a concern especially for anthropologists, with the marker peaking in ANTH at 4.8 occurrences per 10,000 words. The most frequent pairings were respectively *well defined* (22 occurrences), followed by *well established* (16), *well developed* (10) and *well understood* (6):

(30) For any adjacent points a, b in (3.19), there is a *well-defined* element g(a,b) of G that acts as a transposition in at least one of our two symmetric groups Sp+2. MATH

(31) Analysis of pollen grains and phytoliths is *well established* in archaeology (for a summary, see Pearsall, 2000). ANTH

(32) Given the scarcity of functional analyses of Aurignacian stone tools, it is apparent that their use is not *well understood*. ANTH

Some of these collocations appear to be specific to individual disciplines, as in the case of *well characterized* (BIO), *well designed*

(CS), *well individualized* (ANTH), *well managed* (ECO) and *well posed* (MATH):

(33) However, our results also limit the degree to which the *well-characterized* spatial patterns of glomerular activity might participate in odor coding. BIO

(34) Even *well-designed* peripheral displays will occasionally become the focus of their user's attention, but reaching operational use is a central objective in peripheral display design. CS

(35) The mastoid process is large, *well-individualized*, and elongated downward. ANTH

(36) Thus, firms that score below two or above four appear to be genuinely badly or *well managed* rather than extreme draws of sampling measurement error. ECO

(37) As a consequence, for any initial data [EXPRESSION], the critical nonlinear wave equation (1.1) is locally *well posed* in [EXPRESSION]. MATH

Elsewhere *well* is used either to postmodify a verb or to premodify it through the adverbial *how well*. Such options are especially common in CS, where they account respectively for 40% and 12% of all occurrences. The verbs involved tend to flag aspects of the experiment or its methodology that are considered to be 'good' (i.e. desirable) in a given context, the most frequent collocates in this class being *perform*, *apply* and *fit*:

(38) The Twiddler also *performed* surprisingly *well* in our blind-typing conditions relative to results found for typing with limited visual feedback on mobile phones or mini-QWERTY keyboards. CS

(39) Our methods *apply* equally *well* in this setting (where the existence of Julia sets of positive Lebesgue measure is still an open problem). MATH

(40) In both Cambrian and all eight modern webs, the mean niche MEs for 17 properties fall within 61 (Tables 2 and 3), indicating that the niche model *fits* the central tendency of the network structure of all ten webs *well*. BIO

(41) It is also more important to evaluate *how well* the display *fits* with its environment than to evaluate its aesthetic appeal. CS

The only goodness-marking verb in the positive field (i.e. *improve*) also deserves attention. Like *best*, it was found to be unusually prominent in ENG (2.9 occurrences/10,000 words), arguably because of the discipline's emphasis on technological advancement. Whether used transitively or intransitively, *improve* combines more often with inanimate (e.g. *equipment, procedures, results*) than with animate entities (e.g. *researchers*, *subjects*, other agents).

(42) The large rates in those areas are explained by the fact that they are covered by shrub (Fig. 4), having a low ETact rate (Kcb =0.15), *which helps to improve* recharge. ENG

(43) There was significant heterogeneity of the treatment effect across these diagnostic groups, but *dexamethasone significantly improved* survival in the group of patients with definite bacterial meningitis. MED

(44) *Did users improve* their performance in the second trial and was the improvement connected to the type of aid? CS

(45) But despite *party work undertaken to improve* the condition of women, Chinese leaders found it useful to denigrate "feminism". HIST

Compared to positive Group A items, those in the negative field were relatively scant. A majority of these consist of the adjectives *bad* and *poor*, which are entirely absent in MATH and very rare in some of the stronger goodness-marking disciplines, such as ANTH and ENG. Economists are altogether the most likely to signal what is *bad/poor* (1.1 occurrences of each marker/10,000 words), followed by computer scientists, historians and sociologists. In terms of collocates, *bad* tends to qualify *practices*, *managers* and *performance* in ECO, human attributes (*behaviour, intentions, health*) in HIST and experimental features in PHY:

(46) One of the interesting features of the raw data is the substantial fraction of firms that appear to have surprisingly *bad* management *practices*, with scores of two or less. ECO

(47) People might indeed have *bad intentions*, he said, but one could not easily discern them from the outside. HIST

(48) For $\gamma 0 = 0.53$, the *fit* is very good (by definition) on very small redshifts but *bad* on larger redshifts. PHY

Unlike *bad*, *poor* occurs predicatively only in one instance and can be used to post-modify a noun (cf. sentence 50). Albeit often present, its metaphorical source meaning – i.e. lacking in something – is not always retained (51), which makes it synonymous with *bad*. Overall, the most frequent collocate of *poor* was *job*, followed by *information sharing* (in CS).

(49) In addition, while it has been shown previously that a null model that distributes links randomly does a very *poor job* of predicting empirical food-web structure. BIO

(50) For example, Mormons tend to be religiously conservative, but there is little evidence that they are *asset poor*. SOC

(51) Promoting workers who are *poor performers* [...] is likely to lead to lower productivity than considering individual performance when deciding whether to move an employee up the hierarchy. ECO

Two other markers worth mentioning are *worst* and *poorly*. Albeit infrequent in the corpus, the former peaks unusually in HIST, where it underscores (always attributively) the drama inherent in certain elements of human experience:

(52) If others threw themselves into the carefree and relaxed atmosphere of the place, he could find only a sink full of the *worst possible vices*. HIST

(53) Tagore objected to this, not just because he found violence morally unacceptable, but because it copied the *worst feature* of English imperialism. HIST

The adverb *poorly* is noticeable instead for its prominence in BIO (the second least evaluative discipline for goodness) – especially as a premodifier of *resolved*, as shown by example (54) below, but also collocating with *known*, *described* and *suited*. In general, however, its most common collocation was *poorly understood*, which tends to denote the lack of knowledge associated with certain aspects of research.

(54) *Poorly resolved* original-species webs with coarse taxonomic or trophic categories undergo less trophic-species aggregation, because similar taxa are already grouped. BIO

(55) Unfortunately, the precise mechanisms of adherence of residues to tool surfaces or of residue preservation in general remain *poorly understood.* ANTH

5.7.2. Group B

Also in this group most of the words are evaluative attributive adjectives, all encoding the conventional POSITIVE IS GOOD / NEGATIVE IS BAD metaphor drawn from financial accounting. The range of markers is very limited, with only a fraction of adverbs and nouns; my analysis will thus concentrate on the two basic forms *positive* and *negative* used as goodness markers.

Despite its presence in several disciplines, *positive* is less frequent than its antonym. It is noticeably absent in BIO, ENG, MATH and MED – all disciplines that focus on the non-metaphoric meaning of such markers. With very few exceptions (example 57) it qualifies human behaviour, which makes ‘positivity’ a particularly subjective/ emotive variable. A mere 8% of occurrences (58) were predicative.

(56) Individuals high on PA experience stronger *positive emotions* in a videoconference than individuals low on this disposition. CS

(57) The *positive effect* of competition on management practices could work through two possible mechanisms. ECO

(58) However, not all of our adoptees’ *experiences* abroad were *positive.* SOC

The adjective *negative* occurs predicatively only once (61) and collocates mainly with *emotions* (like its antonym) in CS, and with *publicity* in SOC. Again, it is almost invariably associated with human experience:

(59) This is problematic because using this new technology will often lead to technical problems [...] that can arouse many different *negative emotions*, for example, boredom, anger, or fear. CS

(60) As demonstrations, boycotts, and general disorder continued from April through May, graphic incidents of police repression drew enormous *negative publicity*. SOC

(61) In particular, her experiences are consistent with the observation that cultural censure tends to be more intense and *negative* in Korea than in other Asian nations. SOC

5.7.3. Group C

Albeit rare, the two polarities were more balanced in this group, each reaching an average of 0.1 occurrences per 10,000 words. Signalling what if *right* vs. *wrong* appears to be particularly relevant in CS (0.9 occurrences) and HIST (1.0). In the former domain, *right* invariably qualifies the behaviour of computer users interacting with a given software package, as encoded by the phrase *get X right* and other similar realisations; in the latter it is used as a dialectic or moral category:

(62) As for the group arriving at the correct decision after discussion, 10 of the 30 groups got the right answer on the first task, and 7 *got it right* on the second task. CS

(63) Yeats's concern about the direction in which Irish nationalism was heading was such that in 1933 he even told a friend that she *was "right* in comparing De Valera to Mussolini or Hitler". HIST

(64) The Hanafi legal tradition, which had become the preeminent legal school within the Ottoman Empire, had long looked upon them with misgiving. People had to be careful about using them with the *right intentions*. HIST

The adverbial form *rightly* occurs only four times in the whole corpus; three of such realisations are authorial judgements embedded in an evidential, i.e. in a reported claim supporting the RA's line of reasoning:

(65) As Carney *rightly notes*, "Rice and millet dominated the grains that were traded," but Ray Kea's estimate of Axim's rice exports of 100 tons a year would have provided 0.5 lbs of rice per day for a mere 1,000 people. HIST

Unlike its antonym, *wrong* is more often used predicatively than attributively. The latter option was observed only in CS (example 66) where, like *right*, it denotes the behaviour of computer users (*wrong answer/path/expectations*). Elsewhere *wrong* occurs as a moral-dialectic category, often in conjunction with reported knowledge claims, whether integral or non-integral to the text. The only instance of *wrongly* (69) signals a flaw identified by the authors in current knowledge.

(66) [...] users, believing they had taken the *wrong path*, went back to a known position within the menu, consequently reorientating themselves. CS

(67) Yeats *claimed* that the idea that Irish national culture "must come from the Celtic people of the country [...]" was *wrong* because "Ireland is not wholly Celtic any more than England is wholly Saxon, or wholly Catholic any more than England is wholly Protestant." HIST

(68) They pursue a strategy of blurring by emphasizing universal moral qualities that make the division of the world into ethnonational groups appear *wrong* and unjustifiable (Karrer 2002, chap. 12). SOC

(69) Among species in which females and males are misclassified most frequently, less than half of the *wrongly-assigned* specimens seem to be found in the corresponding sister species. ANTH

5.7.4. Group D

This group covers the lexical set built around the noun *problem*, when used to express some kind of unsolved difficulty that deserves attention. In normalised terms, it was most prominent in CS (12.1), followed at a distance by HIST and PHY (4.4 each). In BIO and MATH, on the other hand, its presence is almost negligible. This noun often realises an anaphoric reference by qualifying an earlier claim, with 12% of occurrences (39/336) belonging to the collocations *this problem/these problems* (example 72).

(70) The participants did not make a single mention of erroneous inferences being a *problem*, even when asked what annoyed them or what should be changed. CS

(71) MaVaN models, however, suffer from the *problem* that for some choices of scalar-neutrino couplings and scalar field potentials the combined fluid is subject to an instability once the neutrinos become non-relativistic. PHY

(72) Americans and Mexicans overcame *this* interpretive *problem* by adjusting their gaze, looking less at Indians than through them in search of compelling explanations for Mexico's security crisis. HIST

Among three-word clusters, *the problem(s) of* was found to be the most common option (33/336 occurrences), with a noticeable difference between the singular and plural form: the former tends to introduce the definition of a phenomenon viewed as problematic (example 73) or to name it as such (74), while the latter contextualises it through specification (75-76).

(73) Consider next *the problem of investing in the taste for leisure*, as described by the maximization problem. ECO

(74) One of the significant debates about rapid technology development concerns *the problem of privacy*, which has become a major focus for both academic and popular attention. CS

(75) Eventually, he thought, it would succeed in solving "*the problems of the human race*, national, political, religious," and help give rise to "the nationality of man". HIST

(76) By that time, *the economic problems of the upper classes* – aggravated by falling land rents after 1878 – had become so pressing that land sales reached a massive scope. ECO

The wider trend observed in this respect is a prevalence of *problems*, whose singular counterpart accounts for a marked majority of items only in CS (74%). This finding partly reflects the prominence of two collocations employed only in this domain, namely *organizational problems* (22 occurrences) and *technical problems* (18), which in turn reflect the concern of CS for electronic devices and their operation:

(77) This is problematic because using this new technology will often lead to *technical problems* (e.g., temporal delays, interruption of audio transmission) and *organizational problems* (e.g., with respect to document handling, positioning of the camera) that can arouse many different negative emotions, for example, boredom, anger, or fear. CS

Despite its infrequency, the adjective *problematic(al)* appeared in all domains with the sole exception of MATH. Compared to *problem/s*, it is more common in SOC and in ANTH (which also has the only instance of its adverbial form). Over 70% of occurrences are used predicatively, i.e. in a grammatically prominent position. As illustrated by the examples below, entities qualified as *problematic* range from methodological options (78) to data interpretation (79) and theory building (80):

(78) For example, some evaluation methods, such as experience sampling, inherently call attention to the tool being evaluated, *which is particularly problematic* for peripheral display evaluation because it would violate the very nature of the tool. CS

(79) For this reason, *it is problematic* to attempt to disentangle the relative influence of choices versus constraints, especially using survey data that cannot get at the complex set of factors that might influence individual residential decisions. SOC

(80) The last point *is*, however, *not problematic* from a cosmology point of view since for realistic value of the power-law exponent n it is always true that [EXPRESSION]. PHY

5.7.5. Group E

As the focus of this study is on value marking, also Group E candidates had to be manually inspected to exclude non-relevant meanings – that is occurrences encoding 'statistical' error – which is an inevitable aspect of the procedure employed – as opposed to ‘human/technical’ errors due to misjudgement or bad design and thus marked negatively for goodness. The relevant items in this group (normalized figures) peak in ECO (3.2), followed by CS (1.9) and ANTH (1.2), while in the other disciplines they are scarcely represented or absent altogether. Interestingly, the singular form is used almost exclusively in ECO. The fact that economists are more prone to make *error/s* explicit, largely depends on the topic of one of the ECO papers (the legal-financial implications of ‘medical error’ in childbirth procedures), where the singular form collocates mostly with *rate(s)*, as the RA’s authors assess the benefits of reform in medical liability legislation.

(81) First, conditional upon procedure choice, a decrease in liability leads to less care and hence a higher *error rate*. ECO

(82) These values were computed by taking the intervals for each chord typed in sentences *without any errors* and then averaged for the whole session on a per-user basis. CS

(83) Direct radiocarbon dates, however, proved them to be only 5000 years old, thus demonstrating that *serious excavation errors* obviously occurred during the fieldwork in 1931. ANTH

The link between such errors and their originators is generally concealed, unless the agent is external to the discipline, as in examples (84-85). The only two exceptions to this principle were observed in an Acknowledgements section (86) and in the only instance of *erroneously* (87) documented in the corpus:

(84) We define α as the probability that *a physician makes an error* that results in a potential tort liability. ECO

(85) This metric accounts for both corrected and *uncorrected errors made by the participants* and provides a single total error rate. CS

(86) The data presented here represents a part of my doctoral dissertation and *any errors are entirely my own*. ANTH

(87) Despite these numerous efforts, *many have erroneously relied* on broad terrace sequences, undated geographic differences, and the presence/absence of

> expedient tool-types to determine Soanian technological progression through time. ANTH

This suggests that research errors are too face-threatening to be attributed to a member of the discipline and are therefore rhetorically detached from those responsible. Even in (87) above, which is unique in this respect, the agent is signalled indirectly by an indefinite pronoun that places the onus of naming the culprit on the reader (i.e. *many* → *many scholars*).

5.8. Discussion

The evidence gathered in this chapter is indicative of the most frequent explicit lexis encoding goodness in academic RAs, whether such a value is expressed as an absolute positive, a relative positive (comparative-superlative) or an absolute negative; relative negatives were found to be very rare. The most important findings are summarised and discussed below, with special attention given to variation across disciplines.

5.8.1. Saliency of goodness

If we take into account all the relevant realisations targeted by the analysis, the corpus reveals considerable disparity in the saliency given to goodness, with its markers ranging from 4.2 words per 10,000 tokens in MATH to 35.4 in CS – that is a more than eightfold difference. Goodness would therefore seem to be a considerably more important facet of the academic value system in certain domains than in others. More specifically, normalised counts indicate three levels of intensity, which do not coincide with any of the disciplinary groupings suggested in the literature or with that adopted earlier (i.e. natural sciences, applied sciences, human sciences, social sciences, and mathematical sciences), as shown for example by the fact that CS and

MATH, both classified as 'mathematical sciences', appear at the two extremes of the scale.

Intensity	*Discipline*	*Norm. occurrences*
Strong	CS	35.4
	ECO	26.7
	ENG	25.7
	HIST	20.5
Average	ANTH	16.3
	SOC	15.0
	MED	13.8
	PHY	12.0
Weak	BIO	9.8
	MATH	4.2

Table 7. Goodness-marking intensity by discipline.

The picture therefore is far more varied than initially assumed, being closely related to the type of disciplinary concerns and topics addressed by researchers in a given field. Accordingly, goodness is salient especially in:

- CS as a feature of the interaction between users and computer devices;
- ECO as a feature of economic behaviour and business performance;
- ENG as a feature of the technology adopted and its methodological implications;
- HIST as a feature of human beliefs and actions as they evolve over time.

The fact that RA authors signal goodness more often in these four domains means that their underlying epistemologies justify a strongly evaluative stance. The reader is not simply presented with evidence but constantly reminded of its value along the good-bad axis. Conversely, MED, PHY, BIO and MATH are the four disciplines least likely to signal goodness – a finding that may reflect their emphasis on other values (such as validity or truth) or simply a reluctance to classify experience in terms of good vs. bad.

If the same results are interpreted in terms of polarity, the most 'negative' discipline appears to be CS and the most 'positive' ENG, while in SOC, PHY and MATH the balance between polarities is roughly equal. With the exception of CS, therefore, explicit lexis signalling what is wrong or bad or problematic is generally less common than that referring to what is right or good in the field.

5.8.2. Type of marker and qualified entity

Two thirds of goodness markers (64%) belong to Group A, that is to the core meaning, whether positive or negative, covered by this analysis. The proportion is even higher (i.e. 74%) if Groups B-C, which are also bipolar, are included. This means that around three quarters of markers express the good/bad, positive/negative, right/wrong dyads. Compared to other disciplines, however, ENG has a far higher proportion of Group A items (90%), so it centres almost entirely on the semantic core of goodness, whereas CS has the highest amount of markers (59%) in Groups B-E, which means it has the broadest spread of realisations among those considered.

The results indicate that *good* is used above all attributively (66% occurrences) and, like its antonyms *bad* and *poor*, peaks in ECO. Both *best* and *improve* are most frequent in ENG, while *well* peaks in ANTH (4.8) and is used to qualify a physical or intellectual act subsequent to its performance. Negative Group A items are most common in ECO, followed by HIST and PHY, while *poorly* is most prominent in BIO. Despite being present in more disciplines than its antonym (*negative*), *positive* is less frequent and is noticeably absent in BIO, ENG, MATH and MED, all of which concentrate on the non-metaphoric meaning of this marker. With few exceptions, it qualifies human behaviour, thus making 'positivity' a particularly subjective/emotive variable. The *right/wrong* dyad is prominent only in CS (where it evaluates the behaviour of computer users) and HIST (as a dialectic/moral category). Finally, Group D items peak in CS (12.1) and Group E items in ECO (3.2), followed by CS (1.9) and ANTH (1.2).

Classified by part of speech, there is a predictable prevalence of adjectives (44%), followed by nouns (27%) and adverbs (22%), with a majority of positive markers in each category with the exception of nouns (89% negative). Among high-frequency goodness markers, therefore, positive lexicalisations are unlikely to be expressed nominally. On the other hand, the fact that RA authors are more willing to nominalise faults than positive features, enables them to rhetorically dissociate an undesirable quality from its referent in a way that would not be possible opting for other parts of speech. Disciplinary differences are noticeable also in this respect, with adjectives more prominent in ENG (15.4) than in CS (13.3) – which means that engineers are more prone to adjectivise goodness than would be expected, given that CS has altogether far more markers than ENG (35.4 vs. 25.7). By the same criterion, adverbs are more prominent than expected in ANTH (6.4) and surprisingly in BIO (5.3), while they are under-represented in ENG (4.4) and HIST (3.4). Nouns are particularly scarce in ENG (3.0), which is less likely than other domains to signal *problems* and *errors*. Finally, verbs peak not in CS or ECO but in MED (3.3), thanks to the saliency of *improve* (in line with the discipline's therapeutic orientation).

The wider significance of such data will be assessed in Chapter 9, taking into account evidence from the other three values subjected to analysis. It is at this point to speculate whether the interdisciplinary variation observed so far is specific to goodness markers or extends also to other values. The experience gained in the piloting phase confirms that a complete picture of the corpus is essential for drawing conclusions as to the proclivities of each disciplinary community.

6. Size markers

Unlike goodness, whose axiological significance is relatively unambiguous because it embodies a very central aspect of evaluation, due consideration of *size* as an academic value is justified both by the indeterminacy of claims made along the large-small axis and by the frequency of its markers. Also in the piloting stage, size was among the most frequent explicitly marked values observed in RAs. Lexical items in this category encode judgements that qualify an entity as 'large' or 'small' rather than specifying its exact dimensions: they rely therefore on subjective evaluations whose rationale is shared by RA authors and readers. The propensity to communicate value assessments based on size – whether these target the evidence in hand or other aspects of the knowledge-production process – is also worth investigating because of the disciplinary proclivities that may emerge during the analysis.

The candidate items identified in Chapter 4 – listed again in the table below – loosely cover the semantic field of quantitative assessment. At closer examination, however, the list was found to be excessively heterogeneous, with a clear fault-line separating items that encode the notion of size (e.g. *large, small*) from those that refer instead to quantity (*limited, enough*). The distinction is an important one in this context, as it allows the analyst to focus consistently on lexis marking out a single variable, namely the perceived dimensions of an entity or phenomenon. What is assessed may be quantified literally or figuratively, as the case may be, but should always encode an evaluation of the dimensional boundaries of a referent whose axiological significance derives from the epistemology and specific concerns of each discipline.

Size	*n*
large	615
small	539
larger	261
greater	247
little	184
smaller	165
great	160
limited	150
enough	124
largely	103
substantial	102
Total	*2,650*

Table 1. Candidate items (absolute frequency).

To identify which of these items qualified for analysis, individual concordances were generated for each entry and then scanned to identify its semantic field. The criteria adopted for inclusion and, where relevant, for the addition of further lexis are outlined in the next section.

6.1. Selection of candidate items

When selecting relevant size markers, several of the initial candidates were deemed unsuitable or peripheral to the scope of this chapter and therefore dropped. More specifically, *great* and its derived forms were not included because a large proportion of such items occur in proper nouns (e.g. *Great Britain, Great Lakes, Great War*) or in the phrase *great deal* and because elsewhere they generally mark amount (*great influence, great zeal*) or relevance (*great powers, great opportunity*) rather than size. Similarly, *little* is used almost exclusively for amounts (*little evidence, little hope*) rather than size; the same applies for *enough* (*strong enough, enough cases*).

On inspection, the candidate *substantial* did not qualify either because it is synonymous with 'considerable' and thus partly classifiable as a relevance marker. Finally, *limited* was too problematic for inclusion, being largely equivalent to 'insufficient' and thus encoding amount rather than size, while *largely* was excluded because it is mainly used as an approximator (=roughly) or as a relevance-related marker (=considerably). This means that only the core adjectives encoding size were retained for analysis, though some of their uses also qualified for exclusion:

- *Large, larger.* The only occurrences unsuited to the present study appeared in the prepositional phrase *at large*, whose value as a size marker has been fully lost through lexicalisation.
- *Small, smaller.* There were very few instances that warranted omission – namely three instances of the surname *Small* used in references to the literature.

6.2. Additional items

The first addition for completing lexical sets based on the words listed so far was the superlative of both adjectives, i.e. *largest* and *smallest*. Secondly, a concordance was generated for the near synonym *big*, which (albeit less frequent than its counterpart) is well represented in the corpus. The last addition to this category, in line with the label chosen for the value involved, was the noun *size* and its derived form *sized* (also in consideration of their strong presence throughout the corpus). Taken together, these markers can be organised into four groups:

Group A. *Large, larger, largest*

This lexical set is built around an adjective which, whether in its base form or in the comparative/superlative, clearly encodes the semantic core of the value considered here. Alongside Group B, it tends to form a dyad with its antonyms in Group C.

Group B. *Big, bigger, biggest*

Despite similarities, Groups A and B cannot be considered interchangeable. Corpus variations in their use and distribution will help to explain why scholars draw differently on very similar lexical sets. Only two occurrences involving proper nouns (*Big Mule, Big Three*) were omitted from the count.

Group C. *Small, smaller, smallest*

The opposite polarity is represented entirely by these three forms of the core adjective marking size diminutively. It will be interesting to determine whether these are superimposable to their antonyms in Group A-B or tend to collocate differently across the corpus.

Group D. *Size, sizes, sized*

The importance of *size* as a variable in research may be foregrounded also by these items, whose presence in the RA texts is far from negligible. Whether accompanied by a qualifier or not, all realisations were included in the count as relevant.

6.3. Overall results

After the incorporation of additional value-markers and the subdivision of all items into groups, it was possible to quantify the overall frequency of size markers in the RA corpus. Even considering the first three groups alone, this is greater than that of goodness markers. The most noticeable findings in the results given in Table 2 below is the prevalence of the first two groups over the third, with only 42% (734/1,733) of adjectives marking the 'small' end of the scale. Scholars are therefore more willing to view size in terms of varying degrees of 'largeness' rather than 'smallness'. The contribution of Group D items is also worth remarking, with almost a quarter of all occurrences (546/2,279) belonging to this group.

Group	*Item*	*n*		*Subtotal*
A	large (adj)	(615) 609	65%	
	larger (adj)	261	28%	
	largest (adj)	71	7%	941
B	big (adj)	(51) 49	84%	
	bigger (adj)	5	10%	
	biggest (adj)	4	6%	58
C	small (adj)	(541) 538	73%	
	smaller (adj)	165	22%	
	smallest (adj)	31	5%	734
D	size/s (n)	529	97%	
	sized (adj)	17	3%	546
Total				*(2,290) 2,279*

Table 2. Full list of size markers (by group).

Moving to single lexemes, the most interesting point is the greater prominence of comparative/superlative items in Group A (where they account for 35% of tokens), than in Groups B-C. Not only is *large* in its various forms the preferred size-marker: it is also the one most likely to be used comparatively. In other words, RA authors prefer to describe X as *larger* than Y (or *the largest*), rather than Y as *smaller* than X (or *the smallest*). This does not necessarily imply that 'larger is better' but suggests a tendency to view relative evaluation from the perspective of the larger entity (X) rather than that of its smaller counterpart (Y).

6.3.1. Predicative vs. attributive uses

The WLs generated for Group A-C markers also revealed a certain degree of variation in terms of syntactic positioning. While on average 77% of size-marking adjectives (1,343/1,733) are used attributively, the proportion changes substantially when the results are inspected in greater detail. Table 3 below illustrates such differences with the data divided by group and by form.

Adjectives	*Predicative*	*Attributive*	*n*
Group A	17%	83%	941
Group B	21%	79%	58
Group C	30%	70%	734
Base form	20%	80%	1,196
Comparative	35%	65%	431
Superlative	3%	97%	106
All	*23%*	*77%*	*1,733*

Table 3. Syntactic position of size-marking adjectives (by group and form).

Compared to the mean, predicative uses are rare among Group A adjectives and relatively frequent in Group C, with Group B roughly in between. This means that predicative constructions are particularly unlikely to target 'largeness' and, conversely, show a greater propensity to target 'smallness': it is unusually difficult to write *X is large* and easier on the whole to write *X is small.* Variations between categories of adjectives are even more marked, when the different forms are considered: predicative uses peak at 35% for comparatives, while they almost disappear among superlatives. The two extremes of the range are occupied by *smaller* (predicative in almost half of cases) and *largest* (predicative in only <1%).

The overall prevalence of attributive constructions confirms Soler's data on the use of evaluative adjectives in medical RAs – a phenomenon which shows that "the center of attention is on the noun/object of the construction rather than on the scientist" (2002: 153). The approach taken here, however, does not espouse Soler's argument that size adjectives should be viewed as non-axiological because they are not entirely subjective. Her distinction is itself subjective, given that even the most objective qualifiers are firmly rooted in the subject's real-world experience.

6.4. Distribution across disciplines

The use of size markers was found to vary quantitatively and qualitatively across the corpus, as scholars operating in different disciplinary cultures express claims that serve the interests and goals of their field. The concordances of the target items were scanned to quantify the tokens in each discipline (number in brackets) and the total for each group, as well as the global figure, was normalised by 10,000 words to make figures comparable. The resulting distribution of items is summarised in Table 4, with the last column showing the average number of occurrences in the corpus as a whole.

Item	*ANTH*	*BIO*	*CS*	*ECO*	*ENG*	*HIST*	*MATH*	*MED*	*PHY*	*SOC*	*All*
Group A	22.4	5.4	4.6	14.3	17.0	6.8	3.7	5.2	28.6	6.5	10.0
large	(105)	(27)	(47)	(92)	(81)	(33)	(46)	(16)	(115)	(47)	(609)
larger	(61)	(12)	(11)	(46)	(15)	(30)	(6)	(1)	(54)	(25)	(261)
largest	(17)	(1)	(3)	(10)	(16)	(9)	(6)	(2)	(1)	(6)	(71)
Group B	0.1	-	0.2	0.2	-	0.2	0.9	-	4.5	0.7	0.6
big	-	-	(1)	(2)	-	(1)	(12)	-	(26)	(7)	(49)
bigger	(1)	-	-	-	-	-	(2)	-	(1)	(1)	(5)
biggest	-	-	(2)	-	-	(1)	-	-	-	(1)	(4)
Group C	16.4	5.3	6.3	5.4	8.1	4.5	8.0	5.4	23.1	3.2	7.8
small	(95)	(26)	(69)	(26)	(45)	(38)	(91)	(16)	(103)	(29)	(538)
smaller	(28)	(13)	(15)	(30)	(8)	(7)	(18)	(4)	(33)	(9)	(165)
smallest	(11)	-	-	-	-	(2)	(16)	-	(19)	(1)	(31)
Subtotal	*38.9*	*10.7*	*11.1*	*19.9*	*25.1*	*11.4*	*12.6*	*10.6*	*56.2*	*10.4*	*18.5*
Group D	35.2	7.5	2.5	5.8	2.4	0.4	0.5	3.0	2.4	4.7	5.8
size	(272)	(41)	(28)	(48)	(12)	(4)	(7)	(10)	(14)	(55)	(491)
sizes	(12)	(15)	(5)	(1)	(4)	-	-	-	-	(1)	(38)
sized	(3)	-	(1)	(11)	-	-	-	(1)	-	(1)	(17)
Total	*74.1*	*18.2*	*13.6*	*25.7*	*27.5*	*11.8*	*13.1*	*13.6*	*58.6*	*15.1*	*24.3*

Table 4. Distribution of size markers across disciplines.

Whether or not Group D is included in the count, the results point to three clusters of disciplines: ANTH and PHY, whose value-marking intensity is more than double the overall average; ECO and ENG at or around average; and all the other disciplines well below the average level. This distinction is evident in Figure 1, covering Groups A-C, which lists the ten domains in decreasing order (mean frequency 18.5

occurrences/10,000 words). Thus physicists and anthropologists are those most likely to signal size explicitly, whether through adjectives that encode 'smallness', 'largeness' or (occasionally) 'bigness'. The two disciplines share a concern for quantification which – comparatively speaking – is almost negligible elsewhere, with the sole exception of ENG and ECO.

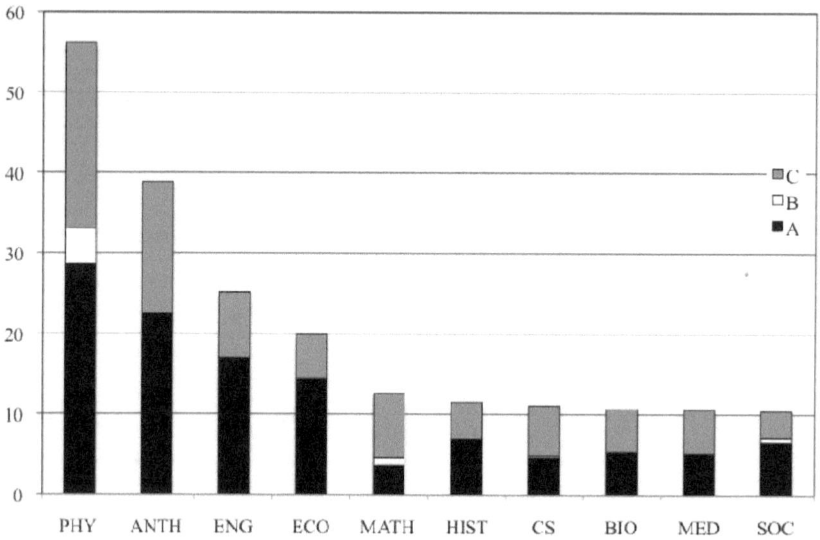

Figure 1. Size markers by group and discipline, in decreasing order (occurrences / 10,000 words).

It is evident that the contribution made by these three groups of markers to each discipline also varies significantly across the corpus. If the two polarities are contrasted by counting the percentage of Gruop A-B items as opposed to Group C items, the balance leans towards *large/big* for ECO, SOC, ENG, PHY and ANTH (in decreasing order), is almost even for BIO and MED, and leans towards *small* in the case of CS and MATH. Economists, sociologists and engineers are thus the most likely to signal the *large/big* polarity over its counterpart, with around 70% of items in Groups A-B. Conversely, computer scientists and mathematicians are more prone to mention 'smallness', with 60% of items in Group C.

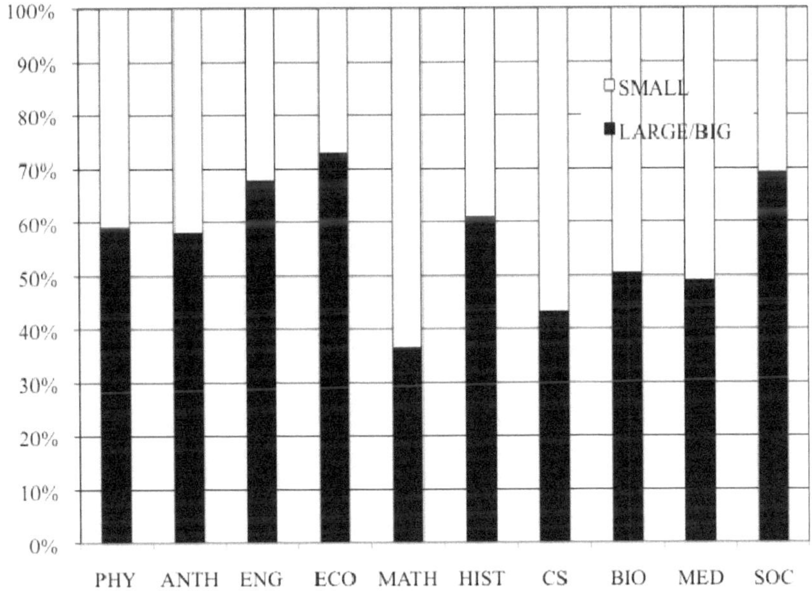

Figure 2. Relative weight of each polarity by discipline (percentage).

If markers in Group D are also considered, the distance between the two domains that top the list and the remaining disciplines in the corpus appears even more striking. ANTH peaks at 74.1 occurrences per 10,000 words, followed by PHY at 58.6 (against an average of 24.3), whereas HIST is lowest in the list at 11.8. The overall picture is that illustrated in Figure 3, with the ten domains listed as usual in decreasing order.

Overall, with the highest number of occurrences appeared in Group D in ANTH (35.2), followed by Group A in PHY (28.6) and Group C also in PHY (23.1). The lowest number, discounting the generally marginal Group B items, was that of Group D items in HIST (0.4) and MATH (0.5).

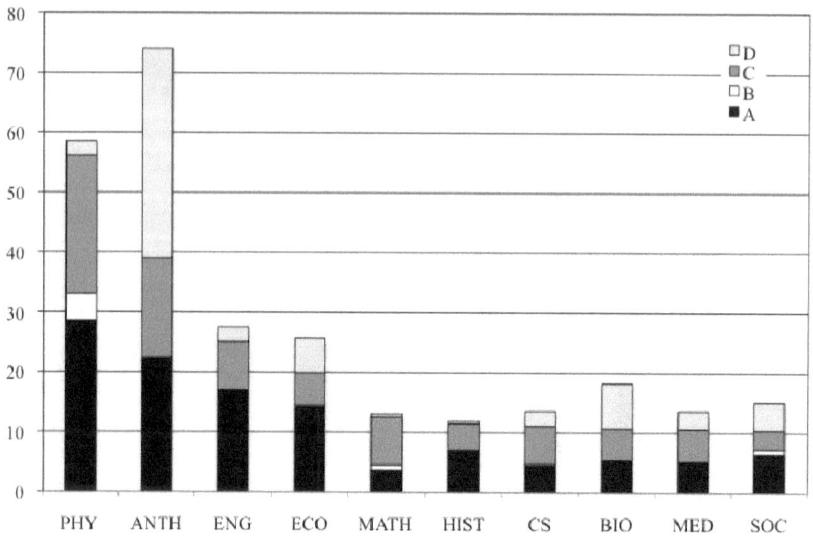

Figure 3. Size markers by group and discipline, including Group D.

Turning to individual markers, there are several interesting deviations from the general pattern outlined above:

- In ECO the base form is, somewhat surprisingly, less frequent than the comparative in Group C (26 *small* vs. 30 *smaller*).
- In HIST the comparative is almost as common as the base form in Group A (33 *large* vs. 30 *larger*).
- MATH has an (roughly) equal number of comparatives and superlatives in both Groups A and C.
- Half of the disciplines have no occurrences of the superlative *smallest* in Group C.

Such quantitative data would be incomplete, however, without an in-depth qualitative exploration of the realisations associated with each size marker. The corpus was therefore further probed for evidence of the contextual factors and discipline-specific motives that underpin the phenomena under scrutiny.

6.5. Qualified entities and realisations

The different realisations of relevant items were identified using WST and manual investigation to identify common patterns of use in terms of (i) the type of referent qualified by size markers across the corpus, and (ii) the wording of target utterances, with special attention paid to their collocates. The subsections that follow illustrate these features in the four groups of size markers and especially amongst the most frequent items in each group.

6.5.1. Group A

All the words in the first group and in the next two are 'evaluative attributive adjectives' (Biber 2004). Of these, the base form *large* is by far the most common, accounting for almost two thirds of occurrences (65%). It is particularly prominent in PHY (20.2 tokens/10,000 words) followed by ANTH (13.2), ENG (12.8) and ECO (9.1), while all the other domains are under the 5.0 mark. This item is associated above all with phenomena recorded by the researcher – its most frequent right collocates in the corpus being *number/s* (56 occurrences), *scale/s* (35), *enough* (16) and *amount/s* (15). A short example from each discipline is given below:

(88) *The mastoid is large* and not well individualized. The supramastoid crest is strongly demarcated. ANTH

(89) Single stellate cell axons (A1) labeled in WT PV-GFP mice showed *large and distinct boutons* that colocalized with GAD65 (A2). BIO

(90) Depending on the experimental condition (see later), the screen of the computer presented either a small or *large picture* of the candidate. CS

(91) There is *a large amount* of heterogeneity in the level of price stickiness across goods. ECO

(92) Along the Sierra Nevada, which is also another region with *large precipitation rates*, Regosols and Cambisols are found. ENG

(93) Throughout the Ottoman Middle East, *large numbers* of people seemed quite receptive to the new pastime, and showed themselves to be open to new sources of fun and excitement. HIST

(94) These equivalence relations *are actually too large*. We will refine them. MATH

(95) The association between *large erythrocyte-rich thrombi* and a TIMI flow grade of 0 or 1 before PCI is consistent with this mechanism. MED

(96) CMB and *large scale structure data* provide constraints on cosmological parameters that help tighten the constraints on H(z). PHY

(97) Blacks, like Hispanics, represent a *numerically large minority group* in the United States. SOC

As shown by these excerpts, the marker is used in ANTH, BIO and CS also to qualify the physical dimensions of an object. Nevertheless, *large* remains prevalently a phenomenological value-marker signalling the researcher's interpretation of empirical data in terms of size. The fact that this is its default meaning, is confirmed in (97) by the disambiguator *numerically*, whereby the RA author signals that *large* is to be understood figuratively. Predicative uses were found to be particularly common in MATH (28%), ECO (24%) and ANTH (19%) but were entirely absent in BIO and appeared only once in HIST. Interestingly, the most frequent L1 collocates were *very* (22 occurrences) and *relatively* (15), which function respectively as an intensifying booster and an approximating hedge:

(98) Because of such low values, the counting uncertainties were *very large* for individual samples, especially for 223Ra and 226Ra. ENG

(99) The OutCast system used a *relatively large* touch-screen display, which would be embedded in a cubicle (office) wall and connected to a computer situated inside the owner's office. CS

The comparative form was also well attested throughout the corpus and far more likely to occur in Group A (relatively speaking) than in Group C, since the *larger/large* ratio is 0.43 while the *smaller/small* ratio only 0.31. In normalised terms, *larger* is actually more prominent in some disciplines than *large* in others, with the former at 9.5 tokens in PHY and 7.7 in ANTH, but it is under 5.0 tokens in BIO, CS, HIST, MATH and MED.

While the qualified entities are, on the whole, very similar to those described earlier for this group, the prevalent R1 collocate – after *brain/s* (16 occurrences, all in ANTH) and *community/s* (7) – is *than*, observed in a total of 18% (48/216) of occurrences. The cluster *larger than* (always used predicatively) peaks percentually in PHY, where it appears in no less than 35% of realisations involving *larger*; what is more, around half of these are intensified by *much*, as observed in example (102) below.

(100) Finally, we predict that *larger brain size* is correlated with extended reproductive lifespan in primates, allowing for a net increase in reproductive output. ANTH

(101) The average participant age was 26, with students composing three fourths of the participants and members of *the larger community* composing one fourth. CS

(102) The instability can possibly occur in these models because the effective mass associated with the scalar field is *much larger than* H. PHY

In line with the pattern in Groups B-C, the superlative was relatively uncommon, with the exception of ANTH (2.1) and ENG (2.5) where, perhaps predictably, it always occurs in the attributive position:

(103) This character set is employed here as it is *the largest and most complete set* of skeletal characters tested among catarrhines. ANTH

(104) As June 1981 was the month with *the largest rainfall*, evapotranspiration and potential recharge, the monthly variability of this year is analyzed in the following section. ENG

6.5.2. Group B

The upper end of the size scale is expressed far less often by items in this group, whose total number is only a fraction (i.e. 6%) of its near synonyms in Group A. The base form (*big*) is again the most common but it is entirely absent in four domains and, most notably, in ANTH (which has the second-highest normalised occurrences of *large*). When it does appear, the qualifier *big* is relatively prominent only in PHY (4.6) and remains under the 1.0 mark in the other disciplines. (Astro)physicists, however, employ it exclusively as part of their terminology (i.e. *big rip, big boost, big brake, big crunch*) – a phenomenon clearly foregrounded by the metadiscoursal 'code gloss' (cf. Hyland 1998a) in example (106) below.

(105) The usual solution to the coincidence problem is to calculate the ratio of the duration of the coincidence state and the lifetime of the universe, assuming that dark energy is phantom-like and the universe will end with *the big rip*. PHY

(106) Second, we will show that this equation, together with the recovery of the general relativistic behavior, can feature a stage of cosmological acceleration followed by *what we call a big boost singularity*. PHY

The only other domain with a sizeable number of tokens is MATH, which mostly (67%) employs the adjective predicatively to qualify a mathematical variable (example 107) or construct (108). This discipline accounts in fact for nearly all the predicative realisations of *big* observed in the corpus.

(107) If κ is *big*, then $\partial M0$ is close to a circle centered at 0, and $f|M1$ is essentially quadratic. MATH

(108) However, when precisely computing the various quantities that appear in Arnold's construction, one observes that there does not exist enough tori in general. More precisely, the gap between tori is *too big*; this is the large gap problem. MATH

The derived forms *bigger/biggest* are seldom employed. They are always attributive and may have either positive (109) or negative associations (110). Coincidentally, both of the following examples are introduced by the same hedge (*perhaps*).

(109) Perhaps *the biggest opportunity* of our descriptive approach for computer-generated models is to mask some of the details that raise privacy concerns while still enabling human interpretation of the computational inferences. CS

(110) Perhaps in the future, *the biggest single theoretical battle* will have to be that between liberationists with a socialist analysis, and feminists with a 'radical feminist' analysis. HIST

6.5.3. Group C

The 'negative' polarity is realised entirely by items in Group C, which accounts altogether for one third of size markers. Almost three quarters of these consist of the base form *small* (73%), followed by the comparative (23%) and the superlative (4%). In normalised terms, *small* peaks in PHY (18.0 tokens/10,000 words) and ANTH (11.9), like its antonym *large*; also the type of qualified entity is very similar. However, if we compare the two markers across disciplines, their distribution shows three types of behaviour: a marked prevalence of *large* in ECO and ENG; a prevalence of *small* in CS and MATH; and a similar proportion of each in the remaining disciplines. The two adjectives also diverge significantly in terms of syntactic prominence, with *small* used predicatively in 26% (138/538) of occurrences, against only 14% (87/609) for *large*. The examples below illustrate such phenomena in each domain:

(111) To soften *small areas* of the sediment, we moistened it with demineralized water or a mixture of water and alcohol (50:50). ANTH

(112) The integrative properties of neurons in piriform cortex appear to be well suited to detecting synchronous inputs from *small ensembles* of OB afferents. BIO

(113) It requires no user interaction and does not interfere with user interaction, although it does present *small indicators* on the phone idle screen as a reminder that data collection is in process. CS

(114) Note that the price declines are indeed *very small* on average – indicating that the pass-through in the short run *is relatively small*. ECO

(115) The slope halfwidth will have *a small (near zero)* value when the sum of the jxij is greater than n. ENG

(116) The worst of all worlds for *the small farmer* would be organized futures markets without bucket shops. HIST

(117) Note that this result also holds irrespective of the sign of the nonlinearity because for *small H1 norms* the energy always controls the H1 norm. MATH

(118) The platelet thrombi were mostly *small or moderate in size*, whereas the erythrocyte-rich thrombi were moderate or large in size. MED

(119) In other words [...] the bare fact of our existence automatically implies that the value of the cosmological constant *should be small* in our Universe. PHY

(120) For example, Jim Moreau's social and work contacts have remained as homogeneous as *the small white town* in which his parents raised him. SOC

It is also worth looking at the top R1 collocates of *small*, which are respectively *number/s* (24 occurrences), *redshifts* (19, all in PHY), *sample/s* (16, all in ANTH and SOC), *screen/s* (11, all CS) and *scale/s* (10). In PHY and CS such collocations are embedded in the discipline's terminology, while in ANTH and SOC they loosely qualify the value of various sampling methods. The top L1 collocates of *small* are *relatively* (31), *very* (27) and *sufficiently* (25, all in MATH) – that is an approximator, an intensifier and an adverb of manner. The finding that all the instances of *sufficiently small* occur in MATH suggests that the discipline is more interested in 'smallness' than its counterparts – a hypothesis confirmed by the fact that it has the highest Group C/A ratio (i.e. 2.1).

(121) Hence [EXPRESSION], provided r *is sufficiently small* (depending on >0), which implies the assertion. MATH

Moving to the comparative, the picture is similar to that observed in the base form. If contrasted with its antonym, *smaller* is particularly prominent only in MATH (1.2 vs. 0.4) and MED (1.1 vs. 0.3). More notably, *smaller* had the highest proportion (48%) of predicative uses among size markers. Such uses are particularly likely to evaluate the quantitative significance of data, empirical parameters and observational phenomena (examples 122-123) and only rarely target the actual physical dimensions of qualified entities (124):

(122) In a subsequent paper [GKKL1] we will show that the constant in Theorems B and B' can be taken to be less than 20 (*and is probably even smaller* than this). MATH

(123) If information about the irregularities of politicians flows better in larger cities, then *the effects of the audits might be smaller*. ECO

(124) If *one's own picture was presented smaller* and less central on the screen, high-anxious students (M=14.6) and low-anxious students (M=14.5) did not differ in their performance. CS

If the concordance list is re-arranged by R1 collocate, it reveals a further tendency across disciplines: 68% (54/79) of predicative uses are built around the *smaller than* collocation. Scholars are therefore particularly prone to complete the *X is smaller* pattern with a term of reference introduced by *than*. When the same parameter is measured for *larger*, the figure is slightly lower, at 63% (47/75). While no other right-collocates of *smaller* were particularly prominent, the L1 list is headed (16 occurrences) by *much*, an option exemplified by the first sentence below:

(125) The table does indicate that the difference between the two in terms of the percentage of workers organized (10 percentage points) is *much smaller than the overall victory rate* (28%). SOC

(126) Lindert (1986, Table 1) documents that in 1810 the average estate of living gentlemen was more than *three times larger than that of merchants and industrial capitalists*. ECO

The superlative *smallest* was instead relatively infrequent, with the exception of ANTH (1.4), where half of the occurrences collocate with *samples*. In line with previous data, it clearly prevailed over its antonym only in MATH (1.1 vs. 0.4).

6.5.4. Group D

Albeit not particularly frequent in the corpus as a whole (where it comes only third, after Groups A and D, in normalised terms), these markers are unique in their distribution across domains. They are strongly represented in ANTH, where they peak at 35.2 tokens, are moderately present in BIO (7.5), ECO (5.8) and SOC (4.7), and are relatively uncommon in the remaining disciplines. Surprisingly, this is the most frequent group (48% of the total) in ANTH, while in PHY – which has the second highest count of Group A and C items – it is relatively rare.

In order to account for such variations, the concordances were scrutinised more closely for further evidence of the underlying rationale. As shown by the examples below, *size* appears to be used almost exclusively in its material sense in ANTH and CS. On the other hand, in ECO and SOC it is generally used figuratively to qualify numeric data:

(127) The emergency-rescue-training mannequin is manufactured with approximately realistic *mass distribution and size.* ANTH

(128) Figure 3 shows a snapshot of the simulated phone, where the *size of the display* corresponded to the original display *size.* CS

(129) The sheer *size of the late-1994 exchange-rate shock* [...] may explain why this paper finds stronger evidence of plant behavioral responses than is typical in the literature using tariff changes. ECO

(130) One line of research on arrest rates suggests that state control of blacks decreases with black *population size*, contrary to the threat hypothesis (Parker, Stults, and Rice 2005). ECO

The exceptional frequency of *size* in ANTH (49%) is largely due to its collocation with *brain* (94 occurrences) and *body* (39). Together the two collocates account for no less than 49% of occurrences in the discipline. The content of the ANTH texts present in the corpus clearly plays a major role in this respect, as they tend to focus on the description of humanoid fossil skeletons (hence the prominence of such features as brain size and body size). After these, the only L1 collocates with >10 occurrences were respectively *sample* (27 occurrences) and *population* (24, mostly in SOC). Finally, among R1 collocates the main option was *of* (70), followed by the pattern *size* (+ modal) + *is/was/be* (40). Nothing remarkable was observed in the (limited) use of the plural form.

(131) The left panel shows the correlation between the parameters and the typical *size of* the bubbles at the end of the phase transition. PHY

(132) The sample *size is* significantly reduced in this analysis, because offices that did not create policies were not at risk of decoupling as defined above. SOC

Finally, the adjective *sized* was concentrated in ECO, where it occurs almost exclusively in the cluster *medium-sized firms*. Group D markers are altogether atypical, insofar as they mention size as a concept rather than an evaluative category and are strongly skewed towards a single domain. Because of this, they will not be included in the data used later for comparative purposes. The reader should therefore refer to the distribution illustrated in Figure 1 rather than that in Figure 3.

6.6. Discussion

The marking of size, both as a concept in its own right and as a quality bounded by two opposite polarities, was found to diverge considerably within the corpus in overall quantitative terms but also as regards the choice of marker employed for this purpose. At the same time, the entities qualified by such lexical items often differed in distribution across domains, as did their top right and left collocates. Concerning this last aspect, Durrant (2009) has recently drawn attention to the importance of academic collocations in different disciplines and their pedagogical significance for EAP students.

6.6.1. Saliency of size

Counting all the relevant realisations considered in this chapter, the saliency given to size is found to vary remarkably across domains. Against an average figure of 24.3 occurrences per 10,000 words, there is a sixfold difference between the two extremes. More specifically, there are two strong size-marking disciplines (ANTH, PHY), three at or around average (ENG, ECO, BIO) and the remaining well below average:

Intensity	*Discipline*	*Norm. occurrences*
Strong	ANTH	74.1
	PHY	58.6
Average	ENG	27.5
	ECO	25.7
	BIO	18.2
Weak	SOC	15.1
	CS	13.6
	MED	13.6
	MATH	13.1
	HIST	11.8

Table 5. Size-marking intensity by discipline.

These subdivisions may be interpreted as indicative not so much of converging academic concerns among different domains but rather of a shared interest in aspects of research that are measurable and hence quantitatively assessable by approximation. While providing specific measurements is not an axiologically relevant act, claiming that something is *large/small* clearly encodes a judgement linked to a variable – or 'parameter', to use Thetela's (1997) term – whose interpretation must be shared, to a certain extent at least, by writer and audience. This variable is marked explicitly, albeit not evaluatively, by the lexeme *size* and its variants (especially in ANTH).

6.6.2. Type of marker

A closer look at the use of size markers within domains highlights several further differences. First of all, the fact that Groups A and B combined (i.e. *large** and occasionally *big**) account for 44% of all occurrences, followed by Group C (*small**) at 32% and Group D (*size**) at 24%. This finding suggests that scholars are generally more willing to view size in terms of varying degrees of 'largeness', rather than 'smallness' or through the evaluatively-neutral markers in Group D. As for the syntactic position of such items – excluding those in Group D, which are either nouns or invariable in word order – their use is attributive in 77% of cases (cf. Table 3). Predicative occurrences were uncommon in Group A (17%) but relatively frequent in Group C (30%), with Group B in an intermediate position. The indication therefore is that attributive constructions are unlikely to encode 'largeness', as compared to 'smallness': in other words, RA authors find it harder to make the subjective statement *X is large* than to say that *X is small*. At the same time, syntactic foregrounding is favoured for less conspicuous entities (i.e. *small* ones), while the same is less likely to occur when an entity is more conspicuous (i.e. *large*).

Turning from general to discipline-specific results, there are several differences worth noting. As mentioned earlier, physicists and anthropologists are far more prone to make this value explicit, through adjectives that encode 'smallness', 'largeness' or (occasionally) 'bigness'. Whether Group D items are included or not, PHY and ANTH share a concern for quantification that is unmatched in other domains. As for the prevalent polarity of such realisations, the *large/big* end of the spectrum prevails most markedly in ECO, SOC and ENG, with around 70% of markers belonging to Groups A-B; conversely, 'smallness' is prevalent in CS and MATH, where Group C items account for around 60% of relevant items.

Group C markers constitute around one third of the total, with 73% of qualifiers in the base form, followed by the comparative (23%) and the superlative (4%). The distribution across disciplines, however, does not always reflect that observed in Group A (see Figure 1) and the balance between polarities varies accordingly, with 'largeness' prevailing in ECO and ENG but 'smallness' prevalent in

MATH and CS, while in the remaining disciplines are roughly equal. As for Group D items, these are particularly frequent in ANTH (35.2 occurrences), where they account for 48% of size markers, moderately represented in BIO (7.5), ECO (5.8) and SOC (4.7) but uncommon elsewhere. In PHY – which has the second highest count for Groups A-C – *size* is seldom mentioned.

6.6.3. Qualified entities and collocations

Group A items are associated above all with the phenomena observed by researchers. Although in ANTH, BIO and CS they often denote the physical dimensions of an object, they are used essentially as value-markers signalling the researcher's interpretation of data in terms of size. The main collocations identified in the corpus, in decreasing order, were *larger than*, *large number/s*, *large scale/s*, *very large*, *relatively large* and *large amount/s*. Group B items were infrequent, with the qualifier *big* prominent only in PHY (4.6), where it occurs exclusively as part of the discipline's terminology, as in *big rip, big boost, big brake, big crunch.*

Within Group C, *small* peaks in PHY (18.0) and ANTH (11.9), like its antonym *large*; the type of qualified entity is also very similar. Its main collocations are *smaller than*, *relatively small*, *very small* and *small number/s*. The fact that all instances of *sufficiently small* occur in MATH suggests that the discipline is more interested in 'smallness' than its counterparts – a hypothesis confirmed by the fact that it has the highest C/A group ratio (i.e. 2.1). *Smaller* also has the highest proportion (48%) of predicative uses among size markers: these are particularly likely to involve the quantitative assessment of data, empirical parameters and observational phenomena but only rarely the actual physical dimensions of qualified entities. Most predicative occurrences (68%) involve the *smaller than* collocation, which means that scholars are most likely to complete the *X is smaller* pattern with a term of reference introduced by *than*. In the case of *larger*, the figure is only slightly lower (63%).

Finally, Group D markers are associated almost entirely with physical dimensions in ANTH and CS, while ECO and SOC generally use them to qualify numeric data. In normalised terms, such items are particularly prominent in ANTH, where the main collocations identified were *brain size* and *body size.*

6.6.4. Vagueness vs. precision

The semantic underspecification inherent in Group A-C qualifiers brings to mind the much-debated phenomenon of *vagueness* in academic lexis. Although indeterminacy is to a certain extent an inevitable feature of human communication (cf. Keefe 2000), modern science emphasises the need to describe the objective, measurable features of experience, which means that linguistic precision and transparency are highly valued. Counter to this trend, a recent study has shown that in academic writing numerical evidence is often introduced by approximators, which serve "to generalize certain tendencies, as well as to refer to proportions, percentages, and exceptionally large or small numbers" (Ruzaite 2004: 244). More surprisingly, their presence was found to be significantly higher in academic texts (5.7 tokens/10,000 words) than in business (2.6), politics (3.5) and leisure-related (3.7) discourse. In line with Ruzaite's data, the main collocates associated with size marking in our corpus included the approximator *relatively*, used to mitigate the truth-value of assessments encoded by the markers *large* and *small.* As a result, such utterances compound two levels of 'fuzziness' (Lakoff 1973), linked on the one hand to the largely subjective nature of the qualifiers involved (how 'large' is *large*?) and on the other hand to the deliberate semantic instability introduced by an approximator (how 'large' is *relatively large*?).

Vague realisations can be interpreted as further evidence of the presence of an underlying principle (the academic value of size) whose significance in context is accessible to both parties, as RA authors and their audience are aware of the axiological variables integral to the discipline and its epistemology. Without this common understanding, such claims as *The pneumatic cells are relatively small* or *The OutCast system used a relatively large touch-screen display* would be meaningless without further specification. Counterbalancing this phenomenon, the main collocates of *large* and *small* also included an intensifier (*very*) that seems to strengthen the truth-value of the proposition. It could be argued, however, that because of the vagueness inherent in the markers it intensifies, the result is not dissimilar to that observed earlier (how 'large' is *very large*?).

7. Novelty markers

The third most frequent group of candidate items identified in Chapter 4 encoded were related to an axiological variable that may be labelled as ‘novelty’. This time-bounded value qualifies a given referent as more or less desirable due to some unprecedented feature viewed as a (potential) improvement on previous referents within the same category. The concept of novelty expresses both continuity and discontinuity with the past and as such is an attribute that can be placed on a cline. Generally speaking, lack of innovation at one end of the cline (maximum continuity, zero discontinuity) is perceived as counterproductive, but the same can be said of the opposite end (minimum continuity, maximum discontinuity), which may too radical a departure from the established order. Finding the right balance between these two extremes is especially important in academic writing when authors and readers negotiate value judgements associated with novelty.

Novelty is linked to the condition of being *new* – which for the OED (2009) primarily denotes something “not previously existing; now made or brought into existence for the first time” or “of a kind now first invented or introduced; novel, newfangled; original”. The lexicographer’s definition is useful insofar as it makes explicit the co-existence of positive (novel, original) and negative (newfangled) connotations in the same qualifier. As mentioned above, novelty is not always equally desirable and its lexical realisations in each discipline are likely to vary in prominence according to the saliency given to this value when interpreting scientific evidence and knowledge claims.

7.1. Why novelty matters

Academic disciplines evolve through a twofold process: on the one hand by extending their insights within existing theoretical/analytical frameworks; and on the other hand by venturing into uncharted ground and challenging (more or less explicitly) existing knowledge. This means that what is 'new' can either be viewed as a mere addition to the discipline or, more ambitiously, as a turning point in its evolution. According to Kuhn (1962) scientific progress is governed by a recurring pattern whereby 'normal science' inevitably accumulates a number or anomalies leading to a crisis that sooner or later produces a new paradigm. At the same time, most researchers are under pressure from the institutions that employ them to maximise their academic productivity (largely in terms of published output). This makes instability an inherent feature of disciplinary communities and their behaviour:

> Unlike some other social systems that seek stability and ritual regularity in their communications (such as churches, island tribes, or lower echelons of bureaucracies) and change only when forced by exigencies (such as climactic change, new populations to proselytize, or political revolution) scientific communities are by their nature committed to new formulations, new knowledge. If they have no new knowledge to create, they cannot be legitimately maintained. (Bazerman 1988: 308)

Throughout their academic career, scholars are accountable to their peers. They acknowledge this by showing familiarity with the literature and interacting with other authors, because ultimately any new knowledge claim must by validated by the disciplinary community. In Bazerman's words again, scientists "must draw on their reading, their empirical experience, and their interactions with their peers so as to use the existing symbol system to point to phenomena previously uncontained by symbols but reliably reproducible, recognizable, and persuasive to peers" (1988: 318). Because of the social networks that underlie disciplines, it is not enough to put forward interesting ideas and/or data – these must also be accepted by fellow researchers as reasonable propositions and be gradually incorporated into established knowledge. Another important factor determining the acceptability of a novel claim is timing: as in other realms of human action, finding the right time-slot can be essential to communicative success. Miller (1992: 323) refers to the time factor as *kairos*, that is "a conceptual or intellectual space, understood as the opportunity provided by explanatory problems, and a social or professional space, understood as the opportunity provided by a forum of interaction". Securing the right slot in an academic debate is no accident but usually the result of careful networking and planning on the author's part.

Research genres and their rhetoric – most notably in the creation of a 'research space' (Swales 1990) where an author can present his/her findings – are instrumental to the dissemination of new knowledge. There is evidence, for instance, that constructing novelty is a priority in letters to academic editors, according to Blakeslee's (1994) investigation of the genre. At the same time, academic discourse is not immune from the influence of journalism, with its emphasis on newsworthiness: Huckin (1987) makes this point in an unpublished paper based on interviews with physicists and biologists, who claim that they search out newsworthy articles when consulting a journal. Mirroring this type of behaviour, is the tendency of RAs to present research in a way that promotes 'surprise value'. Expert writers are particularly proficient in rhetorically balancing the tension between novelty and continuity and "the result of this negotiation is that the literature of a scientific field reproduces itself even in the contributions of those who challenge some of its assumptions" (Myers 1990: 67).

7.2. Selection of candidate items

The WL entries singled out in Chapter 4 as candidates for investigation (listed again below) were all adjectives, with *new* alone accounting for almost half of the occurrences. Even at a quick glance, the semantic area covered by such items is noticeably diverse and not entirely consistent with the value under scrutiny. The concordance of each item had to be inspected therefore to verify whether it qualified for inclusion in the analysis and, if included, to identify which occurrences encoded meanings connected to the idea of novelty outlined earlier – i.e. a certain degree of discontinuity with pre-existing conditions.

Novelty	*n*
new	753
modern	346
recent	188
older	128
novel	122
old	118
Total	*1,655*

Table 1. Candidate items (absolute frequency).

The top entry in the candidate list undeniably qualified for inclusion, with the exception of its use in place names (*New York, New England, New Zealand, New South, New Orleans, New Mexico/Mexican, New World, New Spain, New Jersey*), titles of publications (*New India, New Vision, New Testament, Harper's New Monthly Magazine*) and the names of organisations (*New Man Society*), movements (*New Left*), programmes (*New Deal*) or consumer products (*New Beetle*). The concordance was also checked for instances of *new* meaning 'not used' but none were found.

The next item (*modern*) was almost invariably employed to encode the notion of 'modernity', that is in purely historical terms, as in *modern humans* and *modern Japan*, or in the phrase *modern food webs* (BIO); its more mundane, evaluative meaning was unrepresented in the corpus. As a result, the word was not included in the investigation of novelty markers.

Greater attention was needed in the case of *recent*, which may merely denote a location in time closer to the deictic centre of discourse (in which case it cannot be viewed as a novelty-marker) or, more interestingly, may serve as a positively-connotated qualifier drawing on the idea of novelty. The latter meaning is most prominent in collocations signalling findings or data that add to disciplinary knowledge (e.g. *recent approaches/contributions/evidence*). Because of the evolutionary ethos that underpins scientific enquiry, what is 'recent' is implicitly new and thus very likely to be an improvement on earlier knowledge. With this distinction in mind, purely chronological uses of the adjective (as in *recent fears/imports/ decades/times*) were discounted as irrelevant.

No particular difficulty was encountered in the case of *novel*, which never appeared as a noun (=book-length narrative), while *old* had to be closely inspected to remove age-expressions (e.g. *eight years old, centuries-old*) and occurrences such as *old age, Old World* and *Old South*. This was necessary because of the focus on entries that judge something to be *old* as opposed to 'new' (rather than 'young'), given our interest here in the marking of novelty. By this standard, *older* did not qualify for inclusion since it invariably referred to age rather than (negated) novelty.

7.3. Additional items

The list of core markers conveying the value of novelty was then integrated, as in previous chapters, by completing the lexical sets built around such items and adding, where available, relevant antonyms and/or synonyms. The resulting lexical groups are listed below, complete of further information on the rationale for their inclusion.

Group A. *New, newer, newly, novel, novelty/ies, fresh* | *old, obsolete, antiquated*

To reconstruct the lexical set based on *new*, the WL was searched for instances of its comparative and superlative forms; only a few cases of the former were found. The adverbial *newly* was also included because, though partly overlapping with 'recently' (as in *newly-enacted law*), it also expresses novelty. The set based on *novel* was completed with the introduction of *novelty/ies*. *Fresh* was then added to the group, after removing entries meaning 'not soiled' (e.g. *fresh condition* in ANTH) and 'not salty' (*fresh water system* in ENG). By the same standard, no occurrences of *freshly* (e.g. *freshly excavated, freshly prepared*) were considered. The qualifiers *obsolete* and *antiquated*, which are both loosely synonymous with *old* in the sense targeted here, were then added to the negative end of this group. Like *older*, the superlative *oldest* was excluded because it appeared only in age-related expressions (e.g. *oldest fossils*).

Group B. *Innovate*, innovation/s, innovative, renew**

The second group of items encodes the process of 'innovation', which is interpretable as a subcategory of novelty. The verb *innovate* was thus investigated in all of its morphological variants, along with its nominalised (*innovation*) and adjectival (*innovative*) forms. Linked to this is the verb *renew*, which also qualified for inclusion in the concordance.

Group C. *Recent, recently, latest*

Last in the list is the qualifier *recent* and its adverbial form, both of which were subjected to the same criterion for inclusion applied to Group B items: namely their use as positive markers of new developments in the discipline. Semantically related to this meaning is the superlative *latest*, when it expresses novelty – a case illustrated by the similar collocations *recent research* and *the latest research.* Though surprisingly rare, this lexeme was also included in the group.

7.4. Overall results

The novelty markers selected for investigation account for a total of 1,053 tokens, a result which so far makes novelty third in rank, after size and goodness. If we look at the distribution of individual items, *new* alone accounts for 58% of all occurrences (612/1,053), followed by *recent/recently* at 18% and *novel* at 12%. Negative lexicalisations, limited to Group A, are relatively scarce, merely 4% of the total – a result that underscores the strong desirability of novelty (and the stigma attached to its absence) in research writing. A detailed breakdown of items by group is given below.

	Item	*n*	*Subtotal*
Group A	new (adj)	(753) 612	
	newer (adj)	3	
	newly (adv)	21	
	novel (adj)	122	
	novelty/ies (n)	10	
	fresh (adj)	5	773
	old (adj)	(118) 36	
	obsolete (adj)	2	
	antiquated (adj)	2	40
Group B	innovate* (v)	2	
	innovation/s (n)	29	
	innovative (adj)	6	
	renew* (v)	5	
	renewed (adj)	11	53
Group C	recent (adj)	(188) 126	
	recently (adv)	60	
	latest (adj)	1	187
Total			*(1,328) 1,053*

Table 2. Full list of novelty markers (by group).

It is also interesting to note that the second group of markers are the least frequent, although they are arguably the strongest items (in terms of evaluative force) because of their overt reference to the discontinuity inherent in novelty: something qualified as *innovative* being more of a departure from established order than what is simply qualified as *new*. The use of different parts of speech is also worth considering, as adjectives account for almost the whole of Group A and over two thirds of Group C items, while Group B has a prevalence of nouns (a finding that will be further considered when the analysis focuses on specific realisations within domains).

7.4.1. Predicative vs. attributive uses

As in previous chapters, the position of value-marking adjectives was examined in each concordance to assess the relative weight of predicative/attributive constructions in the three groups considered. The results, summarised in Table 3, show that when signalling novelty (unlike goodness and size) the predicative slot is very marginal, being limited only to a handful of occurrences of Group A adjectives (more specifically *new*, *novel* and *obsolete*).

	Predicative	*Attributive*	*All*
Group A	15	767	782
Group B	-	17	17
Group C	-	127	127
Total	*2%*	*98%*	*926*

Table 3. Syntactic position of novelty-marking adjectives (by group).

On the whole, therefore, novelty hardly ever qualifies for syntactic prominence in the corpus. This may be the case because it is such an obvious quality of academic enquiry that authors are unlikely to foreground it in unmarked contexts.

7.5. Distribution across disciplines

In order to assess the presence and function of these markers in different domains, all the occurrences identified in the corpus were subdivided by discipline. The details are given in Table 4 below, with the total count for each group shown, as usual, in normalised terms. Taken together (cf. bottom line) the figures indicate that the explicit marking of novelty varies considerably from one domain to another: most noticeably, it is particularly intense in HIST (26.0) – at over twice the average – and well below average in ENG, MATH and PHY. The fact that historians are those most interested in this value is perhaps not surprising, given the discipline's focus on the variably predictable aspects of human action and on the amount of innovation/ conservation observed in historical phenomena. Interestingly, the second highest domain in the list is BIO (20.5), which stands out above all for its extensive use of the qualifier *novel*.

Item	*ANTH*	*BIO*	*CS*	*ECO*	*ENG*	*HIST*	*MATH*	*MED*	*PHY*	*SOC*	*All*
Group A	3.9	16.0	8.4	8.1	2.7	23.1	3.1	4.3	3.0	10.1	8.7
new (adj)	(26)	(17)	(93)	(75)	(15)	(201)	(46)	(14)	(18)	(107)	(612)
newer (adj)	-	-	(1)	(1)	-	-	-	-	-	(1)	(3)
newly (adv)	(2)	-	(1)	-	(1)	(8)	(1)	(1)	-	(7)	(21)
novel (adj)	(1)	(97)	(8)	(3)	(2)	(9)	-	(1)	-	(1)	(122)
novelty/ies (n)	-	(4)	(1)	-	-	(2)	(2)	-	-	(1)	(10)
fresh (adj)	-	(1)	-	-	-	(4)	-	-	-	-	(5)
Positive	91%	100%	93%	94%	100%	92%	100%	100%	100%	97%	95%
old (adj)	(3)	-	(6)	(5)	-	(18)	-	-	-	(4)	(36)
obsolete (adj)	-	-	(2)	-	-	-	-	-	-	-	(2)
antiquated (adj)	-	-	-	-	-	(2)	-	-	-	-	(2)
Negative	9%	-	7%	6%	-	8%	-	-	-	3%	5%
Group B	0.4	0.3	-	0.6	0.1	2.3	-	0.3	0.2	1.2	0.6
innovate* (v)	-	-	-	-	-	(2)	-	-	-	-	(2)
innovation/s (n)	(2)	(1)	-	(4)	(1)	(18)	-	-	-	(3)	(29)
innovative (adj)	(1)	-	-	(1)	-	-	-	-	-	(4)	(6)
renew* (v)	-	(1)	-	-	-	(1)	-	-	-	(3)	(5)
renewed (adj)	-	-	-	(1)	-	(3)	-	(1)	(1)	(5)	(11)
Group C	4.2	4.2	1.3	2.1	1.5	0.6	0.8	3.0	2.7	2.2	2.0
recent (adj)	(21)	(24)	(11)	(21)	(8)	(3)	(4)	(9)	(3)	(22)	(126)
recently (adv)	(13)	(7)	(6)	(1)	(2)	(3)	(8)	(2)	(13)	(5)	(60)
latest (adj)	-	-	(1)	-	-	-	-	-	-	-	(1)
Total	*8.5*	*20.5*	*9.7*	*10.8*	*4.4*	*26.0*	*3.9*	*7.6*	*5.9*	*13.5*	*11.2*

Table 4. Distribution of novelty markers across disciplines.

While the lion's share goes to Group A, there were therefore significant differences between domains. These are clearly visible in Figure 1 below, which illustrates the amount of novelty marking across the corpus in decreasing order of frequency. The balance between groups, however, diverges from the overall trend in three domains, as Groups B-C comprise almost half of all markers in MED and PHY, while they are the majority in ANTH. Possible reasons for such behaviour will be explored with the aid of collocational evidence and suitable examples in the next section.

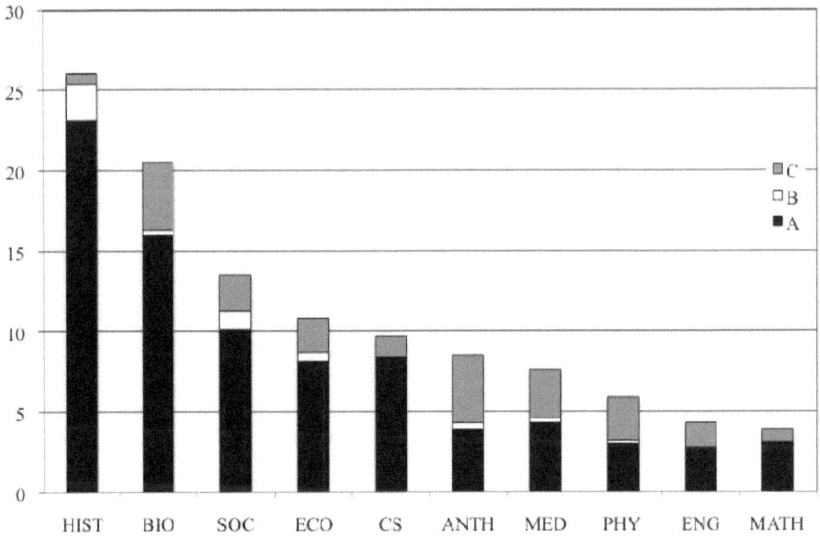

Figure 1. Novelty markers by group and discipline, in decreasing order (occurrences / 10,000 words).

7.6. Qualified entities and realisations

The type of entity qualified by these markers, especially adjectives, is indicative of the prominence given to aspects of research that are interpreted in terms of greater or lesser novelty. When scholars communicate their findings in RAs, one of the axiological variables embedded in their judgements is the value of 'newness', viewed as a key quality in the process of knowledge construction. The assumption made earlier as to the desirability of novelty (in contrast with what is outdated and hence no longer useful or worthy of attention) can only be verified by considering the variety of realisations in the corpus. For this purpose, the concordances generated for the items listed in Table 4 were inspected for evidence of relevant co-occurrences and contextual features. The main findings are described below.

7.6.1. Group A

This is the only group to include negative markers (*old, obsolete, antiquated*) so it is possible to compare the relative weight of the two polarities across domains. While the positive end of the spectrum is strongly prevalent throughout the corpus, there is a clear difference between disciplines where 'oldness', as a proportion of the whole, is totally or virtually absent (BIO, ENG, MATH, MED, PHY, SOC) and those where it accounts for 6-9% of these markers (ANTH, CS, ECO, HIST). The latter disciplines are therefore relatively more prone to signal 'oldness' than other fields represented in the corpus.

Moving to the use of individual items, *new* is clearly the key word in Group A – the only exception being BIO, where the adjective *novel* accounts for 80% of markers. A general reading of the concordance shows that *new* qualifies a wide variety of objects, ranging from the most mundane to the highly abstract. These realisations prevalently involve: (a) aspects of the discipline's methodology and interpretation of phenomena; (b) aspects of the evidence collected. Each case is illustrated below by a pair of examples from each domain, with the qualified entity underlined once for (a) and twice for (b). The impression is that the former implies a greater degree of discontinuity – through more intensely axiological uses of the qualifier *new* – because novelty emerges as a result of deliberation rather than a quality due to the chronological sequence of events.

(133) Recently, *new* methods of cleaning with lasers have been tested (Landucci et al., 2003), although their use is not widespread, and the majority of treatments continue to be done in the traditional manner. ANTH
We had to try to ensure that any fragmentation occurred in a controlled manner along the already existing fracture lines (without creating *new* fragmentation planes). ANTH

(134) Our results reveal *new* developmental roles of MIDA1-like chaperones and HLF-like transcription factors. BIO
Together with structure-based mutagenesis and related biochemical experiments, the *new* TG2 structure provides direct mechanistic insights into isopeptide bond formation by TG2. BIO

(135) After running the experiment with version 1.0, we had *new* questions about behavior and desired to explore different visualizations of face-to-face speaking patterns. CS
When using the *new* system, a group can either view an aggregate of the speaking data over the entire meeting or watch a sliding window of the previous 2 or 5 min for a more dynamic view. CS

(136) This paper proposes a *new* mechanism linking trade and wage inequality in developing countries – the quality-upgrading mechanism – and investigates its empirical implications in panel data on Mexican manufacturing plants. ECO
Therefore the intensive margin of trade was substantially driven by variations in the fraction of trading firms but not by *new* trading partners. ECO

(137) This study proposes a *new* viable eco-remediation technique based on the use of a wide range of natural organic substances (NOS) that characterise the Mediterranean region. ENG
Since the survey boat's average speed was 68km/h and we measured a *new* radon data point every 10 min, the spatial resolution was around 1 km over nearly 200 km of navigation covering both margins of the lagoon. ENG

(138) In reopening the opening of Japan in this way [...] we can attempt to open up *new* dimensions for modern history writing. HIST
Gradually, however, Yeats and Tagore grew uneasy with these *new* nationalist movements and criticized them openly. HIST

(139) Though the second result (Main Theorem II) is more appropriate for applications, the main *new* ideas of the paper appear in section 2 related to the proof of the first result. MATH
Surgering out this circle gives a *new* embedded surface homologous to F1 whose complexity is no greater than that of F1. MATH

(140) Our findings, if confirmed in different settings, will contribute to the assessment of *new* therapeutic and preventive strategies for Africa. MED
In Tanzania, an estimated 74% of *new* HIV infections in men, 22% in women, and 63% in bar and hotel workers are attributable to HSV-2. MED

(141) Some of these ideas were recently generalized in a *new* model of quantum initial conditions for the Universe. PHY
As a direct consequence of this *new* interaction, the neutrino mass mν is generated from the vacuum expectation value (VEV) of the scalar field and becomes linked to its dynamics. PHY

(142) Prominent *new* paradigm theorists Finke and Stark (1988, 1992; see also Iannaccone 1991; Finke, Guest, and Stark 1996) built on Berger and Luckmann's market analogy. SOC
The enactment of the Civil Rights Act of 1964 furnished activists with *new* weapons to impose greater costs upon noncompliant enterprises, but resistance continued. SOC

In most disciplines, *new* qualifies type (a) referents, thus showing a prevalent interest in novelty as a feature of scholarly enquiry, whether in terms of methodological advancement or new theoretical insights. Thus novelty is mainly introduced as a positive value, associated with the scientific community's quest for knowledge. As clearly illustrated by the examples above, this meaning often co-occurs with personal/deictic constructions promoting the authors' findings (e.g. *Our results reveal; This study proposes*) or summarising recent research (*Some of these ideas were recently generalized; Prominent... theorists Finke and Stark*). Though generally dominant in the corpus, the same tendency was not observed in ENG, HIST, MATH or SOC, where novelty qualifies almost exclusively type (b) referents. Based on the use of the main size-marker (*new*), the latter disciplines are arguably less interested in novelty as a feature of research than in something that exists 'out there', awaiting to be observed or acknowledged with hardly any effort on the researcher's part. The co-text of *new* is in line with these findings, since the item's most common right collocates encode both types of qualified entity: *technology/ies* (20 occurrences), *information* (13), *strategy/ies* (11), *way/s* (10) and *opportunity/ies* (9). The only prominent L1 collocates were found to be *this/these* (29).

It is worth adding that, out of 612 occurrences of *new*, only a fraction (i.e. five) are employed predicatively. Because of their rarity, however, they deserve a closer reading:

(143) As if to confirm these fears, the act of smoking "which, from a physical standpoint, was *new* and unconventional" soon expanded to plainly illicit substances such as hashish and opium. HIST

(144) Indeed, although it was Wilson who popularized the term 'self-determination' in the international discourse of the period, the idea behind 'government by popular consent' was hardly *new* or original. HIST

(145) Our results seem to be *new*, even in this vastly simplified case; indeed we are not aware of any nontrivial results concerning the null radius of injectivity for Lorentzian manifolds. MATH

(146) The proof is not *new* (see [LO], for example), but we provide it here for completeness. MATH

(147) We discuss the four such cases separately from the vast majority who explored through activities that were both *new* and interactive. SOC

In three of these, *new* appears within a dyad (*new and unconventional, new or original, new and interactive*) that counterbalances the item's weakness. This may of course be due to its unmarked status, which is at odds with a predicative construction, but the impression is that, like other novelty markers, *new* is weakened by the conventional, down-to-earth quality of the value it communicates. Claiming that something is *new* does not qualify for syntactic prominence even though the value encoded may be of special significance in context, because 'newness' is (within and outside academia) one of the most abused concepts of our age and because it is integral to the evolutionary process of knowledge construction.

Linked to this finding is the absence (apart from three occurrences of *newer*) of comparative/superlative forms in the corpus. The implication may be that, at least in academic discourse, *new* is not gradable, which means that novelty is either present or it is not, with no intermediate options allowed. The marker's non-gradable quality is substantiated by the lack of hedging or intensifying collocates: the only premodifiers employed with *new* (for a total of 6/612 occurrences) were *entirely*, *completely* and *fundamentally*. These modulate the truth value of the claim rather than the intensity of the adjective itself, so that 'newness' is treated as an invariable quality which is more or less present in its referent.

The second most frequent word in Group A is *novel*, a marker concentrated in BIO (13.8 occurrences/10,000 words), with only a fraction in the other domains (all under 1.0) and no tokens at all in MATH and PHY. Unlike *new*, it tends to emphasise discontinuity without evoking the notion of 'recency' (cf. *a new theory* vs. *a novel theory*). This is perhaps reflected, at least in part, by the higher proportion of predicative uses of *novel* (7%) as compared to *new* (1%). However, it is only by looking at specific realisations that this distinction can be tested. The prominence of *novel* in BIO is largely due to a paper entitled 'Rapid encoding and perception of novel odors in the rat', which accounts for all but two of its occurrences in this domain. Interestingly, the paper's authors explain that *novel* means 'not previously presented' (the opposite of *familiar*) and they always employ the term to qualify the experience of the tested subject:

(148) In most trials, the rat has already identified an odorant as *novel* and begun responding to it before peak activity maps have fully developed. BIO

The point-of-view dislocation inherent in such realisations is not inconsistent with the assumption that *novel* underscores discontinuity (assessed here from the perspective of the laboratory rat). The same phenomenon applies to contexts that could justify other interpretations: in the sentence below, for example, *novel trials* are those targeting the perception of 'novel odors' and not a new set of tests.

(149) To further characterize response times to novel odorants, we compared respiratory behavior in all *novel trials* with that in all trials involving the presentation of a learned (CS) odorant. BIO

All the significant right collocates identified in the concordance – namely *odorant/s* (39 tokens) and *trials* (12) – belonged to this article. Only a few instances of *novel* identified in BIO extended to aspects of the research process:

(150) By subsequently combining a secondary RNAi screen with a bioinformatics analysis based primarily on Y2H data, we have identified a MAP complex containing the Skp1 homolog, SkpA, and a *novel* protein we term SkAP. BIO

In the other domains, *novel* qualifies both type (a) and (b) referents. On the surface, many of its occurrences are in fact interchangeable with *new*, albeit (as speculated earlier) with a greater emphasis on discontinuity with previous phenomena. In this respect, the markedness of *novel* is substantiated by its predicative use in several disciplines apart from BIO:

(151) The proposition that brain size is related to life history variables, such as fecundity, age at maturity, and lifespan, is not *novel*. ANTH

(152) Although the notion of reaching operational use of a system is not *novel* to interaction design (John/Kieras 1996), the systems designed using these methods are often focused on conscious, action-level interaction. CS

(153) As *novel* as the drink itself, they became renowned for the loose, worldly atmosphere that they harbored. HIST

Again, premodification was extremely rare, with only two relevant left collocations in the whole corpus (*entirely*, *fundamentally*). The nominalised form *novelty/ies* was also uncommon and largely limited to BIO, though in MATH it is introduced twice by boosters to promote the knowledge claims made by the author:

(154) This definition is certainly one of the *most important novelties* in the present paper [...] This part contains the *main novelties* of our paper. MATH

The last positive marker in this group (*fresh*) had only five relevant tokens in the corpus, four of which in HIST. As in the case of *new*, they either qualify scholarly insights (155) or phenomena/materials (156):

(155) Tracing the relationship between nationalist child welfare activists and the imperial state thus provides a *fresh perspective* on the revolutions of 1918-1919 in East Central Europe. HIST

(156) *Fresh infusions* of African rice consumers and women skilled in rice production are said to have arrived in Suriname via the Dutch slave trade. HIST

The negative polarity of Group A is scantily represented in the corpus, thus suggesting a reluctance to mention 'oldness' in written research because of its extreme negativity (given the almost universal desirability of 'newness'). At the same time, it is reasonable to assume that reference to things that are *old* in this sense may simply be avoided as irrelevant – one of the many instances of textual silence (Huckin 1996) whose presence can only be assessed through qualitative-ethnographic methods of the type employed in Myers's (1990) study of how knowledge is textualised in biology RAs. There were very few relevant instances of *old* and none of *older/oldest*; these occurred mostly in HIST but occasionally also in ANTH, CS, ECO and SOC. It is interesting to note that most of these four domains share an interest in the diachronic dimension of human behaviour, which would account for the emergence of 'oldness' as a feature of human experience rather than scientific judgement. A closer look at the concordance list will help to clarify this point.

Single realisations of *old* show that this qualifier is invariably associated with the observed phenomena (157-159); only once (160) does it qualify aspects of the academic debate. The negotiability of this distinction, however, is signalled at times (161) by the use of quotation marks distancing the author from a problematic conceptual dyad.

(157) The Ottoman state was eager to remove the least doubt about its own religious credentials, which would need occasional burnishing as the *old* assumption of Ottoman military superiority permanently vanished during the eighteenth century. HIST

(158) Just as for the landowners, this creates an incentive to invest in the appreciation of leisure: the industrial dynasties ultimately mimic the tastes of the *old* elite. ECO

(159) Major political events such as imperial conquest or nation-state formation transform the institutional structure, which in turn provides incentives to pursue new strategies of boundary making while letting go of *old* ones. SOC

(160) By the mid-1980s, however, following Joan Scott's influential challenge to apply gender analysis to historical studies and the flowering of cultural studies, new perspectives on individual identity and class consciousness began to dissolve *old* dichotomies. HIST

(161) This new cosmopolitanism is contrasted to most nineteenth- and twentieth-century forms of nationalist thought because it questions the value of nation-states with unique, unitary cultures opposed to all others. At the same time, it also differs from the *'old'* cosmopolitanism or universalism of the eighteenth century. HIST

The only other negative markers found in the corpus were *obsolete* (with two occurrences, both predicative, in CS) and *antiquated* (embedded in citations from Engels and Tagore in HIST). Despite its minimal frequency, *obsolete* is therefore the only marker, among those identified so far, that is always used predicatively. The intensely evaluative orientation of the RAs concerned appears to justify such prominence, at least in CS:

(162) The multicue, icon-laden interface of ContextContacts forces the user to be very selective, because some of the available cues are always irrelevant, *obsolete*, or incomplete with regard to the inferential task at hand. CS

7.6.2. Group B

This group comprises only 0.5% (53/1,053) of all the novelty markers considered, yet its presence within domains is worth exploring because its items are those that most overtly signal discontinuity over time by evoking the notion of *innovation* and *renewal* rather than mere 'newness'. Hence Group B emphasises the cycle of creation, decline and regeneration that underlies both human knowledge and many of the phenomena researched by scientists. As a consequence, it implies (critically) that there was something amiss in the prior state of affairs, awaiting to be rectified. Perhaps the indirectness of such criticism also accounts for the slightly higher number of Group B items (53), compared to negative Group A markers (40).

In normalised terms, the most prominent disciplines were again HIST (2.3 occurrences/10,000 words) and SOC (1.2), while BIO (0.3) is far below average. The type of innovation referred to by such types is largely embedded in the events/phenomena considered:

(163) Modernists' views of history marked a fundamental break with Enlightenment thinking in a way similar to their *innovations* in aesthetic practices. HIST

(164) As Jenness and Grattet (2005) argue, community linkages make an agency more permeable and susceptible to legal *innovations*. SOC

(165) In addition, neocortex size has been shown to be correlated with many measures of cognitive ability, such as rates of *innovation*, social gregariousness, and complex foraging techniques. ANTH

As in the case of *old* (example 161), the precise meaning of *innovation/s* may be negotiable. In the sentence below, quotation marks are used again to signal the conceptual weakness of an evaluation that appeared controversial even in its own day:

(166) Moving on to the more strictly legal arguments, al-Nabulsi found no reason to condemn smoking. Despite the insistence of staunch moralists, he asserted that tobacco was no more an intoxicant than coffee, which had undergone similar legal travails and emerged unscathed. Addressing charges that it was an impious *'innovation'*, he responded that not all innovations were bad. HIST

The only case of *innovation/s* qualifying the research process was found in an ECO text whose authors attribute such a value to the methodology adopted in their study. Because of the claim's face-threatening potential, however, this is aptly hedged by a 'modesty' adjective (cf. Myers 1989):

(167) The county indicators help to account for well-known geographic differences in factors such as access to medical care and physician practice patterns. Although this is a *simple innovation*, most previous studies have not controlled for county-fixed effects. ECO

Likewise, the related markers *innovate** and *innovative* always target the object of research, with one exception (again in ECO, though not from the same RA quoted above) that summarises and commends the authors' approach in the opening sentence of the Conclusions section:

(168) In this paper we use an *innovative* survey tool to collect management practice data from 732 medium-sized manufacturing firms in Europe and the United States. ECO

The last lexical set represented in Group B – consisting of *renew** and *renewed* – is relatively uncommon. There is an inherent ambiguity in its adjectival form, which embraces not only the idea of novelty but also (in varying degrees) that of recurrence, as illustrated by the example below:

(169) The lack of effect of suppressive therapy on HIV acquisition suggests that *renewed* attention should be given to new strategies of HSV-2 prevention and control to prevent HIV infection. MED

7.6.3. Group C

The last group of items are the least explicit markers, for they evoke novelty by the conventional implication that *recent* ideas, methods, research and technology are generally better than those that preceded them. The importance of this group can also be gauged by looking at its relative weight across domains (Figure 2), which is highest in ANTH (approx. 50%) and lowest in HIST (2%).

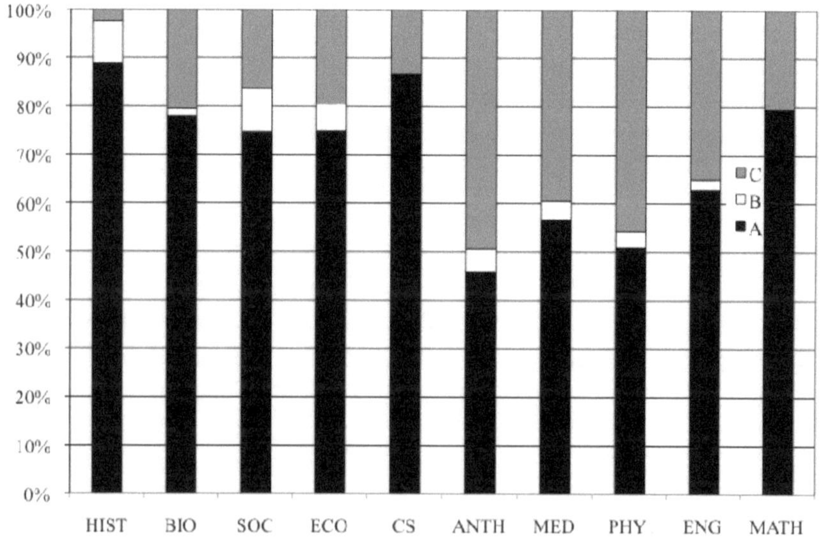

Figure 2. Relative weight of each group by discipline (percentage).

Turning to the distribution of Group C items across the corpus, the most noticeable feature is their prominence in ANTH and BIO (4.2

normalised occurrences), followed by MED (3.0). Yet only one of these domains (ANTH) tops the count for novelty as a whole, which means that Group C is unusually frequent in BIO and MED.

The adjective *recent* qualifies new contributions to the discipline, whether in terms of data, modelling, methodology or technology. In line with this orientation, the main right collocate of *recent* was found to be *study/ies* (33), followed at a distance by *work* (12), *data* (8), *literature* (7) and *research* (6). These collocations are often in thematic position, followed by a 'position verb' (Fløttum *et al.* 2006b) such as *show* or *suggest* indicating how the qualified entity contributes to the ongoing academic debate.

(170) A number of *recent studies have shown* that hierarchical features of food webs related to consumer-resource body-size ratios are important promoters of stability and persistence [52-55], *suggesting* that less-hierarchical arrangements are unlikely to persist over long time scales. BIO

(171) Our *recent work* on exploring visualization techniques is geared to enabling people to understand and manage information that requires attention in a situated social context. CS

(172) The 2000 albedo map was developed only for comparison, as at this moment climatological data were only gathered for up to 1990, but future work will focus on updating the BMHDB with *recent data*. ENG

(173) *Recent research* has revived interest in the association between cultural orientation and wealth by demonstrating that religion and asset ownership are correlated and that some religious groups are much more likely than others to experience persistent asset poverty (Keister 2003a, 2005). SOC

The novelty element is often underscored by the premodifier *more/most*, which is the main L1 collocate (19 occurrences) of *recent*. In both of the examples below, this collocation signals the contrast between older, less reliable references and newer, improved contributions to the literature. Significantly, the adversative connectors *however/although* are often found to the left of this marker (9 occurrences) but only once to its right.

(174) Unlike the early explanations of this defeat, which pointed to squabbles within the movement and poor planning, *more recent* commentary emphasizes

Pritchett's use of nonviolent, legal strategies of repression (McAdam 1982; Barkan 1984). SOC

(175) Although fibronectin crosslinking activity was the original biological function assigned to TG2, *more recent* data suggest that the catalytically active form of mammalian TG2 is a relatively rare species, both in the intracellular and extracellular milieu. BIO

The adverbial form *recently* follows a similar course, being frequently associated with position verbs (e.g. *prove, discuss, report, highlight*) or with the premodifier *more* (8 occurrences). Only in MATH and PHY is it more common than its root adjective. In the two sentences below, for example, its co-occurrence with *new* strengthens the novelty value inherent in each marker:

(176) In addition to modulated scenarios related to the perturbation $\delta\varphi e$, we have *recently* proposed a *new* modulated scenario, modulated inflation [3]. PHY

(177) *Recently*, *new* methods of cleaning with lasers have been tested (Landucci et al., 2003), although their use is not widespread, and the majority of treatments continue to be done in the traditional manner. ANTH

The last Group C item (*latest*) occurred only once as a novelty marker. Like *recent*, its meaning it not entirely transparent in terms of continuity/discontinuity but can be evinced from the context – in this case, the fact that the authors' *latest review* (and not others) is cited as an authoritative source:

(178) In addition, the potential impact of personality was largely ignored in the realm of computer-mediated communication until recently. In their *latest* review, Olson and Olson (2003) summarize this issue as follows. CS

7.7. Discussion

The importance of novelty as an academic value is substantiated by the results described in this chapter, which place it third in rank, after size and goodness, in the RA corpus. Out of 1,053 tokens marking novelty, *new* alone accounts for 58% of occurrences, followed by *recent/recently* (18%) and *novel* (12%), while the contribution of the other items is quantitatively negligible. If these figures are analysed according to the part of speech employed, novelty proves to be an eminently 'adjectival' value (87% tokens), with only 8% of adverbs, 4% of nouns and 1% of verbs – a result largely due to the prominence of *new*. It is thus perceived above all as an attribute and is unlikely to be encoded as a quality in its own right (noun) or an aspect of 'how things get done' (adverb or verb). Unlike goodness and size, however, novelty adjectives are hardly every used predicatively – a finding that suggests scholars are reluctant to give syntactic prominence to such a pervasive, universally acknowledged quality of academic enquiry. Because it is so clearly desirable and lexically unmarked, novelty is seldom foregrounded although it may be of special significance in a specific context. Its centrality (and the stigma attached to negative realisations) is confirmed by the dearth of items encoding the notion of 'oldness' in the corpus (a mere 4% of all novelty markers).

7.7.1. Saliency of novelty

According to corpus data, the saliency of novelty exhibits a considerable degree of variation across domains. When normalised by 10,000 words there is a sixfold difference between the two extremes, namely MATH (3.9) and HIST (26.0). More specifically, novelty is strongly marked in two disciplines (HIST, BIO), around the average level of 11.2 in three others (SOC, ECO, CS) and below average in the remaining domains. The figures are those shown in Table 5 below.

Intensity	*Discipline*	*Norm. occurrences*
Strong	HIST	26.0
	BIO	20.5
Average	SOC	13.5
	ECO	10.8
	CS	9.7
Weak	ANTH	8.5
	MED	7.6
	PHY	5.9
	ENG	4.4
	MATH	3.9

Table 5. Novelty-marking intensity by discipline.

This pattern is not easily interpretable with reference to the disciplinary pairings adopted in the corpus construction stage, apart from the presence of the two *social sciences* (ECO and SOC) in the middle of the intensity-marking range. The fact that HIST tops the list, with over twice the average number of markers, is perhaps not remarkable, given the discipline's interest in what is new vs. pre-existent in historically situated phenomena. On the other hand, the intensity observed in BIO, which was less predictable, depends largely on the topic of one of the papers in the corpus (dealing with the perception of 'novel odors'). Leaving aside the somewhat deviant case of BIO, novelty is most evident in a cluster of disciplines (HIST, SOC, ECO) that share a concern for the social dimension of human action.

7.7.2. Type of marker

When analysing the distribution of novelty markers, it is also important to consider the extent of semantic variation they encode. This is due to the fact that in most occurrences 'newness' qualifies both a position in time (whatever comes last) and, more evaluatively, something that is unique and unprecedented – hence the apparently redundant question 'How new is *new*?'. These two components of novelty are not always discernible and their balance tends to vary from one marker to another. It is thus useful to look at the various markers as separate subcategories of lexically/semantically related items.

The first of these (Group A) consists almost exclusively of adjectives and is the largest contributor to novelty marking in seven out of ten domains: it is less prominent only in MED and PHY (where groups B-C account for almost half of the markers) and in ANTH (where it ranks second, after Group C). The key item is clearly *new*, representing alone no less than 75% of Group A tokens; only in BIO is its prominence overshadowed by another marker in the same category. The second most frequent word (*novel*) accounts for 15% of items in this group and peaks in BIO, at 13.8 occurrences per 10,000 words against an average of only 1.3, but is totally absent in MATH and PHY. Whereas *new* tends to encode novelty as a quality embedded in a sequence of related events, *novel* emphasises discontinuity with the past.

The opposite polarity is seldom signalled lexically in the corpus: a finding that indicates scholars are reluctant to mention 'oldness', as opposed to 'newness', because of its negativity and possibly due to the irrelevance of what is dated or obsolete. There is a marked discrepancy in this respect between domains where 'oldness', as a proportion of the whole, is almost absent (BIO, ENG, MATH, MED, PHY, SOC) and others where it accounts for 6-9% of markers (ANTH, CS, ECO, HIST). The tendency of the latter disciplines to mention also the negative polarity appears more comprehensible if we consider that they share an interest in the chronological evolution of human society or of technology – hence the need to evaluate the 'oldness' of things as well as their 'newness'.

The least common markers are those in Group B, which encodes the strongest meanings in terms of evaluative force. This depends on the overt reference to discontinuity in the evaluation of something as *innovative* rather than simply *new*. Group B emphasises the cycle of creation, decline and regeneration that permeates human knowledge and many of the phenomena dealt with by scientists; it implies that there was something amiss awaiting to be rectified. As in Group A, the disciplines with the highest number of occurrences were HIST and SOC.

Group C contains the least explicit lexical set. Here novelty is signalled by referring to scientific developments that are *recent* –

whether in terms of theoretical insights, methodology or technology. The implication from a researcher's viewpoint is that what is recent is generally better than what came before. Group C items were equally frequent in BIO and ANTH (4.2 occurrences/10,000 words), followed by MED (3.0), while they were almost absent in MATH and HIST. This gap may indicate that the former domains are under greater pressure to innovate, as they push forward the boundaries of disciplinary knowledge, but also – as argued by Tannen (2002) – that there is a greater degree of agonism among such scholars in their quest for academic visibility.

7.7.3. Qualified entities and collocations

The semantic profile of novelty, interpreted as a value underpinning disciplinary research that is made lexically explicit in written discourse, can better be understood by examining the co-text of the markers described above. In particular, it is useful to consider the type of entity to which this value is ascribed, which is linked to the collocational horizon of novelty markers within sentences. The most frequent marker (*new*) is associated with a wide range of objects, ranging from the most mundane to the highly abstract. These generally belong to one of two categories: (a) aspects of the discipline's methodology and/or interpretation of phenomena; and (b) aspects of the evidence observed or collected. The former are prevalent in most disciplines and arguably express a greater degree of discontinuity because they communicate novelty as a result of human judgement and deliberation rather than a feature merely due to the chronology of events. An exception to this tendency was observed, however, in ENG, HIST, MATH and SOC, where *new* is associated almost exclusively with type (b) entities. In such domains novelty is therefore perceived primarily as something that exists 'out there', awaiting to be observed or acknowledged by researchers. The concordance reflects this pattern, with the most common right collocates of *new* being, in order of frequency, *technology/ies*, *information*, *strategy/ies*, *way/s* and *opportunity/ies*.

The virtual absence of comparative/superlative forms, combined with the unusual lack of hedging or intensifying premodifiers, may indicate moreover that (when employed for novelty marking) *new* behaves as a non-gradable adjective. In other words, 'newness' is an either/or feature of disciplinary knowledge that admits no intermediate options. Similar to *new* is the qualifier *novel*, found mainly in BIO. Though on the surface the two markers are interchangeable, the latter places greater emphasis on discontinuity with earlier phenomena – an impression substantiated by its predicative (i.e. structurally marked) use in several disciplines. The opposite polarity (encoded by *old*) was invariably associated with type (b) referents and only once qualified aspects of the academic debate.

The last comparatively prominent marker identified in the corpus signals novelty indirectly, as a quality of *recent* research linked to the RA's topic. Being an implicit improvement on (or deviation from) earlier contributions, recency can thus be understood as synonymous with 'newness' – a perspective consistent with the main right collocates of *recent* (i.e. *study/ies*, *work*, *data*, *literature* and *research*). These collocations are classifiable as evidentials (Biber/Finegan 1989), for they bring in other scholars' claims as an argumentative device underpinning the author's line of argumentation and, accordingly, are often followed by a position verb such as *show, prove, discuss* or *highlight*.

8. Relevance markers

The fourth and last category of markers identified in the global WL centres on the notion of 'relevance', conceptualised here as a quality attached by RA authors to referents deemed to be important/pertinent in a given context. Relevance is a key aspect of the academic value system in that it signals aspects of research deserving special attention on the interlocutor's part. As an analytical category it is dealt with (albeit differently) also elsewhere: Hunston (1994: 199) lists 'relevance' as one of the three *functions* of evaluative speech acts, alongside 'status' and 'value'; more recently, Thompson and Hunston have argued that 'importance or relevance' is one of the four parameters of evaluation (the other three being good/bad, certainty and expectedness) and that its function is largely metadiscoursal:

> It is part of the discourse itself that is evaluated as important, directing the reader towards the main point of the text. This is typically signalled through adjectives and adverbs such as *important* and *significantly.* [...] Evaluation along the importance parameter appears to play a key role in the organization of texts, as indications of the importance or relevance of information are found especially at the beginning and end of paragraphs or discourse sections. (Thompson/Hunston 2000: 24)

Turning from evaluative discourse in general to the explicit lexicalisations of this parameter, it is useful to recall that relevance is also among the seven analytical categories – indicating "how closely related something is to the topic or field being discussed" – identified in Swales and Burke's (2003: 5) study of evaluative adjectives in academic writing and speech. More specifically, it was found to form the most common class of adjectives in RAs and the second most common (after 'size') in the MICASE corpus.

A similar parameter, labelled 'significance', is suggested in Thetela's (1997: 109) account of evaluative claims in RAs, where it indicates "whether, and to what degree, a finding is significant in the research field". Thetela's approach, however, conceptualises this variable more broadly to include the notion of *interest*, which in Swales and Burke's analysis comes under the separate category of 'assessment' because it implies (more or less overtly) an element of subjectivity. Since the view adopted here is consistent with the latter perspective, my analysis will only target items that signal the inherent relevance of qualified entities, i.e. their position in the field rather than their appeal to the parties involved.

Finally, such markers are worth investigating as evidence of an underlying academic value whether or not they operate metadiscursively. This means that relevance will be interpreted inclusively, as a notion including evaluations that are both exophoric (i.e. qualifying an extratextual referent) and endophoric (qualifying an intratextual element), according to the terminological distinction first introduced by Halliday and Hasan (1976: 31).

8.1. Selection of candidate items

A total of seven lexical items potentially classifiable as relevance markers were identified in the global WL. Several of these, namely *important/importance* and *significant/significantly* share the same root words and, unlike the two values examined previously (size and novelty), the list of candidate items includes a noun (*importance*).

Relevance	*n*
important	527
significant	268
major	217
key	172
importance	134
relevant	131
significantly	126
Total	*1,575*

Table 1. Candidate items (absolute frequency).

This list served, as usual, only as a starting point for investigation. It had to be verified by looking at the actual realisations of each item and then expanded through the addition of further lexically/semantically related types. The first step was relatively straightforward, given that very few of the items considered are polysemous or semantically opaque. To avoid the inclusion of unwarranted occurrences, however, a concordance was generated for each word and inspected for contextual evidence of non-relevant uses.

The only problematic cases were the types *key* and *vital*: the former was ignored when used as a noun: e.g. in *classification key, control key, key encryption, the key to* (largely in CS); the latter was ignored only when used onomastically (*the Vital-IT team*) or in its literal meaning of 'related to life': e.g. *Vital Statistics data* (ECO), *religion should be thought of as the vital expression of groups* (SOC). The lack of major obstacles to their classification does not mean, however, that such items are entirely free of ambivalence, as will be explained in the following pages. Specifically, there is an undeniable tension in the lexical set *significant/significantly*, which may be employed in its broader meaning (=important) or as an indicator of mathematical value (=statistically relevant).

8.2. Additional items

Following the procedure adopted in previous chapters, the core markers encoding relevance were integrated with additional types to complete each lexical set and to add, where available, relevant antonyms and synonyms. The resulting groups are listed below, together with further information as to the rationale adopted.

Group A. *Importance, important, importantly* | *unimportant*

This simple and yet extremely pervasive group of markers only required the addition of an adverbial form (*importantly*) and of the negative antonym *unimportant*. Though theoretically available, the types *unimportance/unimportantly* never occurred in the corpus.

Group B. *Major, main, principal, mainly, principally* | *minor*

The next group is built around the qualifier *major*, which combines the notion of relative and absolute prominence – a distinction typically marked by the choice of article (cf. *a major advantage* vs. *the major challenge*). As in the second case it is essentially synonymous with 'main', the additional items included were *main* and its synonym *principal*, followed by the derived adverbs *mainly/principally*. The group was completed by the direct antonym of *major*, i.e. *minor*.

Group C. *Significant, significance, significantly* | *insignificant*

As may be noticed from the list of items in Table 1, this group only lacked the nominalisation *significance* and the antonym *insignificant* (no occurrence of *insignificance* being present in the corpus).

D. *Relevant, relevance* | *irrelevant*

The additions required here were similar to those made to Group C, namely the noun form (*relevance*) and an antonym (*irrelevant*); no instances were found of the types *relevantly, irrelevantly or irrelevance*.

E. *Key, crucial, vital, crucially*

The last group includes the remaining candidate item (*key*), integrated with its near synonyms *crucial* and *vital*. Interestingly, these two qualifiers are listed respectively by Swales and Burke (2003) and by Thompson (2009) among the most frequent evaluative adjectives found in academic writing. The set was completed with the adverb *crucially*, while there were no occurrences of *vitally*.

8.3. Overall results

The number of relevance markers identified by this method is summarised in Table 2, with the figures for each group and item given in terms of absolute occurrences (n). Though infrequent, the negative markers within each group – when available – are listed separately to make the comparison easier. The figures in brackets indicate the total number of candidate items when only a proportion of these qualified for value-marking status.

	Item	*n*	*Subtotal*
Group A	important (adj)	527	
	importance (n)	134	
	importantly (adv)	32	693
	unimportant (adj)	5	5
Group B	major (adj)	217	
	main (adj)	262	
	principal (adj)	61	
	mainly (adv)	88	
	principally (adv)	10	638
	minor	38	38
Group C	significant (adj)	268	
	significance (n)	52	
	significantly (adv)	126	446
	insignificant (adj)	4	4
Group D	relevant (adj)	131	
	relevance (n)	17	148
	irrelevant (adj)	15	15
Group E	key (adj)	(172) 120	
	crucial (adj)	66	
	vital (adj)	(16) 5	
	crucially (adv)	5	196
Total			*(2,261) 2,183*

Table 2. Full list of relevance markers (by group).

Out of a total of 2,183 tokens, more than 80% belong to Groups A-C, which (also in quantitative terms) provide the core lexis of relevance items to the list, showing that 'importance' and 'relative prominence' are the two most common ways of encoding relevance in research writing. Another noticeable point is the infrequency of the negative polarity, which altogether comprises only 3% (62/2,183) of the tokens considered. The reason for this may depend on the one hand on the fact that whatever deserves less notice – i.e. is *not* relevant – tends to be omitted, and on the other hand on the communicative purpose of RAs, which (unlike books reviews, review articles and other eminently evaluative genres, cf. Giannoni 2009b) centre on the construction of new knowledge rather than the appraisal of competing claims.

If classified according to the part of speech involved, such data confirm the major role of adjectives (79% occurrences), followed by adverbs (12%) and nouns (9%). The nominalisation of relevance is thus surprisingly infrequent, compared to its adjectivation, while – as will be seen later – this value is signalled adverbially (above all through a verb-modifier) in a considerable proportion of cases.

	n	*Share*
Adjectives	1,719	79%
Adverbs	261	12%
Nouns	203	9%
Total	*2,183*	

Table 3. Relevance markers (by part of speech).

8.3.1. Predicative vs. attributive uses

As in previous chapters, the position of value-marking adjectives was investigated through their concordance to assess the relative weight of predicative/attributive constructions for each of the five groups considered. The results summarised below show that, when signalling relevance, the predicative position accounts for two out of ten occurrences, with considerable differences between adjectives: in Groups A and D it peaks at 42% (221/527) and 49% (72/146) of realisations respectively, while it is almost negligible in Group B (<1%). The 'stronger' relevance-marking adjectives – i.e. those that warrant syntactic prominence – belong therefore to the *important/ relevant* subgroups, which are arguably closest to the semantic centre of the underlying value.

	Predicative	*Attributive*	*All*
Group A	221	306	527
Group B	5	573	578
Group C	45	223	268
Group D	72	74	146
Group E	31	160	191
Total	*22%*	*78%*	*1,719*

Table 4. Syntactic position of relevance-marking adjectives (by group).

The significance of these considerable differences will be investigated in greater length later in the chapter, drawing also on contextual evidence linked to the evaluative target and collocates of each item.

8.4. Distribution across disciplines

In order to understand variations in the prominence of relevance markers across academic domains, the data summarised in Table 2 had to be broken down by discipline. The total count for each group of items was then normalised per 10,000 words (figures in italics), whereas the absolute number of occurrences of specific markers is given in brackets. For Groups A-D a further distinction was made between lexis encoding the positive polarity and, less often, its negative counterpart. The resulting distribution of relevance-marking items is that detailed in Table 5.

Item	*ANTH*	*BIO*	*CS*	*ECO*	*ENG*	*HIST*	*MATH*	*MED*	*PHY*	*SOC*	*All*
Group A	4.5	4.0	13.6	11.7	6.7	7.4	1.3	7.3	6.2	10.1	7.4
important (adj)	(30)	(21)	(143)	(94)	(24)	(52)	(19)	(21)	(33)	(90)	(527)
importance (n)	(7)	(1)	(38)	(19)	(18)	(14)	(1)	(6)	(2)	(28)	(134)
importantly (adv)	-	(8)	-	(7)	(1)	(11)	-	-	(1)	(4)	(32)
unimportant (adj)	-	-	(1)	(1)	(1)	(1)	-	-	(1)	-	(5)
Group B	7.6	4.8	7.7	5.5	21.4	6.8	3.8	12.7	3.4	6.5	7.2
major (adj)	(20)	(11)	(23)	(14)	(24)	(42)	(3)	(34)	(3)	(43)	(217)
main (adj)	(18)	(12)	(54)	(28)	(59)	(7)	(47)	(5)	(13)	(19)	(262)
principal (adj)	(10)	(4)	(3)	(5)	(17)	(5)	(7)	(4)	-	(6)	(61)
mainly (adv)	(8)	(8)	(19)	(5)	(30)	(9)	(1)	-	(4)	(4)	(88)
principally (adv)	(4)	-	-	(2)	-	(2)	-	-	-	(2)	(10)
minor	(2)	(1)	(4)	(3)	(11)	(7)	(1)	(4)	-	(5)	(38)
Group C	0.4	2.3	15.0	4.7	2.0	4.5	0.6	19.8	5.6	0.3	4.8
significant (adj)	(1)	(13)	(150)	(21)	(5)	(19)	(2)	(36)	(19)	(2)	(268)
significance (n)	-	(1)	(10)	(3)	(2)	(22)	(2)	(11)	-	(1)	(52)
significantly (adv)	(2)	(3)	(40)	(21)	(6)	(7)	(6)	(26)	(14)	(1)	(126)
insignificant (adj)	-	-	-	(4)	-	-	-	-	-	-	(4)
Group D	0.6	0.7	2.6	2.6	0.6	0.4	0.3	3.0	4.5	3.3	1.7
relevant (adj)	(4)	(1)	(28)	(23)	(4)	(3)	(3)	(11)	(22)	(32)	(131)
relevance (n)	(1)	(3)	(4)	(2)	-	-	(2)	-	(1)	(4)	(17)
irrelevant (adj)	-	(1)	(3)	(2)	-	(1)	-	-	(4)	(4)	(15)
Group E	1.5	1.7	2.0	4.3	1.2	3.2	0.9	0.8	1.0	2.9	2.1
key (adj)	(6)	(7)	(13)	(32)	(6)	(19)	(6)	(3)	(2)	(26)	(120)
crucial (adj)	(4)	(6)	(12)	(9)	(2)	(13)	(7)	-	(4)	(9)	(66)
vital (adj)	(1)	-	-	(2)	-	(2)	-	-	-	-	(5)
crucially (adv)	(1)	-	(1)	(2)	-	-	(1)	-	-	-	(5)
Total	*14.6*	*13.6*	*40.9*	*28.9*	*32.0*	*22.4*	*6.9*	*43.7*	*20.7*	*23.1*	*23.3*

Table 5. Distribution of relevance markers across disciplines.

There is a sixfold difference between the two extremes of the range, with MED at 43.7 and MATH at only 6.9 normalised occurrences. Apart from MED, three disciplines – namely CS (40.9), ENG (32.0) and ECO (28.9) – rise above the overall average of 23.3.

The picture becomes as usual more complex when we turn from the total for each discipline to the figures for individual groups of items. Figure 1 clearly shows the extent of inter-group variation observed across the corpus.

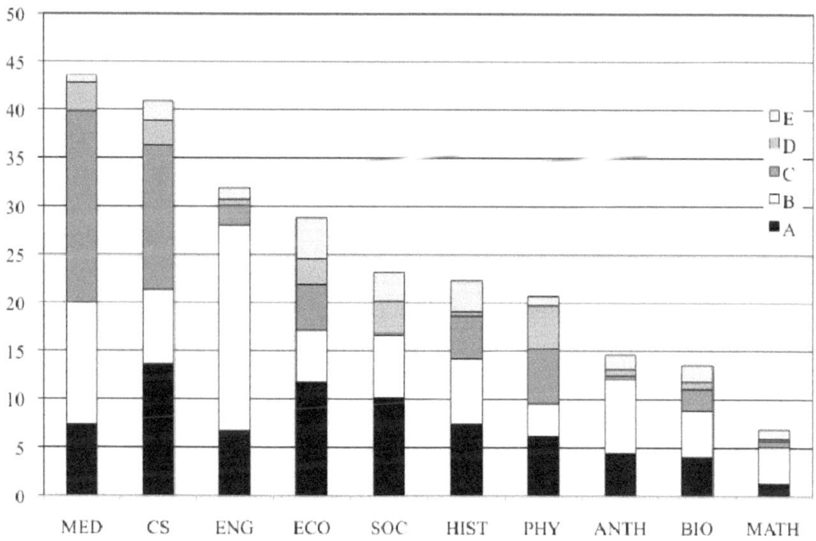

Figure 1. Relevance markers by group and discipline, in decreasing order (occurrences / 10,000 words).

The most frequent markers signalling this relevance belong to Groups A-C. More specifically, the results show that:

- MED is the first domain in Group C (19.9) and the last one in Group E (0.8);
- CS is the first domain in Group A (13.6);
- ENG is the first domain in GroupB (21.4);
- ECO is the first domain in Group E (4.3);
- SOC is the last domain in Group C (0.3);
- PHY is the first domain in D (4.5) and the last in Group B (3.4);
- MATH is the last domain in Group A (1.3) and Group D (0.3);

The greatest extent of variation is observed in Group C (expressing 'significance'), whose contribution to the total is substantial in MED and CS, moderate in ECO and PHY, but very slight in the remaining disciplines. Such behaviour can be ascribed to the special status of Group C items, whose presence often reflects the amount of statistical interpretation appropriate to a given discipline.

8.5. Qualified entities and realisations

The different word groups considered as value markers represent a number of related subvalues, namely 'importance' (Group A), 'relative prominence' (Group B) and 'significance' (Group C). From different perspectives they all communicate the fact that a certain referent deserves special attention and consideration – whatever the specific reason for such a judgement. RA authors use them to signal what is deemed to be relevant to their interests and (by extension) to the discipline they represent. Whether or not the basis for such evaluations is provided, relevance markers flag the aspects of research that most need to be acknowledged.

Unlike the previous three values analysed here, relevance qualifies its target as remarkable with no reference to such 'accessory features' as user perception (goodness), precedent (novelty) or quantitative considerations (size). For this reason it is the least specific of the four values under scrutiny. Again, a closer look at its various realisations is needed in order to appreciate when such value statements are deployed and how they are worded. The following sections illustrate the range of realisations encountered in the corpus, with reference (where available) to parallel findings in the literature.

8.5.1. Group A

Though only marginally, words in this group were the most frequent among those considered, accounting for 28% (698/2,183) of all relevance markers. This agrees with Biber *et al.*'s (2000) findings that the main attributive adjectives employed in academic prose are *good, best, right, important, simple* and *special.* It is also consistent with a recent study of evaluative lexis in student assignments from the British Academic Written English (BAWE) corpus, which concludes that "*important*, *significant* and *useful* are in the top ten most frequent collocates of *very*" and "*important* is the most frequent, and widespread, of the three" (Gardner 2009: 48). At the same time, it is useful to recall work on it+BE+ADJ+to/that patterns in the BAWE corpus, which shows *important* (together with *crucial*) to be one of the most frequent choice of adjectives in undergraduate writing, where it indicates "the values that are esteemed in the discipline (to some extent), and which are promulgated by the student writers at different stages of their development" (Thompson 2009: 55). In our case, 'importance' is signalled above all by authors in CS, ECO and SOC, while it has a low profile (i.e. below the average mark) in ANTH, BIO and MATH. The indication therefore is that this subvalue matters especially to academics in the social sciences (ECO, SOC) and in human-computer interaction (CS).

The qualifier *important* is by far the preferred choice, accounting for no less than 75% (527/698) of Group A markers. After *irrelevant/relevant* (Group D), it is also the most common adjective to be used predicatively (42% occurrences). The examples below show instances of its presence across the corpus, where it overwhelmingly qualifies aspects of the science-making process, i.e. the observation and interpretation of results within the wider context of parallel knowledge claims made in the literature:

(179) Therefore, it is better to limit the use of consolidants to cases in which they are absolutely necessary, and it is *important* to ensure that only the proper (i.e., bone) surface is impregnated. ANTH

(180) A number of recent studies have shown that hierarchical features of food webs related to consumer-resource body-size ratios are *important* promoters of stability and persistence. BIO

(181) Integrating awareness data across devices (from work computer to PDA to home computer) may be *important* for providing a more complete context of users' activities. CS

(182) Manova (2006) is an example of this, highlighting the *important* contribution of the extensive margin of trade in explaining the impact of financial frictions on sectoral trade flows. ECO

(183) Evidently the main driver of aquifer recharge is rainfall, but the soil/plant interaction plays an *important* role on the amount of water available for recharge. ENG

(184) Finally, the place of something in time is not *important* in sinusoidal theories; those features or values that are more recent are not better than older ones, because there is no progress. HIST

(185) The most *important* item is the absorption theorem and a result, Theorem 2.5, which allows us to deduce Theorem 1.5. MATH

(186) However, a small but *important* subgroup of athletes without evidence of structural heart disease may have particularly abnormal ECG patterns. MED

(187) A first *important* difference between the conventional DGP model and the anomaly driven DGP is that the former does not incorporate the self-accelerating branch of the latter. PHY

(188) This finding is *important* because some movement sympathizers have denied that Zapatistas sought mere economic compensations. SOC

In most of the above sentences, *important* serves to flag aspects of research deemed to be particularly noteworthy. However, the grounds for such a judgement are only seldom (184, 188) made immediately explicit: as the claim merely rests the author's authority, it is harder to prove or to disprove. A special feature, noticeable in (179), is the *it is/was important to* + verb pattern (cf. Thompson 2009) that underlies most of the predicative constructions involving this qualifier. By communicating to readers what is/was important to do, the researcher signals procedural decisions recommended to the disciplinary community as advisable. In the present tense, the string encodes a directive speech act whose deontic force is only slightly weakened by generalisation (a total of 66 occurrences of this pattern were counted in the corpus). In several instances, however, it is simply used as a rhetorical device foregrounding (metadiscursively) its object by means of such cognitive verbs as *note, consider* and *acknowledge*:

(189) It is *important to consider* the possibility that plants are subject to time-varying productivity shocks in addition to the time-invariant level of productivity represented by λ. ECO

The collocational horizon of this adjective yields further contextual information worth reporting here. Predicative and attributive constructions are distributed more or less equally across domains. Among the former, the most frequent R1 collocates of any interest, with 28 occurrences each, are *for/in* + noun phrase (example 190) or occasionally a verb (191). Only nine instances of *because* (192) and two of *since* introducing a reason clause were counted in this position.

(190) Politics, race, and related extralegal factors become increasingly *important for departures and enhancements* that entail more ambiguity and allow for more discretion. SOC

(191) For certain sectors and activities, there is indeed evidence that prior experience was *important in determining* who would become an entrepreneur. ECO

(192) Distraction is *important because* it affects the user's ability to carry out his or her primary action and will likely influence their qualitative reactions to using the display. CS

These collocations contextualise the relevance claim by specifying its territory. They make explicit the value's denotational range within a given setting and, albeit rarely, signal on what basis an evaluation is being made. The latter aspect is rather surprising, insofar as it means that the vast majority of relevance judgements involving this qualifier provide no immediate justification: the reason is either given elsewhere in the text or simply left unsaid.

Finally, the left collocates were searched for negative realisations – that is statements of what is considered to be *not important* – but only a total of eight occurrences (with *not* either in L1 or L2 position) were found:

(193) These two additional assumptions are *not important* for our qualitative results and serve to simplify the algebra. ECO

(194) Components 3-5 are *not as important*, and each of these three components explains about the same amount of variance, between 12% and 13.2%. ENG

Among the attributive constructions, R1 collocates were then searched for evidence of what is qualified as *important*. The only relevant item with a sizeable presence was *role/s* (27 occurrences). In keeping with the earlier observation that importance is attached primarily to the science-making process, the string *important role* is linked to the functional interpretation of observed phenomena and is mostly used within the standard phrase *play a role*, as illustrated by the following sentences:

(195) MTs *play diverse and important roles* in many cellular processes. BIO

(196) Platelets are thought to *play an important role* in embolization and microvascular dysfunction. MED

This collocate is followed at a distance by *factor/s, issue/s*, *source/s* (9 each), *criterion/criteria, difference/s*, *information* (7 each) and *feature/s, implication/s, part*, *point/s* (6 each), which together account for a third of all attributive realisations:

(197) The transport of food and/or tools may also have been an *important factor* in the evolution of bipedalism. ANTH

(198) Interview participants said user awareness of information is an *important criterion* for evaluating peripheral displays. CS

(199) The currency in which prices are rigid has *important implications* for exchange rate pass-through and cross-country spill-over effects of monetary and fiscal policy. ECO

It s worth looking at the L1 premodifiers associated with this qualifier. Interestingly, the most frequent were *more/most* (30 occurrences each) and *very* (10). Of these, *more important* collocates in a third of cases with *than*, thus making explicit its term of comparison (example 200). The data show then that importance is seldom premodified and that, when it is, its purpose is to highlight the merits of a qualified entity contrastively rather than by modulating its denotative force.

(200) However, there are social forces beyond those emerging from specific social contexts that make certain levels of categorical distinction *more important than* others for a person's overall life chances. SOC

(201) Construction of invariant geometric measures is probably the *most important* traditional problem of ergodic theory. MATH

The second contributor to Group A, by frequency, is *importance*. It accounts on average for 19% of markers, although the proportion is much lower in BIO and MATH and highest in ENG and SOC. It is followed in 73% (98/134) of cases by a prepositional phrase, generally qualifying methodological aspects of research, introduced by *of*:

(202) Compared to the *importance* of the other two measures, time and effectiveness, the accounted variance by age was rather small. CS

(203) Both the EVA-3S and SPACE studies, together with ours, point to the *importance* of completion of randomized trials. MED

The third way of signalling this subvalue is through the sentence-adverb *importantly*, but it is relatively infrequent and totally absent in certain domains. As shown by the next two examples, it serves as an 'attitude marker' of interpersonal discourse (Hyland 1998a) and can be paraphrased as *It is important (for me) to say that*. In line with this function, *importantly* occurs in sentence-initial position in around half of cases (example 204). Moreover, it is often premodified by *more/ most*, which act as logical connectives comparatively linking the claim to previous propositions in the text (205).

(204) *Importantly*, along the polarized BG cells, CHL1 was mainly localized to the apical radial fibers and processes. BIO

(205) Suspicious of Santa Anna and, *more importantly*, facing acute threats from Apaches and Comanches, none of the three sent any men. HIST

Instances of the negative form *unimportant*, albeit documented in the corpus, were negligible. As argued for other markers, its absence may be justified on the one hand by the fact that whatever lacks importance tends to be ignored not only in the research but also in its description and, on the other hand, by the centrality of a trait whose absence is too critical to be stigmatised under normal circumstances (a point confirmed by the very limited use of *not important*).

(206) As opposed to other developing countries with similar income per capita, the low level of education in Brazil makes newspapers an *unimportant* source of local news. ECO

(207) However, in MaVaN models the effective mass of the scalar field mφ H sets the scale, m−1φ, where these processes and the associated gradient terms become *unimportant*. PHY

8.5.2. Group B

Comparable in frequency to the previous items are those in Group B, which signal relevance in terms of 'relative prominence' among a range of options. They account for 31% (676/2,183) of all relevance markers and, among these, for 34% (578/1,719) of adjectives. In four domains (ANTH, BIO, ENG and MATH) this is the most widely-represented class of markers, with ENG recording the highest normalised figure (21.4 occurrences). Qualifying something as *main*, *major* or *principal* implies a comparative value judgement that presents the target entity as more relevant than others. As remarked earlier, however, *major* (217 occurrences) is semantically opaque in this respect because it combines the notion of comparative and absolute value. i.e. of 'particularly important' and 'most important'. Though often marked by the choice of article, this distinction is not always evident:

(208) The *major* challenge ahead that this paper has identified and tried to address is to comparatively explain the emergence, stabilization, and transformation of these various forms of ethnicity. SOC

Rather than speculating on the item's polysemy, it is more advisable to concentrate on the type of entity it qualifies. Unlike *important*, which targets the science-making, *major* mainly qualifies the status of empirical evidence assembled by researchers. In all the domains considered it singles out phenomena which, among others, deserve special consideration:

(209) General observations reveal most locations to be in the frontal zone within a radius of 1 km from *major streams* that represented the sources of raw material. ANTH

(210) The median values of the *major ions* were used to determine a median groundwater type for each cluster. ENG

(211) Wilson remained, at least until the spring of 1919, the only *major figure* in the international arena who appeared to have both the will and the power to promote the implementation of self-determination. HIST

(212) In the preceding section, I outlined the *major mechanisms* that stabilize a boundary by reducing the range of strategic options from which actors choose. SOC

Even more frequent (especially in CS, ECO, ENG, MATH and PHY) is the qualifier *main*. Its L1 context is particularly notable for the prominence of *our* (49 occurrences), used almost exclusively in ECO and MATH as a cataphoric (example 213) or, occasionally, an anaphoric (214) metatextual device foregrounding elements of the authors' research:

(213) In this paper we do not wish to explore the reasons that price durations can differ across market and nonmarket transactions. So, for the rest of this paper, *our main focus* is on market transactions. ECO

(214) *Our main result* provides unexpected answers to the following questions: how many relations are needed to define G, and how short can these relations be? MATH

On the other hand, *main* tends to qualify abstract nouns linked less to the evidence itself than to its interpretation. Confirmation of this trend is provided by R1 collocates with >10 occurrences, namely *result/s* (24), *effect/s* (24) and *theorem* (12, all in MATH):

(215) The *main result* of our paper is that the diffusion of the probability to measure a given value [...] may indeed be suppressed in the parts of the landscape where the number of nearest neighbors for any given vacuum is small. PHY

(216) Several *main effects* for seeing one's own picture in the videoconference were found, as across all conditions anger, dislike, and shame were intensified. CS

(217) The following two corollaries are immediate consequences of the *main theorem* and the definitions. We omit the proofs. MATH

The use of *principal* (a very near synonym of *main*) is not dissimilar, apart from the absence of first-person collocations used metatextually. Consistent with the latter finding, *principal* appears to qualify aspects of research that lack a direct link to propositions made earlier or later in the RA – its most frequent R1 collocate being *component/s* (19 occurrences). The following sentences are an apt illustration of this:

(218) A *principal components* factor analysis with Varimax rotation was conducted to examine the factor structure of these items in this sample. CS

(219) The *principal white representative* for the merchants likewise concluded in retrospect that it was the boycott that "ended that whole era". HIST

(220) Malaria is commonly considered to be a *principal cause* of severe anemia in Africa. MED

Before moving on to the adverbs in Group B, it is worth mentioning the only marker (*minor*) representative of the negative polarity. Albeit not common, this is present in all domains except PHY and tends to qualify factual information involving the dimensions of phenomena (examples 221-222); only less often (223-224) does it target the actual interpretation of data:

(221) Strokes were classified as major or *minor* on the basis of the National Institutes of Health Stroke Scale. MED

(222) We expect them to be relatively insensitive to any changes in *minor* denominations, cults, and marginal movements. SOC

(223) The performance of the single tasks was of *minor importance* in this context. CS

(224) Rice played a *minor role* in the so-called 'agricultural renaissance' of Brazil in the second half of the eighteenth century. HIST

Another remarkable aspect of this adjective is its predicative use (cf. 221). It is indeed the only Group B item – apart from one instance of *major* – to admit such a construction. The severity of evaluating something as *minor* would therefore seem to warrant its syntactic prominence in a way that is not available when other (less marked) lexicalisations are employed.

Finally, the type of meaning encoded by *main/principal* may be realised adverbially – an option that tends to qualify events (through a verb modifier) or the qualities of an object (through an adjective modifier) rather than the object itself. The preferred choice here – especially frequent in ENG – is *mainly*, which modifies a verb in 77% of cases (example 225), an object in 13% (226) and an adjective in 10% (227):

(225) Stellate and basket cells *occupy mainly* the upper or lower half of the ML, respectively. BIO

(226) Samples of C5 are located in the buried valleys, *mainly St. Hermas Valley*, and in intermediate locations between recharge zones and "stagnant" valley centers. ENG

(227) Even if a nurse is *mainly responsible* for an error, the physician supervising her work will usually be named in any suits arising from the error. ECO

Because of the adverb's syntactic mobility, there are cases where distinguishing the modified part of speech is anything but straightforward. In (228) below, for instance, the onus is on the reader to decide whether the referents are *mainly indigenous Mexicans* or, alternatively, *mainly indigenous Mexicans*:

(228) Politicians ambivalent about or even opposed to the war also talked about raiding, but they incorporated Indians into arguments against a cession – for example, invoking the "well-known fact" that raiders had "encroached upon and broken up many of the settlements of the Spaniards" in the north, leaving behind *mainly indigenous Mexicans* unfit for American political life". HIST

8.5.3. Group C

Markers in this group foreground 'significance' either: (a) in its broader sense (=important), or (b) as an indicator of mathematical value (=statistically relevant). As the latter meaning is prevalent and varies according to the amount of statistical analysis carried out in each domain, Group C exhibits the greatest degree of interdisciplinary variation, from <1 occurrence per 10,000 words in ANTH and SOC to 19.8 in MED and 15.0 in CS. Accordingly, it constitutes the largest group of relevance markers for MED and CS but the smallest for ANTH and SOC.

These results are very close to those of an exploratory study of value-related lexis in RAs (Giannoni 2010), which recorded a peak of 'significance' markers in MED (at 16.2 occurrences) while ECO only reached 6.6 (the figure here is 4.7). Interestingly, meaning (a) is entirely absent in MED and rare (8%) in ECO, though the distinction may be arduous to make with no explicit indication that the 'significance' intended is of a statistical nature. Further evidence of the pervasiveness of this group is provided by Thetela (1997), who identified *significant* as the most frequent evaluative adjective in a multidisciplinary RA corpus. More recently, Gardner (2009) has shown that *significant* (alongside *important* and *useful*) is one of the top three qualifiers in the BAWE corpus of undergraduate writing.

Predictably, the adjective *significant* accounts for the majority – namely 60% (268/450) – of markers in this group. Sentences (229-230) illustrate meaning (a) and (231-232) meaning (b), whereas (233) is an example of the overlapping/ambiguous realisations mentioned above:

(229) Beginning in the 1890s, however, many nationalists, including Tagore and Yeats, began to question the ability of politicians to make any *significant* changes. HIST

(230) The absence of *significant* costs imposed on vulnerable business interests, the reticence of the federal government, and the corresponding intransigence of local public officials made even modest gains elusive. SOC

(231) The estimated rate ratio for acyclovir was smaller than 1 for the high-adherence category and increased with lower adherence, but neither the trend nor any of the within-category rate ratios were statistically *significant*. MED

(232) There was no *significant* difference in error rates between the practice and evaluation sessions for either the highlighting-off group, F(1, 54) = 2.88, p = .10. CS

(233) The lack of such instances tentatively suggests that errors in inferences are not a *significant* barrier for the use of mobile awareness. CS

In example (232), unlike the one that precedes it, meaning (b) is not made explicit by the premodifier *statistically* but elicited by the data that follows. This is most often the case with statistical relevance, as shown by the fact that while almost all of the realisations in the corpus – outside HIST and SOC – communicate meaning (b), only 8% (21/268) of occurrences are disambiguated by this premodifier. Even in a discipline like CS, where statistical significance is the norm, there were instances such as example (233) where both meanings are contextually viable.

It would be unwise, however, to insist too much on the semantics of such realisations, because ultimately the two meanings are conjoined. The very notion that 'significance' can be statistically determined is in fact debatable, as argued by McCloskey for the field of economics:

> The abuse of the word 'significant' in connection with statistical arguments in economics is universal. Statistical significance seems to give a standard by which to judge whether a hypothesis is true or false, that is independent of any tiresome consideration of how true a hypothesis must be to be true enough. [...] Significance in statistics, however useful it is as an input into economic significance, is not the same thing as economic significance. The point is not that levels of significance are arbitrary. Of course they are [...] Most texts on econometrics do not mention that the goodness or badness of a hypothesis is not ascertainable on merely statistical grounds. (McCloskey 1983: 497-498)

The prevalence of meaning (b) in our corpus shows that *significant* is associated overwhelmingly with the interpretation of experimental evidence, its top R1 collocates – apart from *difference/s* (27 occurrences) – being *interaction/s* (21), *effect/s* (14) and *change/s* (10). All of these occurred in CS and MED:

(234) Of soldiers without PTSD, the proportion with a high PHQ-15 score was much lower and also showed no *significant differences* according to type of injury. MED

(235) The final model showed a *significant interaction* (P=0.005 by the likelihood ratio test). MED

(236) It was found that there was a *significant effect* of group size on the percentage of information shared in a group's second task discussion. CS

(237) No *significant change* was observed in the mean maximum carotid-artery intima-media thickness. MED

Among premodifiers, the top L1 collocate is *no* (44), followed by *statistically* (20), with all other options having less than ten occurrences each. The relatively high proportion of negative realisations – where 'significance' is ruled out rather than affirmed – is confirmed by the finding that the *There* BE *significant* pattern (50 occurrences) is negated in 70% of cases.

(238) We conclude that the rapid oscillations of the Ricci scalar have *no significant* impact on the scale factor for models in which RF”(R)<<1. PHY

(239) An analysis on the overall workload did not reveal any interesting effects. There was *no significant* main effect for highlighting, phrase set, or session. CS

Compared to this qualifier, the noun *significance* is relatively uncommon and, because of its strong presence in HIST, has a sizeable proportion of meaning (a) uses. The most frequent R1 collocate (*of*), which accounts for no less than 40% of occurrences, is typical of HIST texts (cf. examples 240-241). Accordingly, there is a marked tendency to qualify significance as *statistical* (23% of occurrences) when meaning (b) is intended (242):

(240) The issues raised by the pits, however, surpassed the *significance of* a single exchange, signaling a turning point in the history of capitalist exchange relations. HIST

(241) The borderlands scholarship has obscured the geopolitical *significance* of the interethnic violence of the 1830s and 1840s. HIST

(242) Analyses are two-sided, with a P value of 0.05 considered to indicate *statistical significance*. MED

The noun would thus appear to cover a broader semantic area than the qualifier, insofar as it can more easily be deployed (if suitably contextualised by an *of*-phrase) to encode non-statistical meanings within Group C.

The last item (*significantly*) is instead particularly prominent, being the most frequent adverb among all relevance markers. Unlike other relevance-focused adverbs, it is present in all domains – but especially so in MED, followed at a distance by CS, PHY and ECO. *Significantly* prevalently modifies a past participle (243) or the comparative of a dimensional qualifier (244). However, there were only two instances of the word used (parenthetically) as a metadiscoursal device (245).

(243) Thus, compared to other firms in the same country and industry, and after controlling for a range of firm-level characteristics, higher import penetration is *significantly associated* with better management scores. ECO

(244) Although substantial efforts were made to improve the reliability of the system, some users encountered a *significantly lower* level of reliability than others. CS

(245) So long as firms' capabilities across all management practices are positively correlated – which they are, *significantly*, within the eighteen practices examined – our measure based on a subset of practices will provide a proxy of the firm's true management capabilities. ECO

These results are substantiated by inspection of the adverb's most frequent R1 collocates, which are respectively *associated* (11), *correlated* (8), *higher/lower* (17) and *more/less/fewer* (12). In a majority of cases, *significantly* is preceded by copula *be*, whose subject is either a statistical variable (example 246) or, more directly, the object under investigation (247):

(246) However, *the percentage* of infants who received intensive care *was not significantly* greater for singletons than for multiples (83% and 84%, respectively). MED

(247) Across all columns, the conclusion emerged that tougher *product market competition is* associated with *significantly* better management practices. ECO

As for negative lexicalisations, these were limited to four instances of *insignificant*. Because of their marked semantic value in this context, they are nevertheless worth mentioning. They all occurred in ECO as statistical qualifications of the author's quantitative data (*scores, coefficient, estimates, relationship*):

(248) Using average managerial hours worked as a basic proxy for effort, we find an *insignificant relationship* between tougher competition and longer managerial hours. ECO

8.5.4. Group D

Only 7% (163/2,183) of items belonged to this group, despite its coincidence with the label chosen for the value dealt with in this chapter. Its variation across domains was rather limited, with a peak (normalised figures) in PHY (4.5), followed by SOC (3.3) and MED (3.0), while ANTH, BIO, ENG and HIST were all under the average 1.7 mark. As usual, adjectivation is the standard lexical option chosen for this purpose, with the qualifier *relevant* accounting for 80% of tokens. Something endowed with this quality, which belongs to the semantic core of relevance marking, is considered to be pertinent (and thus of special significance) in a given context. The saliency of *relevant*, when compared to other adjectives, is confirmed by its unusually frequent predicative use (46% of occurrences), which is more than twice the mean (22%) for relevance-marking adjectives reported in Table 4.

The concordance shows a prevalence of realisations qualifying the status of empirical evidence as variably useful to knowledge production (249-250). Less often it defines the methodological assumptions/approaches adopted by RA authors (251) or in the literature (252).

(249) If the ground state $\psi 0(n)$ is not normalizable (such as in the case of an infinite landscape of vacua), higher k eigenstates are *relevant* in determining the late-time asymptotics. PHY

(250) This finding is *relevant* because it illustrates that, contrary to previously expressed concerns, an array of claims within a frame does not undermine a movement's cause. SOC

(251) In Section 2, we give some of the background for the link Floer homology from [25], with special emphasis on the part of the theory *relevant* to us for our present purposes. MATH

(252) Neuroeconomic research following up on the DRPE hypothesis has the potential for providing economists with much *relevant* information. ECO

In line with the item's frequent predicative use, its top R1 collocate is *to* (27 occurrences), followed by *information* (14) and *for* (10). On the other hand, it is premodified by adverbs that contextualise (*clinically, politically*) or modalise (*especially, immediately, particularly, really*) its meaning, or else by comparative evaluative adverbs (*more, most, less*):

(253) This meeting was convened by University of Michigan and CDC investigators, and the critical margin was based on what was considered to be *clinically relevant*. MED

(254) We use instead the more precise, if jargonistic, term pluralistic deobjectivation to describe the sociological process *most relevant* to the diversity tradition. SOC

The nominalised form *relevance* is far less common and totally absent in three domains (ENG, HIST and MED). Since the last of these had a relatively high occurrence of the adjective, it may be argued that medical researchers are, comparatively speaking, those most likely to mention what is *relevant* rather than *relevance* itself. More often than not, the noun is qualified either with regard to its object (introduced by an *of*-phrase), its impact (introduced by a *to*-phrase) or both:

(255) To investigate the physiological *relevance of the open form* of TG2 described above, we sought to characterize the closed (GTP-bound) and open (inhibitor-bound) conformations of TG2 in solution.

(256) With the absence of role models who have achieved a stable, middle-class lifestyle through steady employment, this model loses its *relevance to youths*. SOC

(257) The main relevance *of the quality-upgrading hypothesis to policy debates* may lie in its identification of a new dimension of relative winners and losers from trade in developing countries. ECO

The only negative lexeme in this group is *irrelevant.* It appears occasionally in the corpus but is striking for its predicative position in 80% of occurrences. The fact that irrelevance is normally predicated rather than attributed means, as suggested for other negative markers, that its severity is high and thus inconsistent with the (unmarked) attributive slot. It qualifies above all experimental variables (258-259), though there is one instance, in HIST, where it extends to interpretative/theoretical aspects (260):

(258) Scaling analysis again shows that disorder of V (n) is *irrelevant* for arbitrary effective numbers of dimensions N. PHY

(259) These logs, with *irrelevant* information sifted out, are the primary source of data discussed in this article. CS

(260) In the Black Atlantic, the frontier thesis might seem *irrelevant*, but there, too, the literature on creolization [...] saw the historiographical pendulum swing toward an emphasis on the discontinuity of the transatlantic experience. HIST

8.5.5. Group E

These are the most polarised relevance markers with a sizeable presence in RAs. They not only signal the noteworthiness of something, but qualify it as indispensable. With the exception of the last item (*crucially*), Group E markers are all qualifiers, used above all attributively (84% of times). Only fourth in terms of frequency, after Groups A-C, they peak in ECO (4.3), HIST (3.2) and SOC (2.9), which tend to be the most argumentative – and at need polemical – domains represented in the corpus. Because of their polarisation, they convey authorial stance (cf. Biber/Finegan 1989) as well as ideational meaning.

By far the most pervasive item (61% of markers), *key* is the only Group E qualifier present in all domains. It is seldom if ever used predicatively (only 3% of occurrences), and only in the phrase BE *key to/for* (cf. example 263 below). As a rule, it qualifies aspects of the research interpreted as particularly important; this is reflected in its R1 collocates, of which the most frequent across texts were respectively *feature/s* (7 occurrences), *element/s* and *role/s* (5 each), *actors, aspect/s* and *variable/s* (4 each):

(261) Although SAP fosters the transmission of information through marketing, the *key features* of our model apply here. ECO

(262) A fundamental assumption of our argument about strategic adaptation is that developments and other actors in the contested arena and the signals they send play *key roles* in shaping the movement group's tactical choices. SOC

(263) Learning to minimize movement of the center of mass may be *key to* reducing the cost of locomotion when carrying head-supported loads. ANTH

Turning to the item's L1 collocates, there is an interesting balance between instances of *the key* (27 occurrences) and *a key* (26) + singular noun, that is between qualifications signalling relevance as unique (example 264) or not (265):

(264) This allows us to demonstrate that conformal measures exist for any $\delta \geq \delta^*$, which is *the key step* of the proof (see also Theorem E). MATH

(265) Developing an effective design language for expressing rhythmic patterns is *a key aspect* in making them useful and understandable. CS

Albeit less frequent, *crucial* is also well documented (outside MED) in the corpus, with HIST and ENG at the two extremes of the range. It is also among the top adjectives observed in undergraduate writing, alongside *important*, by Thompson (2009), who significantly found that, compared to engineering, history texts were twice as likely to use this item in predicative evaluations. Unlike *key*, *crucial* is used primarily in conjunction with interpretative variables, as suggested by its main R1 collocates *role* (7 occurrences, all preceded by *play*), *question/s* (3), *difference, importance* and *link* (2 each):

(266) As it is well known the boundaries $N\pm(p)$ play a *crucial role* in understanding the causal structure of Lorentzian manifolds. MATH

(267) As we mentioned above, there is a *crucial difference* between multi-field (double) inflation and modulated perturbation scenarios. PHY

About a third of realisations (24/66) are predicative and most of these introduce a prepositional phrase with *to/for/in* that specifies the scope of the qualification:

(268) Second, the model does not deal with one additional important fact about mutual fund advertising, namely that it rarely includes data on management fees (Cronqvist 2005), data that are arguably *crucial to assessing future returns*. ECO

(269) This barrier to recombination between the X and Y was *crucial for their differentiation* and therefore marks the origin of these sex chromosomes. BIO

The last two types considered were *vital* (example 270) – whose presence is negligible, with only 5 occurrences qualifying *areas, costs, insights* and *numbers* – and the sole adverb in this group (*crucially*). The latter is also rare but worth mentioning for its role as an attitude marker, since it engages the reader by flagging the relevance of specific parts of the discourse. In four out of five instances, it qualifies what is about to be said (i.e. cataphorically) (271):

(270) Once planters learned how to use land and water to grow rice [...] increasing numbers of rice growers were not *vital* to their success. HIST

(271) *Crucially*, we assume that coarse thinkers do not have a separate mental representation for s=0 and that they cannot group s=0 together with both s=1 and s=2 at the same time. ECO

8.6. Discussion

The lexis examined in this chapter centres on relevance, conceptualised as a quality attached by scholars to whatever is considered noteworthy in a given setting. Interestingly, it is among the analytical categories used to classify "how closely related something is to the topic or field being discussed" in Swales and Burke's (2003: 5) analysis of evaluative adjectives in academic writing and speech. Relevance is an essential aspect of the academic value system, insofar as it brings to the attention of readers evaluations based on shared interpretations instrumental to the negotiation of knowledge claims.

At the same time, the fact that most relevance judgements appear to lack direct justification suggests that scholars tolerate a considerable degree of subjectivity in this area. In other words, it is appropriate for authors to flag elements of their research (and discourse) by reminding the readership and themselves of its importance, without necessarily providing reasons for such evaluations. As for their target, the examples listed so far clearly show that relevance can be attached to a well-known fact (readily acknowledged by the reader), a personal statement (within the ongoing academic debate) or a call for change (subject to compliance by peers). In each case, the markedness of the claim depends on extratextual as well as textual factors.

Compared to the other values considered here, relevance is the least specific because it does not hinge on such 'accessory features' as user perception, precedent or quantitative considerations. Moreover, most of its markers reflect a range of related subvalues: namely 'importance' (Group A), 'relative prominence' (Group B) and 'significance' (Group C), all of which signal that a given qualified entity deserves special consideration.

8.6.1. Saliency of relevance

Measured in terms of lexical prominence, relevance appears to be particularly salient in the applied sciences (MED, ENG) and CS (i.e. human-computer interaction). The three disciplines share a strong focus on the tangible benefits of technological improvement, which explains their frequent use of items signalling what deserves special attention or, conversely, what is unremarkable. The normalised count for each domain in Table 6 shows that ANTH, BIO and MATH fall well below the average mark (i.e. 23.3), while the remaining disciplines are around average; there is a sixfold difference between the two extremes of the range. The eminently descriptive nature of

ANTH/BIO/MATH, combined with their linear argumentative style and avoidance of overt polemics, may account for the dearth of relevance markers in such domains.

Intensity	*Discipline*	*Norm. occurrences*
Strong	MED	43.7
	CS	40.9
	ENG	32.0
Average	ECO	28.9
	SOC	23.1
	HIST	22.4
	PHY	20.7
Weak	ANTH	14.6
	BIO	13.6
	MATH	6.9

Table 6. Relevance-marking intensity by discipline.

Predictably the vast majority of markers were adjectives (79%), while nouns only played a negligible role (9%). Among qualifiers, however, there is considerable variation in terms of syntactic prominence, with almost 40% of Group A and D items and <1% of Group B items used predicatively. This means that the 'stronger' adjectives are those signalling the subvalues of 'importance' and 'relevance', which are closest to the value's semantic core. Another noticeable point is the infrequency of the negative polarity (only 3% of markers); this may be due on the one hand to the fact that whatever deserves less notice – i.e. is *not* relevant – tends to be omitted, and on the other hand to the communicative purpose of RAs, which (unlike book reviews, review articles and other eminently evaluative genres) is the construction of new knowledge rather than the appraisal of competing claims.

8.6.2. Type of marker

Quantitatively speaking, the first three groups account for 83% of the lexical items considered. This means that 'importance' and 'relative prominence', followed by 'significance', are by far the most common ways of encoding relevance in research writing. The distribution of markers is indicative of the disciplinary proclivities in the value's lexical visibility across the corpus. It is therefore useful to look at patterns of use taking into account the type of marker most likely to occur in each domain as well as the normalised figures for each group.

Group A (importance) is most represented in CS, ECO and SOC, while it drops below average in ANTH, BIO and MATH. It hinges on the qualifier *important*, which accounts for no less than 75% of occurrences. Interestingly, *important* is (after *irrelevant/relevant*) the main relevance-marking adjective to be used predicatively – a finding that confirms its significance in marked as well as unmarked contexts. The adverb *importantly*, which is absent in certain domains, is instead relatively uncommon and always appears as an attitude marker targeting the interpersonal plane of discourse. Finally, the negative form *unimportant*, although documented in the corpus, was very seldom found.

Group B (relative prominence) is slightly more frequent than the previous and signals relevance in relation to a range of options. Its markers account for 31% of items and, among these, for 34% of adjectives. In four domains (ANTH, BIO, ENG and MATH) this is the most widely represented group, with ENG recording the highest normalised figure (21.4). The adjectives *main* and *major* were the most frequent options in this group.

Group C (significance) encodes 'significance' either in its broader sense (=important), or as an indicator of mathematical value (=statistically relevant). The latter meaning is widely prevalent and varies with the amount of statistical analysis appropriate to each domain. Accordingly, this group has the widest range of inter-disciplinary variation, from <1 occurrence in ANTH and SOC to 19.8 in MED and 15.0 in CS. It represents the largest subvalue among relevance markers in MED/CS but the smallest in ANTH/SOC.

Group D (relevance) accounts only for 7% of relevance markers, although its name coincides with the value investigated here. Things endowed with this quality are considered to be pertinent (and thus of special significance) in a given disciplinary context. The saliency of *relevant*, when compared to other adjectives, is confirmed by its unusually frequent predicative use (46% of occurrences) – more than twice the mean for relevance-marking adjectives.

Group E (polarised realisations) has the most extreme relevance markers with a sizeable presence in the corpus; apart from *crucially*, they are all qualifiers. Of these, *key* is both the most common and the only item present in all domains. Albeit less frequent, *crucial* is also well documented in the corpus (apart from MED), with HIST and ENG at the two extremes of its range.

The overall picture emerging from these results (cf. Figure 1) points to the centrality of relevance especially in the applied sciences, as compared to the pure sciences. Normalised figures are highest in MED, CS, ENG and ECO, while they are lowest in BIO and MATH. The breakdown by group shows further levels of variation, especially among items signalling the subvalue of significance. In conclusion, evidence-based disciplines, whose task is as much to collect quantitative data as to identify suitable (and sustainable) techniques/ technologies, are those most likely to foreground what is deemed to be pertinent to a given purpose. The textual cue to this essential link is provided by relevance markers – hence the value's frequency in the corpus and its considerable fluctuation between domains.

8.6.3. Qualified entities and collocations

The significance of such items hinges on the type of qualified entity as much as on their relative frequency. A summary of how different markers tend to co-occur with other lexemes is given below, taking into account also left collocates when relevant to a marker's usage.

Within Group A, *important* primarily qualifies aspects of the science-making, that is of the observation and interpretation of results in the light of other knowledge claims in the literature. However, the grounds for such judgements are only seldom made explicit, which suggests that the claim rests on the author's authority (making it harder to prove or to disprove its validity). Reflecting the functional interpretation of phenomena, the top R1 collocates of *important* were *role/s*, *factor/s*, *issue/s* and *source/s*. Surprisingly there were only nine occurrences of *because* in R1 position, which suggests that relevance claims involving this adjective tend to offer no immediate justification for its use (the reason being either mentioned elsewhere in the text or simply left unsaid). Finally, *important* is seldom premodified and when it is, it highlights the relevance of a qualified entity contrastively – its top L1 collocates being *more* and *most*, with *more important* followed in a third of cases by *than*. The number of negative realisations (*not important*) was negligible.

Group B markers are less consistent in terms of qualified entity. Whereas *major* usually targets the status of empirical evidence, *main* generally qualifies abstract nouns linked less to the evidence itself than to its interpretation (its top R1 collocates being *result/s*, *effect/s* and *theorem*). Moreover, *main* is notable for the prominence of L1 *our*, used as a cataphoric or, occasionally, an anaphoric device foregrounding elements of the authors' research. Though similar to *main*, *principal* tends instead to target aspects of research with no direct link to propositions made earlier or later in the RA. The only marker representative of the subvalue's negative polarity (*minor*) was found in all domains except PHY and is applied to factual information involving the dimensional nature of phenomena. The fact that it is the only Group B item to occur predicatively suggests that the severity of evaluating something as *minor* deserves far greater syntactic prominence than when other, less marked lexicalisations are used.

Among Group C markers, almost all the occurrences of *significant* outside HIST and SOC encode statistical relevance, yet only 8% are disambiguated by the premodifier *statistically*, leaving the reader to infer this meaning from the co-text. As its most common L1 collocate is *no*, there is a sizeable proportion of cases (16%) where significance is ruled out rather than affirmed. The noun *significance* appears to cover a broader semantic area than the adjective, insofar as it is used more often (suitably contextualised by an *of*-phrase) to encode non-statistical meanings. More frequent than any other relevance-marking adverb, *significantly* modifies above all past participles and comparatives of dimensional adjectives. *Insignificant*, on the other hand, occurs only in ECO for statistical assessments of the authors' quantitative data (i.e. *scores, coefficient, estimates, relationship*).

Among Group D items, the saliency of *relevant* is confirmed by its frequent predicative use (46% of cases), which is more than twice the average figure for relevance-marking adjectives. Its concordance shows a prevalence of realisations qualifying empirical evidence as variably useful to knowledge production. The noun *relevance* is relatively infrequent and, more often than not, qualified either with regard to its object (introduced by an *of*-phrase) and/or its impact (introduced by a *to*-phrase). *Irrelevant* appears occasionally and is most striking for its predicative position in 80% of occurrences, which makes it by far the most marked qualifier considered here. This finding arguably reflects the severity of value claims that deny relevance and are thus inconsistent with an (unmarked) attributive slot.

Finally, all the items in Group E are qualifiers, with the exception of *crucially*. Despite their polarised position among adjectives, they are mainly used attributively (in 84% of cases). The most frequent marker (*key*) is almost always in attributive position and tends to qualify aspects of the research viewed as particularly prominent, as shown by its top R1 collocates *feature/s*, *element/s*, *role/s*, *actors, aspect/s* and *variable/s*. On the other hand, around a third of realisations of *crucial* are predicative and most of these introduce a prepositional phrase with *to/for/in* specifying the scope of the qualification. The variation observed within this group provides further evidence that the semantic value of lexical items is constrained by syntax and quasi-formulaic collocational patterns, so that words which at first sight appear to be synonymous are in fact seldom interchangeable.

9. General discussion

9.1. Analytical basis

The analysis of disciplinary variation in academic writing conducted in this volume is inspired by recent research in applied linguistics as well as the sociology of science. More specifically, it takes on board the literature dealing with academic genres (e.g. Bazerman 1988; Swales 1990, 2004) and the disciplinary cultures that underlie such texts (Becher 1981; Becher/Trowler 2001), with a focus on the wording of evaluative speech acts (Hunston/Thompson 2000) investigated through linguistic corpora and discourse analysis (as in Biber *et al.* 2004). In this context it is essential to realise that, within academia, each branch of knowledge forms a separate world in terms of "goals, methods and beliefs, [...] conventions, histories or values" (Hyland 2000: 9). A discipline can thus be conceived as a relatively well-established subdivision of academic research with its own norms of enquiry and communication and a minimum degree of recognition from academic institutions and other disciplines.

Among the variables that define work carried out by academics there are aspects (whether of the research process, theoretical argumentation, or written presentation stage) to which the parent disciplinary community assigns an interpretation whose polarity reflects its current standards, beliefs and practices. These signal the axiological variables favoured by each discipline within a wider academic value system. As Hyland aptly explains, "what counts as relevant issues, convincing evidence, valid inference and appropriate interpersonal conduct is grounded in disciplinary values transmitted via socialisation and secured through a system of peer judgement. The principal realisation of this schema is the research article" (1997: 22).

There is an inevitable relationship between the written expression of scholarship and the values and priorities pursued by researchers, for written texts are "not merely an epiphenomenon on the boundaries of academic practice" but offer "a window on the practices and beliefs of the communities for whom they have meaning" (Hyland 2000: 5). The discourse communities that coalesce around such texts share "assumptions about what objects are appropriate for examination and discussion, what operating functions are performed on those objects, what constitutes 'evidence' and 'validity', and what formal conventions are followed" (Porter 1986: 39). The most prestigious type of academic publication is undoubtedly the *research article* (RA), a term used here for any contribution to a journal comprising new experimental evidence (where envisaged by the discipline) coupled with an element of theoretical speculation.

The three research questions guiding my exploration of how such values are textualised in academic writing, were respectively:

- RQ1. What academic values are signalled in the discourse of research articles belonging to different disciplines?
- RQ2. What lexical resources are employed to signal such values and to what degree are their lexicalisations transparent?
- RQ3. With what evaluated entities do academic values tend to correlate, both within and across disciplines?

In order to answer these questions, a corpus of 100 RAs was assembled from top-ranking international journals covering ten disciplines representative of five scientific areas:

NATURAL SCIENCES	Biology	Physics
APPLIED SCIENCES	Medicine	Engineering
HUMAN SCIENCES	History	Anthropology
SOCIAL SCIENCES	Sociology	Economics
MATHEMATICAL SCIENCES	Mathematics	Computer Science

Albeit not large by current standards, the corpus measures almost one million words (cf. Appendix 2) and is thus suited to the combined quantitative/qualitative methodology suited to the investigation of value-marking lexis.

9.2. Evaluative lexis and value markers

All the explicitly evaluative lexemes (mostly adjectives) with ≥100 occurrences in the RA corpus were extracted from the global WL and set aside for investigation as potential value markers or *candidate items* (Appendix 3). Because they often shared the same semantic field, it was then possible to group many of these into four categories linked to different axiological variables: namely goodness, size, novelty and relevance. The concordance of each candidate item was then inspected to assess whether and to what extent that specific word was used evaluatively. This significantly reduced the number of markers pertaining to each value. Subsequently further items related formally (in terms of word stem) or semantically (synonyms and antonyms) to such markers were added, in order to integrate the explicit lexis pertaining to the four values. As a result, all the markers considered belonged to groups of formally/semantically-related words within each axiological category.

Before turning to the type of realisations observed and to the frequency of such markers, it is worth looking at the evaluative nature of the four most prominent values identified in the corpus. When a text signals that something is *good*, *large*, *new* or *important* (or their opposite), it provides information as to:

- the evaluated entity, whose assessment operates on a continuum from highly factual (object internal) to highly contextual (object external);
- the observer's perception of that entity, which also operates on a continuum ranging from highly subjective (observer dependent) to highly objective (observer independent).

While distinguishing between these two facets of evaluation can be arduous and lead to endless debate, their contribution to the four values singled out for analysis is clearly different. The diagram below is an attempt to illustrate this relationship:

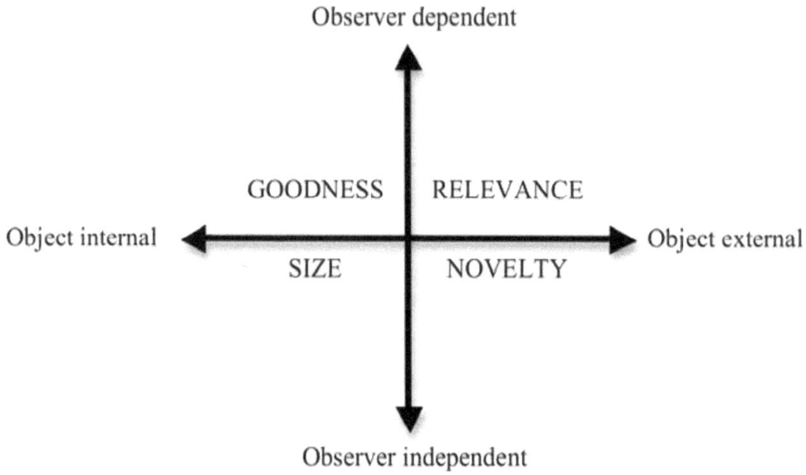

Figure 1. Planes of evaluation and targeted values.

Within this framework, size and novelty are the two more observer-independent values, because their perception is less a matter of personal opinion than the evaluation of goodness and relevance. Along the horizontal axis, relevance is arguably less dependent upon factual (i.e. object internal) information than goodness, and novelty less so than size. The fact that evaluation combines an element of externality and one of subjectivity is indirectly recognised by Soler's remark that the "interpretation/evaluation – certainty/observational fidelity sequence seems to parallel the subjectivity/objectivity continuum in scientific discourse, and adjectives seem to have a very important role in this respect" (2002: 154). Though only an approximation of the complexity inherent in evaluative speech acts, the fact that different values tend to draw differently on each plane is relevant to the data gleaned from the corpus. Accordingly, the interests and methods of enquiry typical of a given discipline, as reflected in the distribution of value markers, are likely to favour one or the other half of these two planes.

9.3. Academic values signalled in the corpus (RQ1)

Relevance, size, goodness and novelty (in that order) were found to be the four most frequent values encoded overtly in the lexis of academic RAs. Taken together they accounted for 6,677 tokens in a 986,185 word corpus, which (once the results are normalised by discipline) means a total of 74.5 occurrences every 10,000 words. There is, however, a considerable distance between the first two values and the latter, with relevance more than twice as frequent as novelty. It is interesting to note that relevance and size also top the list in Swales and Burke's (2003) analysis of evaluative adjectives in the Hyland RA corpus, while in spoken academic English (MICASE data) the order is reversed. Though less prominent than here, relevance and novelty markers have also been observed in such a minor academic genre as the book blurb (Gesuato 2007). On the whole, therefore, RA authors foreground primarily what is considered to be important/relevant, followed by dimensional considerations (whether factual or figurative), evaluations along the good/bad axis, and finally by references to what is new or novel.

Before considering how far these axiological variables are typical of each domain examined, it is important to remember that their presence is inextricably bound to the type of genre chosen for investigation (i.e. the research article), whose main purpose is to describe new scientific findings and assert congruity with a discipline's existing cognitive framework. Had the corpus consisted of book reviews or another typically evaluative genre, the results may have been markedly different: in article acknowledgements, for example, the top qualifiers targeting the perceived quality of contributions are *helpful*/*valuable*, both of which stress the utilitarian, interpersonal dimension of academic value (cf. Giannoni 1998).

9.3.1. Interdisciplinary variation

A full breakdown of results is given in the table below, with figures above the average for each value shaded in grey.

	Relevance	*Size*	*Goodness*	*Novelty*	*Total*
CS	40.9	11.1	35.4	9.7	*97.1*
PHY	20.7	56.2	12.0	5.9	*94.8*
ENG	32.0	25.1	25.7	4.4	*87.2*
ECO	28.9	19.9	26.7	10.8	*86.3*
HIST	22.4	11.4	20.5	26.0	*80.3*
ANTH	14.6	38.9	16.3	8.5	*78.3*
MED	43.7	10.6	13.8	7.6	*75.7*
SOC	23.1	10.4	15.0	13.5	*62.0*
BIO	13.6	10.7	9.8	20.5	*54.6*
MATH	6.9	12.6	4.2	3.9	*27.6*
Average	*24.7*	*20.7*	*18.0*	*11.1*	*74.5*
SD	*11.2*	*14.7*	*8.8*	*6.8*	-

Table 1. Relative prominence of values by discipline (normalised data).

The disciplines are listed here according to their total frequency (last column), which ranges from a maximum of 97.1 (CS) to a minimum of 54.6 (BIO), followed at a distance by MATH at 27.6. With the exception of MATH, therefore, the difference between the two ends of the spectrum is less than twofold. A far greater degree of variation is observed instead in the marking of the single values that make up such totals, as shown by the standard deviation (SD) from the mean for each variable. The figures indicate that novelty and goodness are on the whole far less discipline-specific than size and relevance, which means that dimensional evaluations and statements of what is deemed to be relevant vary significantly across domains.

Another way of measuring the clustering of value markers is to calculate their normalised presence in the top/bottom three domains of a hypothetical 100,000 word sample of the corpus containing 10,000 tokens from each discipline, which shows the following pattern:

Value	*Top 3 Disciplines*	*Bottom 3 Disciplines*
Relevance	MED+CS+ENG (47%)	MATH+BIO+ANTH (14%)
Size	PHY+ANTH+ENG (58%)	SOC+MED+BIO (15%)
Goodness	CS+ECO+ENG (49%)	MATH+BIO+PHY (14%)
Novelty	HIST+BIO+SOC (54%)	MATH+ENG+PHY (13%)

Table 2. Clustering of domains at each end of the scale.

Whereas the bottom three domains have an almost identical proportion of markers (around 14% of the total) for all the values considered, the top three account for a majority of markers only in the case of size (58%) and novelty (54%). Compared to the latter, relevance and goodness appear therefore to be less clustered at the high end of the range. It should be added that all domains feature at least once both in the top cluster (with the sole exception of MATH) and in the bottom one (except for CS). The tentative hypothesis made in Section 4.1 of a link between the level of value marking and lexical density, as measured by the STTR index, is not corroborated by these results.

The interdisciplinary variation detailed in Table 1 can be better visualised by plotting such data in a chart (Figure 2) with a separate bar reserved for each value. While the general pattern follows the sequence based on total scores, several peaks (and troughs) are noticeable along the way.

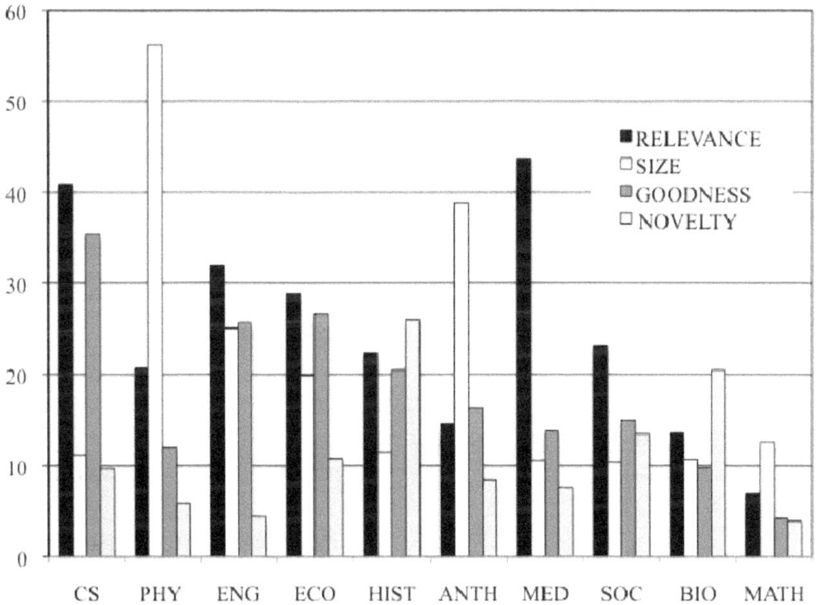

Figure 2. Value markers by discipline, in decreasing order (norm. occurrences).

The overall trend is more evident in the next chart, where each value is plotted as a stacked layer. The different domains are arranged again in decreasing order, with CS at the high end of the curve and MATH at the low end:

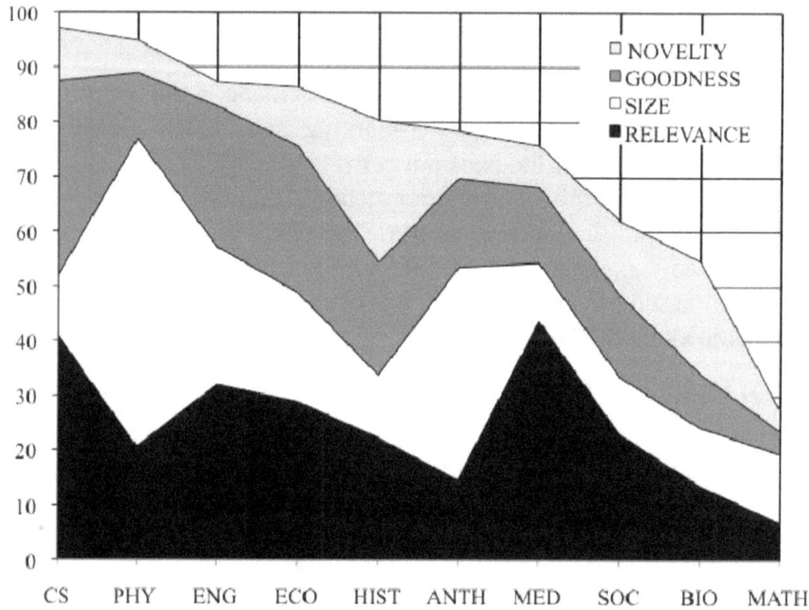

Figure 3. Distribution of values across disciplines (norm. occurrences).

The shading helps to distinguish between the general trend and individual variations. In particular, it shows that the closest disciplines (namely ECO/ENG on the one hand, and HIST/SOC on the other hand) are those with relatively comparable value levels. Conversely, CS, PHY and MED stand out for the prominence given respectively to goodness, size and relevance.

The overall saliency of these academic values across disciplines is seemingly unrelated to the pairings adopted in the corpus construction phase. Most notably, none of the five domains included in the upper half (or in the lower half) of Table 3, based on total counts, belongs to the same scientific area:

Relevance		*Size*		*Goodness*		*Novelty*	
MED	43.7	PHY	56.2	CS	35.4	HIST	26.0
CS	40.9	ANTH	38.9	ECO	26.7	BIO	20.5
ENG	32.0	ENG	25.1	ENG	25.7	SOC	13.5
ECO	28.9	ECO	19.9	HIST	20.5	ECO	10.8
SOC	23.1	MATH	12.6	ANTH	16.3	CS	9.7
HIST	22.4	HIST	11.4	SOC	15.0	ANTH	8.5
PHY	20.7	CS	11.1	MED	13.8	MED	7.6
ANTH	14.6	BIO	10.7	PHY	12.0	PHY	5.9
BIO	13.6	MED	10.6	BIO	9.8	ENG	4.4
MATH	6.9	SOC	10.4	MATH	4.2	MATH	3.9

Table 3. Ranking of disciplines within each value (norm. occurrences).

If we turn to the prominence of individual values, however, the following behaviour is observed: the APPLIED SCIENCES (MED/ENG) rank among the top five disciplines for relevance, the HUMAN SCIENCES (ANTH/HIST) for goodness and the SOCIAL SCIENCES (ECO/SOC) for novelty as well as relevance; size is the only value that does not appear in any pairing. This means that, despite the unique axiological profile of each discipline, the SOCIAL SCIENCES are on the whole those most likely to signal the values underlying their research, with a focus on what is deemed to be good/bad (goodness) and new/old (novelty) in the field. Goodness is also prominent in the HUMAN SCIENCES, while the APPLIED SCIENCES tend to underscore what is important/unimportant (relevance).

A slightly different picture of variation across scientific areas emerges in Table 4 below, which lists the average number of markers calculated for each disciplinary pairing. From this perspective:

- Relevance is highest in the APPLIED SCIENCES.
- Size is highest in the NATURAL SCIENCES.
- Goodness is highest in the SOCIAL SCIENCES.
- Novelty is highest in the HUMAN SCIENCES.

	Relevance	*Size*	*Goodness*	*Novelty*	*All*
APPLIED SCIENCES	37.8	17.8	19.7	6.0	81.4
HUMAN SCIENCES	18.5	25.1	18.4	17.2	79.3
NATURAL SCIENCES	17.1	33.4	10.9	13.2	74.7
SOCIAL SCIENCES	26.0	15.1	20.8	12.1	74.1
MATH. SCIENCES	23.9	11.8	19.8	6.8	62.3
Average	*24.7*	*20.7*	*18.0*	*11.1*	74.5

Table 4. Prominence of values across scientific areas (norm. occurrences).

While the four axiological variables identified in this volume are well represented in all the domains considered and may thus be said to belong to the broader *academic value system*, their prominence has thus been shown to vary considerably from one discipline to another and (to a lesser extent) between scientific areas.

9.3.2. *Intradisciplinary variation*

The figures in Table 1 showed how the marking of each variable deviated from the average level observed across disciplines, that is interdisciplinary variation from the mean. But it is also useful to look at *intradisciplinary* variation, that is the extent to which values deviate from the mean observed within disciplines. This perspective is illustrated below, with above-mean counts highlighted again in grey.

	CS	*PHY*	*ENG*	*ECO*	*HIST*	*ANTH*	*MED*	*SOC*	*BIO*	*MATH*
Relevance	40.9	20.7	32.0	28.9	22.4	14.6	43.7	23.1	13.6	6.9
Size	11.1	56.2	25.1	19.9	11.4	38.9	10.6	10.4	10.7	12.6
Goodness	35.4	12.0	25.7	26.7	20.5	16.3	13.8	15.0	9.8	4.2
Novelty	9.7	5.9	4.4	10.8	26.0	8.5	7.6	13.5	20.5	3.9
Average	*24.3*	*23.7*	*21.8*	*21.6*	*20.0*	*19.6*	*18.9*	*15.5*	*13.6*	*6.9*
SD	*14.0*	*19.5*	*10.4*	*7.0*	*5.4*	*11.5*	*14.5*	*4.7*	*4.2*	*3.5*

Table 5. Distribution of values within disciplines (norm. occurrences).

The most evident difference here is that, proportionally speaking, relevance makes an above-average contribution in six out of ten domains, size and goodness in four each and novelty only in two

(HIST and SOC). This finding confirms the prominence of relevance as the dominant value in most disciplines, with the exclusion of PHY, ANTH, BIO and MATH. The same data can be plotted as a percentage of the total count of each value:

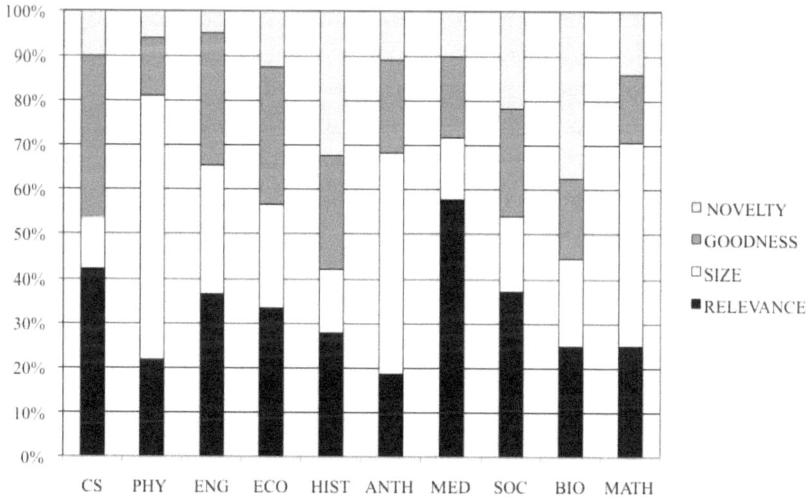

Figure 4. Proportional contribution of each value across disciplines.

Although SD naturally tends to rise when value marking is stronger, it does not always follow this trend. Notably, ECO and HIST exhibit less variation in their values than might be expected, whereas ANTH and MED have more. The axiological profile of the first two is thus flatter, compared to the latter, which indicates that they tend to discriminate less between these four values.

9.3.3. Axiological profile of disciplines

By taking into account both the overall level of value-marking intensity and the prominence of specific values in each domain, disciplines can be described in a way that captures the essence of their axiological profile. The evidence summarised in Tables 1 and 5 shows strong disciplinary proclivities in explicit value marking which –

though perhaps inconspicuous to the reader – constitute a measurable feature of academic writing, linked to the epistemological standards that guide scientific enquiry in the disciplines.

The descriptions below illustrate these variables in terms of *focus* (relative prominence of specific values) and *explicitness* (value-marking intensity) for each of the ten domains considered:

- ANTH is size-focused and moderately explicit;
- BIO is novelty-focused and scarcely explicit;
- CS is relevance/goodness-focused and highly explicit;
- ECO is relevance/goodness-focused and highly explicit;
- HIST is balanced and highly explicit;
- ENG is balanced and highly explicit;
- MATH is size-focused and scarcely explicit;
- MED is relevance-focused and moderately explicit;
- PHY is size-focused and highly explicit;
- SOC is relevance-focused and scarcely explicit.

These profiles are not inconsistent with Becher and Trowler's (2001) description of the qualities of knowledge in different disciplinary groupings outlined in Chapter 2 (Table 1). In particular, their claim that the pure sciences are particularly concerned with quantity is arguably reflected in the finding here that PHY and MATH are both size-focused. Similarly their argument that the humanities and social sciences are 'value-laden' is partly confirmed by the high degree of value marking in HIST and ECO.

9.4. Lexical resources encoding value (RQ2)

In keeping with the evaluative function of the lexis considered, adjectives constitute the majority of markers identified in the corpus, accounting altogether for over three quarters (77%) of items. They are followed by nouns (11%), adverbs (9%) and occasionally verbs (3%). The importance of investigating the obvious link between adjectivation and academic values is described as follows in a small-scale study of adjectives in biochemistry/neurochemistry RAs:

> Adjectives allow scientists to describe and qualify phenomena observed during the experimental stage and to anticipate agreements or oppositions to claims with caution and strategic consideration of the opinions and views of peers. This observation is directly related to the role of adjectives with an evaluative purpose in scientific discourse because evaluation, though personal, depends on the value-system of the scientific community in which discourse is generated. (Soler 2002: 149)

The use of adjectives as a yardstick for describing texts in different disciplines should not be underestimated. Work by Losee (1996) on the statistical significance of lexicogrammatical features in multi-disciplinary corpora suggests that adjectives are (after foreign words and nouns) the part of speech that most discriminates between theory-based and applied, practice-based disciplines.

The data in Table 6 below reveal, however, that if each value is taken separately, the role of adjectivation varies considerably: from 100% for size to less than half (44%) for goodness, which has the most balanced range of markers. The figures in brackets are, as usual, non-normalised occurrences:

	Relevance	*Size*	*Goodness*	*Novelty*	*All*
Adjectives	79% (1,719)	100% (1,733)	44% (759)	88% (926)	77% (5,137)
Nouns	9% (203)	-	27% (468)	4% (39)	11% (710)
Adverbs	12% (261)	-	22% (369)	1% (7)	9% (637)
Verbs	-	-	7% (112)	7% (81)	3% (193)
Total	*(2,183)*	*(1,733)*	*(1,708)*	*(1,053)*	*(6,677)*

Table 6. Weight of different parts of speech in value marking.

These results may partly be explained by the limited availability in English academic discourse of parts of speech encoding certain values (e.g. '*largeness* or '*smallness*' in the case of size) but are also a consequence of how authors drawn on the unmarked lexical repertoire of their field. The much more balanced range of parts of speech associated with goodness marking – almost half of which are either nouns or adverbs – can be ascribed to the fact that this value has the broadest meaning and, as a result, the widest range of lexicalisations. Another interesting difference regards relevance, which is the only value to favour adverbs over nouns/verbs, mainly because of the pervasiveness of *significantly*. As for verbs, these are more prominent than nouns/adverbs only in the case of novelty – a finding linked to the intentional, agentive element incorporated in this variable.

9.4.1. Syntactic position of adjectives

For each of the values considered, the corpus was scanned to identify different adjectival constructions, distinguishing between predicative and attributive uses. While the latter were clearly prevalent, their proportion varied both between values and within groups of markers, as described in the previous chapters. The overall results condensed below show that attributive qualifiers account for around three quarters of the total in the case of size and relevance but reach almost 100% of the total for novelty.

Adjectives	*Predicative*	*Attributive*	*All*
Relevance	22%	78%	1,719
Goodness	14%	86%	759
Size	23%	77%	1,733
Novelty	2%	98%	926

Table 7. Syntactic position of value-marking adjectives.

The significance of such data stems from the fact that "The presence of the scientist is more evident in predicative adjectival constructions [...] i.e. the speaker/writer is more openly visualized as the source of the qualifying statement" (Soler 2002: 153). The relatively high proportion of predicative uses among relevance qualifiers (22%) may thus agree with my earlier argument that relevance is a subjective, observer-dependent value (cf. Figure 1). On the other hand, the frequent predicative use of size qualifiers – which constitute the largest group of value-marking adjectives in the corpus – is less easy to explain: while their frequency clearly indicates that size judgements are also interpersonally salient, it partly reflects the high proportion (35%) of comparative size-markers employed predicatively. As for individual items, predicative constructions were found to be prevalent only in a small number of negative and/or polarised qualifiers (*wrong, worse, problematic, obsolete, irrelevant*).

These results may be interpreted as evidence that writer involvement is adjusted not only to match the type of value encoded by a qualifier but also its markedness, as confirmed by the rarity of predicative constructions among some of the most common qualifiers (e.g. *new, positive, better, large*) in the corpus.

9.4.2. Lexical transparency of markers

Establishing the status of value markers in a corpus is an arduous task. The potentially unlimited number of evaluative lexemes and phrases capable of encoding, more or less directly, meanings related to the academic value system "makes a fully systematic and comprehensive account of evaluation extremely difficult, perhaps even impossible" (Römer 2008: 127). It is possible, however, to critically explore meanings-in-context by combining corpus-analysis tools and manual investigation of WLs/concordances in a way that is both quantitatively and qualitatively significant. The results described in Chapters 5-8 often report the difficulty of dealing with lexical items that are polysemous and may involve no value marking at all. The methodology employed here attempts to balance the often-opposing demands of systematicity and workability. One advantage of concentrating on *explicit* markers, to the exclusion of more opaque or indirect realisations, is that it allows the analyst to examine a relatively small number of realisations, singling out candidates closer to the semantic core of the target values (see Appendix 3).

The challenges faced in this respect were posed by two categories of words: (i) items that may or not count as value markers because of their ambiguity; (ii) items that are clearly value markers but allow different interpretations. The former include such words as *negative* (relevant if it encodes an evaluation of goodness; irrelevant if it expresses an arithmetic concept), *new* (relevant if it expresses novelty; irrelevant when it means 'not used') and *error* (relevant when it does not refer to 'statistical error'). The latter are represented by *significant* (which may encode 'importance' or 'statistical relevance') and *major* (that can mean 'particularly important' or 'most important').

It is comforting to speculate that some of these interpretive dilemmas are shared by expert readers and, at times, are a deliberate feature of academic discourse. The most explicit realisations remain of course those involving extreme or polarised markers, but there is a general tendency in academic writing to avoid such forms, especially in RAs (cf. Swales/Burke 2003). The only polarised items with a sizeable presence (*key* and *crucial*) encoded relevance, i.e. the most prominent of the four values investigated in the corpus.

9.5. Variation among qualified entities (RQ3)

The working hypothesis suggested in the piloting stage of this study (cf. Chapter 4, Table 3) of a correlation between values and evaluated entities was not borne out by the results. Regularities were observed instead in the tendency of specific lexical items to qualify a certain type of axiological target or *referent*, and these pairings were in turn dependent upon the discipline(s) involved: the picture is thus far more complex than initially assumed. The pages that follow provide an overview of such evidence for each category of value markers, taking into account, where relevant, also the contextual information embedded in their right and left collocates.

9.5.1. Goodness referents

The qualifier *good*, which is never premodified, generally targets on the procedural value of data, statistical tools or modelling techniques, as shown by its top R1 collocates (*example/s*, *agreement*, *approximation*, *fit* and *representation*). Most of the collocations in ECO, on the other hand, centre on the term *management*. Also *best* tends to qualify procedural aspects of research (*alignments, fit, outcomes, predictors*) in all domains, with the exception of HIST. The comparative form *better* co-occurs with the past participle of verbs that describe research (*endowed, placed, suited*), its performance (*absorbed, studied, supported*) or interpretation (*understood, documented*). The adverb *well* collocates most notably with *defined*, *established*, *developed* and other adjectives, some of which specific to individual disciplines: e.g. *characterized* (BIO), *designed* (CS), *individualized* (ANTH), *managed* (ECO) and *posed* (MATH). Also *improve* (like *best* and *well*) was found to be unusually prominent in ENG, arguably because of the discipline's focus on technological advancement; it co-occurs above all with inanimate subjects (*equipment, procedures, results*). Finally, the adjective *positive* qualifies almost exclusively human behaviour, which makes 'positivity' a particularly subjective/emotive variable.

Negative lexicalisations of goodness were more varied in terms of referent. Thus *bad* often qualifies *practices*, *managers* and *performance* in ECO, human attributes (*behaviour, intentions, health*) in HIST, and experimental features in PHY. The adverb *poorly*, on the other hand, frequently occurs in cognitive evaluations, its main collocate being *understood*, followed by *known*, *described* and *suited*. Entities qualified as *problematic* range from methodological options to data interpretation and theory building; *error* focuses instead on faults due to misjudgement or bad design, with the link between such errors and their originators normally concealed, unless the agent is external to the discipline.

9.5.2. Size referents

The adjective *large* (like *larger*) targets primarily the data available to researchers: its most frequent collocates in the corpus were *number/s*, *scale/s* and *amount/s*. Although in some domains (ANTH, BIO and CS) it often qualifies the actual physical dimensions of an object, *large* remains prevalently a phenomenological value-marker, signalling the researcher's perception/interpretation of data in terms of size. Its main L1 collocates were respectively an intensifier (*very*) and a hedge (*relatively*). The second most common size marker (*small*) shared the same kind of referent.

An interesting difference observed between domains is the marked prevalence of *large* in ECO/ENG and of *small* in CS/MATH, with a similar proportion of the two in the remaining disciplines. The most obvious implication of this finding may be that the former domains favour an empirical perspective which, comparatively speaking, is more concerned with macrophenomena than minor referents. Thus *small* collocates often with *number/s*, *sample/s*, *scale/s, screen/s* (CS) and *redshifts* (PHY), with the last two firmly embedded in disciplinary terminology. Its top L1 collocates were *relatively* and *very* (as for *large*, but in reverse order), followed by *sufficiently* (MATH). The fact that *sufficiently small* is limited to MATH suggests that this domain has a high regard of 'smallness', a hypothesis confirmed by the finding that it had the highest ratio (2:1) of 'smallness' to 'largeness' markers among disciplines.

9.5.3. Novelty referents

The qualifier *new*, which accounts for over 60% of items signalling novelty, is associated with a wide variety of referents, ranging from the most mundane to the highly abstract. There is, however, a prevalence of occurrences targeting either aspects of a discipline's methodology and interpretation of phenomena, or aspects of the evidence collected. Entities of the first type prevail in most domains, the impression being that these realisations signal a greater degree of discontinuity, with novelty presented as a result of deliberation rather than a quality merely arising from the chronological sequence of events. *New* is very seldom premodified and hardly ever used in the comparative form, which suggests that novelty is a non-gradable value in academic settings.

The referents of *recent* tend to be new contributions to the discipline, whether in the form of data, modelling, methodology or technology. In line with this finding, its main right collocate was *study/ies*, followed at a distance by *work*, *data*, *literature* and *research*. The adverbial form *recently* qualifies the same type of entity. Finally, the negative polarity, largely represented by *old*, is infrequent and concentrated in HIST, where the qualifier invariably targets the phenomena under investigation; only once does it evaluate the ongoing academic debate.

9.5.4. Relevance referents

The most frequent relevance marker (*important*) stands out for its markedness, being employed predicatively in over 40% of occurrences. It largely qualifies aspects of the science-making process, that is of the observation and interpretation of results within the wider context of knowledge claims made in the literature. Its main R1 collocates with a sizeable presence were *role/s, factor/s, issue/s* and *source/s*, while premodifiers were rare and when they did occur they mainly qualified their referent contrastively (*more important than*) rather than by modulating its evaluative force. The noun *importance* was followed in almost three quarters of occurrences by an *of*-phrase that tends to qualify methodological aspects of research.

There were significant differences also in the referents of other relevance markers: *major* mainly targets the status of empirical evidence and in all of the domains considered it singles out phenomena deserving special consideration. On the other hand, *main* and *principal* tend to qualify abstract nouns associated less with the evidence itself than its interpretation. This finding is corroborated by the R1 collocates of *main* with most occurrences in the corpus: namely *result/s*, *effect/s* and *theorem*.

A special case is the adjective *significant* and other items within the same lexical group. This may be used in its broader sense (=important), or as an indicator of mathematical value (=statistically relevant). Although the two meanings are not always distinguishable and may in fact overlap, the latter is clearly prevalent, with *significant* overwhelmingly targeting the interpretation of experimental evidence – its top R1 collocates were *difference/s*, *interaction/s*, *effect/s* and *change/s*. The relatively high proportion of negated forms (where significance is ruled out rather than affirmed) is substantiated by the finding that the sequence *There* BE *significant* belonged to negative realisations in 70% of cases. The adverb form *significantly* is most often preceded by a copula whose subject (i.e. its referent) is either a statistical variable or, more directly, the object under investigation.

After *significant*, the most common marker was *relevant*, whose predicative prominence (49% of occurrences) is evidence of the marker's saliency. It prevails in realisations that qualify the status of empirical evidence as more or less useful to knowledge production. Less often it defines methodological assumptions/approaches adopted by the RA author(s) or in the literature. *Relevant* tends to be pre-modified either by adverbs that contextualise (*clinically, politically*) or modalise (*especially, immediately, particularly, really*) its meaning, or by comparative evaluative adverbs (*more, most, less*).

The adjectives *key* and *crucial* peaked in ECO, HIST and SOC, showing these to be the most argumentative (and at times polemical) domains represented in the corpus. The polarisation of such items means that they convey authorial stance as well as ideational meaning. Thus *key* qualifies interpretive variables considered to be particularly important – a fact reflected by its top R1 collocates *feature/s*, *element/s* and *role/s*. The referents of *crucial* are very similar, as shown by it main R1 collocates (*role*, *question/s* and *difference*).

9.6. Final remarks

The analysis of academic RAs conducted in this volume offers insights into how scholars with different disciplinary backgrounds construct and negotiate what counts as scientific knowledge by drawing on a common repertoire of shared notions, assumptions and norms of interaction. The methodological approach developed for this purpose rests on the assumption that evaluative speech acts not only convey information about the author/writer's stance and identity but also communicate something about the axiological parameters or *values* that inspire scientific enquiry. These are embedded in evaluations that "are construals of experiences in context on binary scales between positive and negative: good (plus value) vs. bad (minus value), desirable vs. undesirable, important vs. not important, lovely vs. hideous etc." (Downes 2000: 104). Each value is a facet of what constitutes 'worthiness' (cf. Thetela 1997) amongst scholars affiliated to the same (sub)disciplinary community.

The patterns identified both across disciplines and in the various referents associated with each lexical item indicate that authors (more or less consciously) write within a web of unwritten rules that constrain their linguistic options. While none of the markers examined is specific to the discourse of academics, their use is 'academic' insofar as it evokes shared meanings that are both acceptable and comprehensible to scholars even without supporting evidence. When RA authors claim that something is good, new, large or important they draw on a semiotic-axiological system of values in a way that, *per se*, is neither scientific nor systematic. Yet it would be unwise to assume that the significance of such markers simply replicates that observed in general English. At the same time, the fact the such values are not limited to academia means that RAs cannot be separated from the wider textual world in which their readers are immersed. There is indeed growing evidence (cf. Gross 2000; Giannoni 2008) of concerted efforts on the part of editors and publishers to narrow that gap by introducing elements of popularised science and commercial publications into the rhetoric of academic publications.

By foregrounding what counts as value-laden (i.e. desirable or undesirable) in their midst through explicit lexicalisations, researchers signal to peers their awareness of the academic value system, as implemented in a given disciplinary culture. In so doing, they claim an axiological common ground with their peers and strengthen the collegiate, communal dimension of research. Although not all axiologically-relevant meanings are expressed explicitly, those which are most important to the discipline can be reasonably assumed to occur more frequently and be more lexically prominent than others.

It may of course be argued that the values mentioned most often are those associated with controversy and the negotiation of tensions within the process of knowledge construction. The data collected here, however, does not corroborate this hypothesis, as only a fraction of negative realisations and/or markers were linked to such values. Instead, the intensity and distribution of value marking differed considerably across domains, suggesting that what counts as a value is inextricably linked to the methodology as well as the content of a discipline.

Such findings are, of course, not devoid of limitations. The first concerns the construction of the corpus, based on disciplinary pairings linked to five scientific areas. The results show that, apart from certain general divergences observed between these areas, differences in value marking are generally stronger between single disciplines. What is more, the texts chosen for each domain inevitably reflect the specific interests of the host journal and the level of subdisciplinary specialisation that governs contemporary science. It is virtually impossible to select a journal that represents any of the major disciplines across the board, as the competition for readership and exposure presses editors towards new, increasingly discrete, research niches to be filled.

Another aspect that cannot be ignored, as mentioned earlier, is the role of high-frequency markers signalling the most explicit (i.e. lexically prominent) values. While quantitatively significant, the level of value-marking intensity measured across the corpus does not only reflect the centrality of a given axiological variable but may also depend in part on the level of explicitness appropriate to each discipline. After all, journal articles do not tell the whole story – they are only the *public face* (Hyland 1997: 21) of science and such 'academic values' as personal integrity, competitiveness and cost efficiency mainly lead an extratextual life.

Despite these limitations, RAs are a unique source of linguistic evidence reflecting the beliefs and priorities of disciplinary communities. Being published texts, they reach well beyond the small entourage of fellow researchers familiar with their authors and mediate between different interests and branches of learning within domains. At the same time, the genre's emphasis on knowledge construction through well-established procedures sanctioned by its parent community means that RAs are strongly compliant with (and thus representative of) a discipline's linguistic inventory.

10. Conclusions

10.1. Theoretical insights

The results of this study shed some light on a small but highly prominent group of variables embedded in the discourse of research, whose presence shows how authors flag fundamental aspects of knowledge linked to the value system shared by the members of a given disciplinary community. The phenomenon is consistent with Reed's (1996) interpretation of values as 'regulatory mechanisms' that mediate between the self and its social environment, reflecting an individual's stage of socialisation as well as his/her personal growth. The lexical evidence yielded by the RA corpus assembled here suggests that by simply mentioning such variables, an author:

- recognises their role as *basic evaluative parameters* applicable to the discipline and its judgements;
- claims the presence of an *axiological common ground* among researchers in the discipline despite their different approaches and orientations;
- signals potential *tensions in the research process*, that is aspects whose interpretation is controversial and thus negotiable.

Though often mentioned in the literature on academic discourse, few applied linguists have attempted to define the notion of 'value' and, what is more, its analytical implications remain largely unexplored. Among EAP specialists there is, however, a general recognition that academic literacy includes an awareness of the values that orientate research. Paltridge, for example, argues that learning to write in the academy is "learning to acquire a repertoire of linguistic practices which are based on complex sets of discourses, identities, and values" (2004: 90). Hyland warns that analysts should not underestimate the variability and instability of such phenomena, for "if we see communities as real, stable groups conforming to rules and values and upholding a consensus we are clearly obscuring the potentially tremendous diversity and variety of members' roles, allegiance and participation in their disciplines" (2000: 9). Greater interest in the axiological content of language is shown by the literature on intercultural communication, which is particularly pertinent in the light of Hyland's (2000) argument that disciplines constitute separate *cultures* within academia. The relationship between cultural values and discourse is described by Corson in the following terms:

> A value is an attitude or an interest that people in a cultural group cherish for its own sake, or perhaps cherish instrumentally as something that is essential to the maintenance of the group itself. Cultural values provide structures or mechanisms that affect the behaviour of the members of a group; they influence the way people behave and interact. There seems [to be] a simple analytical relationship between the idea of a norm in language use and the idea of a cultural value. While there are many aspects of language use that seem to be universal, other aspects vary across cultures and grow from cultural learning processes that establish socially appropriate norms of communicative behaviour. (Corson 1995: 187)

The values embedded in research writing embrace therefore both a social dimension, linked to the specific scientific community of which the author is a member, and a cultural dimension given by the discipline itself. The assumption made in Chapter 4 that these variables can be reconstructed from the linguistic cues contained in a corpus has underpinned my investigation of the four values most frequently marked by academic texts (in decreasing order, relevance, size, goodness and novelty). The number and distribution of explicit markers drawing attention to such variables tend to vary from one discipline to another according to their salicency. At the same time, the fact that a certain value is mentioned more/less often could be linked to its degree of 'negotiability' in a given setting – with authors more likely to assert qualities whose presence is problematic rather than those taken for granted by the disciplinary community.

At first sight, relevance, size, goodness and novelty may not recall what in common parlance is understood as a 'value', because of their apparent lack of moral or personal connotations. The literature on evaluation, however, has developed an approach that embraces any variable encoded in speech acts conveying some kind of judgement. As Thompson and Hunston make clear, "evaluation is the broad cover term for the expression of the speaker's attitude or stance towards, viewpoint on, or feelings about the entities or propositions that he or she is talking about. This attitude may relate to certainty or obligation or desirability or any of a number of other sets of values" (2000: 5). Taken together, the four variables described here can be assigned to the 'value set' of *desirability*, because they all qualify aspects that are desirable (or not) from a researcher's viewpoint. Even size – i.e. the evaluation of something as large or small – inevitably recalls criteria and expectations conducive to desirability. At the same time, relevance, size, goodness and novelty are interpretable as aspects of 'attitudinal stance', according to Conrad and Biber's (2000) framework, insofar as they express feelings or judgements about a proposition.

Variation in the prominence assigned to such values across domains may also be partly explained in the light of Cole's hypothesis that the amount of evaluation carried out in a discipline reflects the balance between its core knowledge (well-established theories and analytical tools) and its research frontier (ongoing work in the field), because "our opinions of what good science is and who has done good work are based on judgments made by other people or the evaluation system in our field" (1983: 136). Using the age of textbook citations as a parameter, Cole concludes that consensus is far greater, and thus evaluation less prominent, in the natural sciences than in the social sciences – a result that agrees with my finding that relevance and goodness are far less marked in the natural sciences compared to the social sciences.

The corpus analysed here contains textual evidence of the axiological variables that guide research in the disciplines, providing authors and readers alike with a yardstick for interpreting prior/new knowledge claims. Because of their pervasiveness in published academic discourse, such variables deserve close scrutiny also in view of pedagogic applications geared in particular to novice researchers, who may be native speakers of English or part of the wider ELF (English as a Lingua Franca) community. Awareness of the values expressed in RAs could help to empower weaker members of academia that are still learning to master the genre's conventions (cf. Christie 1989; Martin 1989). It is particularly important for postgraduate students, who "need to learn to work within the value-systems of their target communities" (Swales 1990: 219).

One way of doing this is to engage learners in an assessment of the four categories of value markers identified here, as employed in their writing and in a comparable sample of texts produced by experts in the field. After measuring the relative prominence of each axiological variable in terms of value-marking intensity, and the range of lexical items employed for this purpose, the results could then be debated with/among learners to enhance their awareness of the function and significance of such markers in a given genre. At the same time any major differences between the two groups of texts could be investigated as potentially problematic deviations from the norm on the learners' part, especially if a given value is over-represented or under-represented. Attention should also be drawn to general trends in the syntactic position of value-marking qualifiers (which may be used quite differently in other languages or genres) and to limitations in the range of marker-referent pairings available to authors.

The purpose of such tasks is to form an 'axiologically proficient' academic writer, capable of signalling value-related judgements through lexis that is normally unmarked, but may occasionally be marked for negativity or intensity. This is especially important for doctoral students or junior researchers who are keen to improve their writing skills for publication. In the case of less advanced learners, however, the primary concern is to critically assess the scientific value of a publication as *readers*. For their benefit, the classroom can be used to explore the function(s) of value markers in a given text, focusing on their contribution to the author's argument vis-à-vis the topic and competing claims in the literature. Recognition that readers' perception of such realisations may be influenced by such factors as their cultural background, language and career is a good starting point for consciousness-raising activities. As observed by Swales (2004c: 20), the insights of corpus linguistics can help students to acquire "greater confidence and competence in both their written expressiveness and their capacity to reflect upon it".

The lexical resources that signal academic values are also of interest for their collocational behaviour, which is largely related to discipline-specific content and rhetorical conventions. Attempts to compile lists of academic collocations to improve EAP vocabulary learning (cf. Durrant 2009), for example, might benefit from a focus on value-related lexemes as indicators of particularly sensitive meanings. As undergraduates and novice writers do not always appreciate what aspects of research deserve to be prized or stigmatised through appropriate evaluative acts (Mei 2006a, 2006b), explicit instruction as to which elements in a researcher's narrative are likely to be evaluated in terms of relevance, size, goodness or novelty may make learners more aware of the pairings of values and referents in their discipline.

10.2. The role of academic values

As published accounts of ongoing contributions to the field, RAs play a central role in the construction and dissemination of new findings to fellow researchers; they "embody the social negotiation of disciplinary enquiry, revealing how knowledge is constructed, negotiated and made persuasive" (Hyland 2000: 3). The relationship between discourse and the academic community is mutually constitutive, in that the socio-cognitive practices endorsed by scholars in a given field shape and are shaped by their use of language. The purpose of a RA is to present knowledge claims in a way that is both persuasive and consistent with previous research, while offering readers information that is sufficiently novel and central to the field (i.e. of scholarly interest). This does not mean that authors are driven exclusively by an intellectual appetite for knowledge: in a competitive, tightly-controlled environment, academics are also under constant pressure to publish a suitable number of papers in international peer-reviewed journals each year, to prove they are sufficiently productive and respected scholars in their field. The result is that "this desire to gain reputation therefore acts as a system of social control as it encourages conformity to the approved discursive practices of the discipline" (Hyland 2000: 171).

The variables identified as values in this study are closely related to the practices endorsed by each discipline and to the rhetorical features of the RA genre. By signalling to peers what is remarkable in terms of relevance, size, goodness or novelty, authors not only promote their own views/findings but also show compliance with an established body of knowledge sanctioned by peers. In this sense, the values themselves exert a form of power over the members of a discipline, who become recipients as well as agents of their authority. Ultimately, the presence of certain values in academic discourse is not remarkable *per se* but as evidence of the axiological system present in each discipline and duly reaffirmed by its members in their published interactions.

The nature of this system clearly deserves greater attention, as it remains largely unexplored. A large part of the literature on values approaches the concept from an individual psychological perspective. The most influential model (Schwartz 1992, 1994) claims the existence of a 'universal structure of values' based on two bipolar dimensions: openness to change vs. conservation, and self-transcendence vs. self-enhancement. Schwartz's taxonomy deals essentially with *motivational value types*, that is with the psychological needs that guide individual behaviour across cultures. Its main purpose is to conceptualise the fundamental opposition between the self and others – an aspect that is inherent in the rhetoric of RAs, as authors carefully position their claims within a wider framework provided by the literature. Academic value judgements seek to strike a balance between opposing needs. The degree of openness/conservation and self-transcendence/enhancement will depend on the broader context in which a value is evoked, with more junior scholars veering perhaps towards the first option and their more senior colleagues towards the second option in each pair.

When a model like this is adopted as a basis for empirical research, however, the analyst runs the risk of searching for proof of pre-conceived variables rather than letting the evidence speak for itself. Bilsky and Koch (2002) for example, speculate as to whether Schartz's values are universals or only 'methodological artefacts' elicited by the questionnaires and self-reported data collected by researchers; they conclude that the model's structure (i.e. its bipolar organisation) is sound but fails to prove its taxonomical validity.

Closer to the concerns of this study is a very useful (though relatively obscure) paper entitled 'A cognitive approach to values', published in the *Journal for the Theory of Social Behaviour*. Its authors join the debate by acknowledging that "value is among the most fuzzy concepts of the social sciences. It seems to play the role of a passe-partout in the explanation of a number of phenomena, either intrapsychic or interactional or macrosocial" (Miceli/Castelfranchi 1989: 169). Despite the subject's complexity, they attempt to define the conceptual boundaries of these 'mental and social objects', whose presence permeates human experience. The main difference observed between values and evaluations is that the former are only general, vague judgements which tell us that something (e.g. honesty) is good or bad without explaining why:

> Believing and remembering that honesty is 'good', and behaving in accordance with this belief, is much easier and effective than trying to evaluate whether honesty is good in that particular instance, for that specific goal. From a social point of view, this is exactly why values are so precious for the maintenance of social cohesion: the individual will not bother himself/herself and others by questioning at any given time whether honesty should be pursued. He/she will believe honesty should be always pursued. (Miceli/Castelfranchi 1989: 191)

From this perspective, therefore, values are neither goals nor standards but unquestionable entities that cannot be disproved, and as such belong ultimately to the realm of irrational thought; more importantly, they play a normative role based on the individual's relationship with authority. The absolute nature of values means that they are imposed by the social environment rather than selected systematically: thus individuals may find it difficult to justify their value system and possible conflicts arising between different values. The social role of these axiological constructs is particularly relevant to academic communication, because it implies that disciplinary communities need to exercise pressure and control over their members in order to ensure stability and cohesiveness. This function is clearly consistent with the view that values are a component of ideology, alongisde identity, aims, norms and group relations (see, among others, van Dijk 1998).

The very nature of values – and especially their unchallenged introjection on the recipient's part – makes them, unlike evaluations, far less noticeable to the analyst. They are so well camouflaged within discourse as to appear merely an integral part of the lexis. The fact that academic values are (like many other features of discourse) not unique to academia but merely more or less prominent, contributes to this impression. Relevance, size, goodness and novelty are evoked in almost every sphere of human interaction, and as such may be discounted by the analyst as too mundane for in-depth examination, but the discursive-argumentative power of these variables originates to a large extent from their apparent insignificance.

The corpus evidence presented in this volume indicates that disciplinary cultures draw differently from the value system in both quantitative and qualitative terms. In so doing, authors not only comply with a framework that meets the expectations of their peers but also exploit a range of widely-accepted axiological variables strategically, to forward their own knowledge claims. This also seems to be the case in other academic genres, as shown by Blakeslee's finding that readers' letters to journals tend to emphasise 'newsworthiness' by foregrounding such elements as novelty and usefulness, to the point that "in keeping with their function of announcing innovations, letters have come to resemble journalistic accounts of scientific findings" (1994: 91).

The fact that only the four most frequently marked values were selected for analysis does not mean they are unrelated; their tendency to co-occur and follow similar patterns of variation both across and within disciplines suggests that they are part of an *academic value system* whose exact boundaries await investigation. As observed earlier, this system consists of mental as well as social objects, which means it functions in ways that are linguistically measurable only in part. At the same time, it may include variables that are seldom if ever made explicit or are never socialised in writing.

10.3. Methodological considerations

The results reported in this study are an example of how corpus analysis can be used to probe a system which, inevitably, remains both open-ended and unavailable for full examination. Academic values are never asserted overtly (e.g. *X is a value*), but rather evoked through markers drawn from their semantic field (*A has X*). The methodology adopted here seeks to reconcile a purely lexical perspective, such as that adopted by Biber (2004) and Biber *et al.* (2004a, 2004b), with the strongly pragmatic, but rather pessimistic, approach to the quantification of evaluative language propounded by Hunston (1993b, 1994). It rests therefore on the dual assumption that the explicit marking of evaluative categories classifiable as 'values', is in itself an analytically meaningful feature of academic lexis, and that a large part of such marking is performed by single words. When the focus is placed on values rather than evaluative acts, the claim that "the word is perhaps not the most useful unit of analysis in the search for evaluative meanings" (Römer 2008: 121) can perhaps be set aside, without denying that evaluative meanings are conveyed by phrases and structures as well as individual words (Stubbs 2001).

Because of their straightforward, largely unqualified lexicalisations, values are easier to identify in a corpus than the complex, pragmatically-embedded realisations investigated by the literature on evaluation in academic discourse (cf. Hunston/Thompson 2000; Del Lungo Camiciotti/Tognini Bonelli 2004). At the same time, however, the analysis of value-marking items cannot be restricted to words in isolation but should extend to co-occurrences on each side of an item. This implies an examination of collocations embodying the phraseology and topical content of academic texts, combined with a focus on how value markers are interpreted by researchers in different fields.

While most of the initial corpus data was obtained automatically using a well-known concordancer (Scott 2006), further analysis would have been impossible without manual inspection of individual WLs and concordances. The inevitable polysemy of many items, and their occurrence in spurious contexts such as proper names, made this an essential element of the methodology adopted here. Manual inspection also allowed the identification of qualifiers used predicatively (as compared to attributively) and of 'qualified entities', that is of the referents to which a certain value is ascribed. These were generally located in the immediate co-text but at times, especially with predicative constructions, they were further removed from the item under scrutiny. The procedure followed here may thus provide a viable solution to the problem envisaged by Durrant, who warns that manual analysis of the function of collocations in a corpus "may prove a prohibitively labour-intensive task" (2009: 9-10). The size of the corpus (just under one million words) helped to make the task feasible without undermining its representativeness. The result is a compromise which hopefully fits the purpose of this study, though the criteria adopted inevitably imply a degree of subjectivity (whose soundness can be judged both from the methodological procedure and the examples quoted in each chapter).

As in any other investigation of language in context, there are issues that remain open for debate. One of these is the classification of academic domains into discrete categories whose stability, however, is being eroded by mounting specialisation and new (often interdisciplinary) areas of enquiry. Moreover, each of the journals sampled for the corpus is not only the expression of a certain branch of research within its discipline (or subdiscipline) but also of the interests of its editor and/or of the publisher's marketing strategy. Another issue is the weight of single RAs in a medium-sized corpus employing ten texts per discipline and, related to this, the fact that "the disciplines themselves are far from homogeneous" (Hunston 1993a: 132), in terms of variation between individual texts. Had the corpus been larger, its representativeness could have been verified by dispersion counts (measuring spread across texts) for each domain, but the number of texts considered did not justify the use of dispersion as a statistically significant variable.

There were also issues linked to the type of item under scrutiny. The relationship between axiology (encoded by value markers) and terminology (which includes 'dead evaluators') is one of these dilemmas, as exemplified by the decision made in Chapter 5 to exclude *best practices* (a fully lexicalised, dead evaluator) from the count. The fact that most of the relevant markers involved a certain degree of underspecification or vagueness means that their interpretation often depended on contextual information, which explains the decision to opt for a systematic manual investigation of all items. Typical examples of vagueness were the qualifiers *new* (whose meaning ranges from 'not used' to 'novel') and *significant* (from 'important' to 'statistically relevant'). As in other corpus-based studies, the analysis conducted in this volume incorporates the observations of its author, who albeit a member of the academic community is not affiliated to any of the disciplines considered. Even the insights of a non-insider, however, can lead to "a global understanding of the viewpoints and values of a community" (Fasold 1990: 47).

10.4. Directions for further research

Far from exhausting its subject, this study opens up four main avenues – partly linked to the novelty of the approach – for further enquiry. The first of these would be to extend the same investigation to other academic genres: a recent small-scale study of metaphoric value markers in four academic domains (Giannoni 2009a) appears to confirm the importance of inter-generic variation, with value marking peaking in editorials and book reviews, as compared to abstracts and RAs. Such differences clearly reflect the intensely evaluative orientation of the first two genres and their exploration could shed light, contrastively, on the diatypic determinants of axiological variation. It would also be interesting to determine whether a given value varies across genres in response to their content and communicative purpose. Swales and Burke's (2003) analysis, for example, indicates that qualifiers expressing relevance are far more common in RAs than in lectures and other spoken texts, while those stressing size and assessment are far less frequent. Finally, the corpus assembled here treats the RA as a single text without distinguishing between its different sections, but if a narrower analytical focus were adopted, relevant markers could be analysed across the IMRD sequence to account for the values associated with each (sub)genre. Research of this type might provide contextual evidence for Swales's (2004b) argument that an item's evaluative force varies according to its position in a text.

Another possible development would be to investigate the same variables over time, using a diachronic corpus covering various decades of research output in the same disciplines (or, where available, in the same journals). The increasing number of digitalised back issues made available by most journals to subscribers makes this option both easier and cheaper than in the past. Its findings would be of great help because so little is known about diachronic variation in academic values, though there is strong evidence of substantial changes in evaluative practices over the last two centuries (Salager-Meyer 1999; Salager-Meyer *et al.* 2003).

A third option would be to assess such phenomena inter-linguistically (a variable covered by the two studies cited in the previous paragraph). A comparison of the academic values signalled most often in different languages, could provide useful evidence of how far their presence is a feature of the discipline considered and/or of the rhetoric of a specific linguistic community and its culture(s). Such evidence would be particularly welcome in the light of the ongoing controversy on the dominance of English and the threat to the rhetorical integrity of other languages posed by the Anglicisation of academic communication (cf. Mauranen 1993a, 1993b; Canagarajah 1999, 2002a, 2002b).

The last direction for further research is of a more ethnographic nature and requires a corpus capable of distinguishing between RA authors along such variables as gender, seniority, affiliation, scientific impact and cultural background. Its analysis could lead to a deeper understanding of the relationship between axiology and non-linguistic factors whose impact on academic discourse is already an object of considerable interest (cf. Fløttum *et al.* 2006a; Tse/Hyland 2006; Dressen-Hammouda 2008). A similar approach, spearheaded by Hyland (2008, 2009) is to focus on the writing of specific scholars, based on individual corpora representative of their respective output.

Much of the information required in such cases is of an extratextual nature, which means that the analyst has to rely on insider knowledge, where available, or make probabilistic assumptions about the authors' specific profile.

In conclusion, I trust that the present volume holds something of interest for different types of reader – the discourse analyst and EAP practitioners, postgraduate international students but also linguistically-conscious scholars across the disciplinary spectrum. Its publication will be fully justified if other authors join this discussion and accept the challenge of mapping the linguistic dimension of academic values. By testing its methodology and/or assessing the significance of its insights also in other contexts, future contributions can only add breadth and depth to the approach suggested here. Which means that comments are welcome and, *ça va san dire*, all errors are mine.

References

AAUP (American Association of University Professors) 1999. On Collegiality as a Criterion for Faculty Evaluation. Statement adopted by the Association's Council, Washington DC, November 1999. Retrieved 10 March 2008 from <http://www.aaup.org>.

Allen, Michael W. / Ng, Sik Hung 1999. The direct and indirect influences of human values on product ownership. *Journal of Economic Psychology* 20/1, 5-39.

Ali, S. Nazim / Young, Harold C. / Ali, Nasser M. 1996. Determining the Quality of Publications and Research for Tenure or Promotion Decisions: A Preliminary Checklist to Assist. *Library Review* 45/1, 39-53.

Alm-Arvius, Christina 2006. Live, Moribund, and Dead Metaphors. *Nordic Journal of English Studies* 5/1, 7-14.

Anderson, Laurie 2004. The Collaborative Construction of an Appraisal in a Graduate Seminar: An Analysis from Different Research Perspectives. In Anderson, Laurie / Bamford, Julia (eds) *Evaluation in Oral and Written Academic Discourse*. Rome: Officina Edizioni, 97-116.

Anderson, Laurie / Bamford, Julia (eds) 2004. *Evaluation in Oral and Written Academic Discourse*. Rome: Officina Edizioni.

Anderson, Robert David 2004. *European Universities from the Enlightenment to 1914*. Oxford: Oxford University Press.

Atkinson, Dwight 1999. *Scientific Discourse in Sociohistorical Context. The Philosophical Transactions of the Royal Society of London, 1675-1975*. Mahwah, NJ: Erlbaum.

Badger, Richard 2004. The Agonism and the Ecstasy: Conflict and Argument in Applied Linguistics. In Baynham, Mike / Deignan, Alice / White, Goodith (eds) *Applied Linguistics at the Interface*. London: BAAL & Equinox, 11-28.

Bazerman, Charles 1988. *Shaping Written Knowledge. The Genre and Activity of the Experimental Article in Science*. Madison, WI: The University of Wisconsin Press.

Bazerman, Charles / Paradis, James (eds) 1991. *Textual Dynamics of the Professions. Historical and Contemporary Studies of Writing in Professional Communities*. Madison, WI: The University of Wisconsin Press.

Becher, Tony 1981. Towards a Definition of Disciplinary Cultures. *Studies in Higher Education* 6/2, 109-122.

Becher, Tony / Trowler, Paul R. ^{2}2001. *Academic Tribes and Territories*. Buckingham: SRHE & Open University Press.

Bednarek, Monika 2006a. Evaluating Europe: Parameters of Evaluation in the British Press. In Leung, Constant / Jenkins, Jennifer (eds) *Reconfiguring Europe. The Contribution of Applied Linguistics*. London: BAAL & Equinox, 137-156.

Bednarek, Monika 2006b. *Evaluation in Media Discourse: Analysis of a Newspaper Corpus*. London: Continuum.

Bednarek, Monika 2008. 'An Increasingly Familiar Tragedy'. Evaluative Collocation and Conflation. *Functions of Language* 15/1, 7-34.

Berkenkotter, Carol / Huckin, Thomas N. 1993. Rethinking Genre from a Sociocognitive Perspective. *Written Communication* 10/4, 475-509.

Berkenkotter, Carol / Huckin, Thomas N. 1995. *Genre Knowledge in Disciplinary Communication. Cognition Culture Power*. Hillsdale, NJ: Erlbaum.

Berkenkotter, Carol / Huckin, Thomas N. / Ackerman, John 1991. Social Context and Socially Constructed Texts. The Initiation of a Graduate Student into a Writing Research Community. In Bazerman, Charles / Paradis, James (eds) *Textual Dynamics of the Professions. Historical and Contemporary Studies of Writing in Professional Communities*. Madison, WI: The University of Wisconsin Press, 191-215.

Bex, Tony 1996. *Variety in Written English. Texts in Society: Societies in Text*. London: Routledge.

Bhatia, Vijay K. 1993. *Analysing Genre. Language Use in Professional Settings*. London: Longman.

Bhatia, Vijay K. 1997. The Power and Politics of Genre. *World Englishes* 16/3, 359-371.
Bhatia, Vijay K. 2002. LSP and Professional Practice: Negotiating Disciplinary Conflicts. In Gotti, Maurizio / Heller, Dorothee / Dossena, Marina (eds) *Conflict and Negotiation in Specialized Texts*. Bern: Peter Lang, 41-57.
Bhatia, Vijay K. 2004. *Worlds of Written Discourse*. London: Continuum.
Biber, Douglas 2004. Variation among University Spoken and Written Registers: A New Multi-Dimensional Analysis. In Leistyna, Pepi / Meyer, Charles F. (eds) *Corpus Analysis: Language Structure and Language Use* [Language and Computers 46]. Amsterdam: Rodopi, 47-70.
Biber, Douglas / Conrad, Susan M. / Reppen, Randi 1998. *Corpus Linguistics. Investigating Language Structure in Use*. Cambridge: Cambridge University Press.
Biber, Douglas / Conrad, Susan M. / Reppen, Randi / Byrd, Pat / Helt, Marie / Clark, Victoria / Cortes, Viviana / Csomay, Eniko / Urzua, Alfredo 2004a. *Representing Language Use in the University: Analysis of the TOEFL 2000 Spoken and Written Academic Language Corpus*. Princeton, NJ: Educational Testing Service.
Biber, Douglas / Csomay, Eniko / Jones, James K. / Keck, Casey 2004b. A Corpus Linguistic Investigation of Vocabulary-Based Discourse Units in University Registers. In Connor, Ulla / Upton, Thomas A. (eds) *Applied Corpus Linguistics. A Multidimensional Perspective* [Language and Computers 52]. Amsterdam: Rodopi, 53-72.
Biber, Douglas / Finegan, Edward 1989. Styles of Stance in English: Lexical and Grammatical Marking of Evidentiality and Affect. *Text* 9/1, 93-124.
Biber, Douglas / Johansson, Stig / Leech, Geoffrey / Conrad, Susan / Finegan, Edward 1999. *The Longman Grammar of Spoken and Written English*. London: Longman.
Biglan, A. 1973. The Characteristics of Subject Matter in Different Scientific Areas. *Journal of Applied Psychology* 57/3, 195-203.
Bilsky, Wolfgang / Koch, Mareike 2002. On the Content and Structure of Values: Universals or Methodological Artefacts? In Hox, Joop / de Leeuw, Edith / Schmidt, Peter / Blasius, Jörg (eds) *Social Science*

Methodology in the New Millennium. Updated and Extended Proceedings of the Fifth International Conference on Logic and Methodology. Leverkusen: Leske & Budrich [CD-ROM].

Black, Thomas R. 1993. *Evaluating Social Science Research. An Introduction*. London: SAGE Publications.

Blakeslee, Ann M. 1994. The Rhetorical Construction of Novelty: Presenting Claims in a Letters Forum. *Science, Technology, & Human Values* 19/1, 88-100.

Bondi, Marina 2005. Metadiscursive Practices in Academic Discourse: Variation across Genres and Disciplines. In Bamford, Julia / Bondi, Marina (eds) *Dialogue within Discourse Communities. Metadiscursive Perspectives on Academic Genres*. Tübingen: Max Niemeyer, 3-29.

Braxton, John M. 1989. Institutional Variability in Faculty Conformity to the Norms of Science: A Force of Integration or Fragmentation in the Academic Profession? *Research in Higher Education* 30/4, 419-433.

Breivega, Kjersti Rongen / Dahl, Trine / Fløttum, Kjersti 2002. Traces of Self and Others in Research Articles. A Comparative Pilot Study of English, French and Norwegian Research Articles in Medicine, Economics and Linguistics. *International Journal of Applied Linguistics* 12/2, 218-239.

Brodkey, Linda 1987. *Academic Writing as Social Practice*. Philadelphia: Temple University Press.

Brown, Penelope / Levinson, Stephen C. ^{2}1987. *Politeness. Some Universals in Language Usage*. Cambridge: Cambridge University Press.

Brumfit, Christopher 1995. Educational Linguistics, Applied Linguistics and the Study of Language Practices. In Blue, George M. / Mitchell, Rosamond (eds) *Language and Education* [British Studies in Applied Linguistics 11]. Clevedon: Multilingual Matters & BAAL, 1-15.

Brumfit, Christopher 1997. Theoretical Practice: Applied Linguistics as Pure and Practical Science. *AILA Review* 12, 18-30.

Burnard, Lou (ed.) 2007. *Reference Guide for the British National Corpus*. Oxford: British National Corpus Consortium. Retrieved

10 March 2008 from <http://www.natcorp.ox.ac.uk/XMLedition/URG>.

Cameron, Lynne / Deignan, Alice 2006. The Emergence of Metaphor in Discourse. *Applied Linguistics* 27/4, 671-690.

Canagarajah, A. Suresh 1999. *Resisting Linguistic Imperialism in English Teaching*. Oxford: Oxford University Press.

Canagarajah, A. Suresh 2002a. *A Geopolitics of Academic Writing*. Pittsburgh: University of Pittsburgh Press.

Canagarajah, A. Suresh 2002b. Multilingual Writers and the Academic Community: Towards a Critical Relationship. *Journal of English for Academic Purposes* 1/1, 29-44.

Channell, Joanna 2000. Corpus-Based Analysis of Evaluative Lexis. In Hunston, Susan / Thompson, Geoff (eds) *Evaluation in Text. Authorial Stance and the Construction of Discourse*. Oxford: Oxford University Press, 38-55.

Charteris-Black, Jonathan 2005. *Politicians and Rhetoric. The Persuasive Power of Metaphor*. Basingstoke: Palgrave Macmillan.

Christie, Frances 1989. *Language Education*. Oxford: Oxford University Press.

Cole, Stephen 1983. The Hierarchy of the Sciences? *The American Journal of Sociology* 89/1, 111-139.

Conrad, Susan / Biber, Douglas 2000. Adverbial Marking of Stance in Speech and Writing. In Hunston, Susan / Thompson, Geoff (eds) *Evaluation in Text: Authorial Stance and the Construction of Discourse*. Oxford: Oxford University Press, 55-73.

Corson, David 1995. World View, Cultural Values and Discourse Norms: The Cycle of Cultural Reproduction. *International Journal of Intercultural Relations* 19/2, 183-195.

Coulmas, Florian 1992. *Language and Economy*. Oxford: Blackwell.

Coxhead, Averil 2000. A New Academic Word List. *TESOL Quarterly* 34/2, 213-238.

Crawford Camiciottoli, Belinda 2004. Metaphor as Evaluation in Business Studies Lectures. In Anderson, Laurie / Bamford, Julia (eds) *Evaluation in Oral and Written Academic Discourse*. Rome: Officina Edizioni, 53-71.

Crystal, David 2003. Final Frontiers in Applied Linguistics? In Sarangi, Srikant / van Leeuwen, Theo (eds) *Applied Linguistics*

and Communities of Practice [British Studies in Applied Linguistics 18]. London: Continuum & BAAL, 8-24.
van Damme, Dirk 2002. *Outlooks for the International Higher Education Community in Constructing the Global Knowledge Society.* Paris: United Nations Educational, Scientific and Cultural Organization.
Dijk, T.A. van 1998. *Ideology: A Multidisciplinary Approach.* London: SAGE Publications.
DDC 2003. *Dewey Decimal Classification and Relative Index. Edition 22.* Dublin, OH: OCLC Forest Press.
Diani, Giuliana 2004. Evaluation in Academic Review Articles. In Partington, Alan / Morley, John / Haarman, Louann (eds) *Corpora and Discourse.* Bern: Peter Lang, 189-203.
Del Lungo Camiciotti, Gabriella / Tognini Bonelli, Elena (eds) 2004. *Academic Discourse – New Insights into Evaluation.* Bern: Peter Lang.
Downes, William 2000. The Language of Felt Experience: Emotional, Evaluative and Intuitive. *Language and Literature* 9/2, 99-121.
Dressen, Dacia 2003. Geologists' Implicit Persuasive Strategies and the Construction of Evaluative Evidence. *Journal of English for Academic Purposes* 2/4, 273-290.
Dressen-Hammouda, Dacia 2008. From Novice to Disciplinary Expert: Disciplinary Identity and Genre Mastery. *English for Specific Purposes* 27/2, 233-252.
Dudley-Evans, Tony 1995. Genre Models for the Teaching of Academic Writing to Second Language Speakers: Advantages and Disadvantages. *TESOL France* 2/2, 181-192. Reprinted in Miller, Tom (ed.) 1997. *Functional Approaches to Written Text: Classroom Applications.* Washington: USIS.
Dudley-Evans, Tony 1997. Genre: How Far Can We, Should We Go? *World Englishes* 16/3, 351-358.
Durrant, Philip 2009. Investigating the Viability of a Collocation List for Students of English for Academic Ourposes. *English for Specific Purposes* 28/3, 157-169.
Duszak, Anna 1997a. Cross-Cultural Academic Communication: A Discourse-Community View. In Duszak, Anna (ed.) *Culture and Styles of Academic Discourse.* Berlin: Walter de Gruyter, 11-39.

Duszak, Anna (ed.) 1997b. *Culture and Styles of Academic Discourse*. Berlin: Mouton de Gruyter.

Duszak, Anna 2005. Between Styles and Values: An Academic Community in Transition. In Cortese, Giuseppina / Duszak, Anna (eds) *Identity, Community, Discourse. English in Intercultural Settings*. Bern: Peter Lang, 69-94.

Ebeling, Signe O. / Heuboeck, Alois 2007. Encoding Document Information in a Corpus of Student Writing: The British Academic Written English corpus. *Corpora* 2/2, 241-256.

Evensen, Lars Sigfried 1997. Applied Linguistics within a Principled Framework for Characterizing Disciplines and Transdisciplines. *AILA Review* 12, 31-41.

Faber, Brenton 2003. Creating Rhetorical Stability in Corporate University Discourse. Discourse Technologies and Change. *Written Communication* 20/4, 391-425.

Fairclough, Norman 1993. Critical Discourse Analysis and the Marketisation of Public Discourse: The Universities. *Discourse & Society* 4/2, 133-168.

Fairclough, Norman 1995. *Critical Discourse Analysis: The Critical Study of Language*. London: Longman.

Fasold, Ralph W. 1990. *The Sociolinguistics of Language*. Oxford: Basil Blackwell.

Felices Lago, Ángel / Hewitt, Elaine 2004. Personal Qualities of Job Advertisements: Axiological and Lexical Analysis of Samples in English from the Spanish Press. *LSP & Professional Communication* 4/2, 8-26.

Feingold, Mordechai (ed.) 2000. *History of Universities*. Ongoing Series. Oxford: Oxford University Press.

Fishelov, David 1993. *Metaphors of Genre. The Role of Analogies in Genre Theory*. University Park: Pennsylvania State University Press.

Fløttum, Kjersti 2006. The Typical Research Article – Does It Exist? In Suomela-Salmi, Eija / Dervin, Fred (eds) *Perspectives interculturelles et inter-linguistiques sur le discours académique. Cross-cultural and Cross-linguistic Perspectives on Academic Discourse*. Vol. 1. University of Turku, Finland: Publications du département d'études françaises, 16-44.

Fløttum, Kjersti / Dahl, Trine / Torodd, Kinn 2006a. *Academic Voices. Across Languages and Discplines*. Amsterdam: John Benjamins.

Fløttum, Kjersti / Kinn, Torodd / Dahl, Trine 2006b. "We Now Report on..." versus "Let Us Now See How...": Author Roles and Interaction with Readers in Research Articles. In Hyland, Ken / Bondi, Marina (eds) *Academic Discourse Across Disciplines*. Bern: Peter Lang, 203-224.

Flowerdew, John 2000. Discourse Community, Legitimate Peripheral Participation, and the Nonnative-English-Speaking Scholar. *TESOL Quarterly* 34/1, 127-150.

Flowerdew, John 2001. Attitudes of Journal Editors to Nonnative Speaker Contributions. *TESOL Quarterly* 35/1, 121-150.

Fortanet-Gómez, Inmaculada 2004. Verbal Stance in Spoken Academic Discourse. In Del Lungo Camiciotti, Gabriella / Tognini Bonelli, Elena (eds) *Academic Discourse – New Insights into Evaluation*. Bern: Peter Lang, 99-119.

Francis, Gill 1993. A Corpus-Driven Approach to Grammar: Principles, Methods and Examples. In Baker, Mona / Francis, Gill / Tognini-Bonelli, Elena (eds) *Text and Technology: Essays in Honour of John Sinclair*. Amsterdam: John Benjamins, 137-156.

Gardner, Sheena 2009. Evaluation across Disciplinary Groups in University Student Writing: The Critique Genre Family as Texts and Text. In Edwardes, Martin (ed.) *Proceedings of the BAAL Annual Conference 2008. Taking the Measure of Applied Linguistics*. CR-ROM. London: Scitsiugnil Press.

Gea Valor, Maria Lluïsa 2000. *A Pragmatic Approach to Politeness and Modality in the Book Review Articles*. Valencia, Spain: Universitat de València.

Gesuato, Sara 2007. Evaluation in Back-Cover Blurbs. *Textus* 20/1, 83-102. Special issue on "(R)evolutions in Evaluation" edited by Marina Dossena and Andreas H. Jucker.

Giannoni, Davide S. 1998. The Genre of Journal Acknowledgements: Findings of a Cross-Disciplinary Investigation. *Linguistica e Filologia* 6, 61-84.

Giannoni, Davide S. 2005. Negative Evaluation in Academic Discourse. A Comparison of English and Italian Research Articles.

Linguistica e Filologia 20, 71-99. Available online at <http://hdl.handle.net/10446/150>.
Giannoni, Davide S. 2006. Expressing Praise and Criticism in Economic Discourse: A Comparative Analysis of English and Italian Book Reviews. In Del Lungo Camiciotti, Gabriella / Dossena, Marina / Crawford Camiciottoli, Belinda (eds) *Variation in Business and Economics Discourse. Diachronic and Genre Perspectives*. Rome: Officina Edizioni, 126-138.
Giannoni, Davide S. 2007. Metatextual Evaluation in Journal editorials. *Textus* 20/1, 57-82. Special issue on "(R)evolutions in Evaluation" edited by Marina Dossena and Andreas H. Jucker.
Giannoni, Davide S. 2008. Popularizing Features in English Journal Editorials. *English for Specific Purposes* 27/2, 212-232. Special issue in Honor of John Swales, edited by Ann M. Johns.
Giannoni, Davide S. 2009a. Disciplinary Values in English Academic Metaphors. *Linguistica e Filologia* 28, 173-191. Available online at <http://hdl.handle.net/10446/379>.
Giannoni, Davide S. 2009b. Negotiating Research Values across Review Genres: A Case Study in Applied Linguistics. In Hyland, Ken / Diani, Giuliana (eds) *Academic Evaluation: Review Genres in University Settings*. Basingstoke: Palgrave Macmillan, 17-33.
Giannoni, Davide S. 2010. Metaphoric Values and Disciplinary Identity in English Research Articles. In Archibald, James / Garzone, Giuliana (eds) *Discourse, Identity and the Professions*. Bern: Peter Lang.
Gilbert, Nigel G. / Mulkay, Michael 1984. *Opening Pandora's Box. A Sociological Analysis of Scientists' Discourse*. Cambridge: Cambridge University Press.
Gordon, Michael 1984. How Authors Select Journals: A Test of the Reward Maximization Model of Submission Behaviour. *Social Studies of Science* 14/1, 27-43.
Gosden, Hugh 1995. Success in Research Article Writing and Revision: A Social-Constructionist Perspective. *English for Specific Purposes* 14/1, 37-57.
Gotti, Maurizio / D'Angelo, Larissa 2008. CADIS: A Corpus for the Analysis of Identity Traits in English Specialised Discourse. In Di Martino, Gabriella / Polese, Vanda / Solly, Martin (eds)

Identity and Culture in English Domain-Specific Discourse. Naples: ESI, 311-324.
Graddol, David 1997. *The Future of English? A Guide to Forecasting the Popularity of the English Language in the 21st Century*. London: British Council.
Graddol, David 2006. *English Next. Why Global English May Mean the End of 'English as a Foreign Language'*. London: British Council.
Gross, Alan G. 2000. The Science Wars and the Ethics of Book Reviewing. *Philosophy of the Social Sciences* 30/3, 445-450.
Gross, Alan G. / Harmon, Joseph E. / Reidy, Michael 2002. *Communicating Science. The Scientific Article from the 17th Century to the Present*. Oxford: Oxford University Press.
Halliday, M.A.K. / Hasan, Ruqaiya 1976. *Cohesion in English*. London: Longman.
Halliday, M.A.K. / Martin, J.R. 1993. *Writing Science. Literacy and Discursive Power*. London: The Falmer Press.
Hartley, James / Sotto, Eric / Fox, Claire 2004. Clarity across the Disciplines. An Analysis of Texts in the Sciences, Social Sciences, and Arts and Humanities. *Science Communication* 26/2, 188-210.
Harwood, Nigel 2005. 'Nowhere Has Anyone Attempted... In This Article I Aim to Do Just That'. A Corpus-Based Study of Self-Promotional *I* and *we* in Academic Writing across Four Disciplines. *Journal of Pragmatics* 37/8, 1207-1231.
Hasan, Ruqaiya 1978. Text in the Systemic-Functional Model. In Dressler, Wolfgang U. (ed.) *Current Trends in Textlinguistics*. Berlin: Walter de Gruyter, 228-246.
Hasan, Ruqaiya 1989. The Structure of Text. In Halliday, M.A.K. / Hasan, Ruqaiya (eds) *Language, Context and Text: Aspects of Language in a Social-semiotic Perspective*. Oxford: Oxford University Press, 52-69.
Headland, Thomas N. / Pike, Kenneth L. 1990. *Emics and Etics: The Insider/Outsider Debate*. London: SAGE Publications.
Herndl, Carl G. / Fennell, Barbara A. / Miller, Carolyn R. 1991. Understanding Failures in Organizational Discourse. The Accident at Three Mile Island and the Shuttle Challenger

Disaster. In Bazerman, Charles / Paradis, James (eds) *Textual Dynamics of the Professions. Historical and Contemporary Studies of Writing in Professional Communities*. Madison, WI: The University of Wisconsin Press, 279-305.
Hickey, Raymond 2003. *Corpus Presenter Software Suite*. London: John Benjamins.
Hinds, John 1987. Reader versus Writer Responsibility: A New Typology. In Connor, Ulla / Kaplan, Robert B. (eds) *Writing Across Languages: Analysis of L2 Text*. Reading, MA: Addison-Wesley, 141-152.
Hoey, Michael 2000. Persuasive Rhetoric in Linguistics. A Stylistic Study of Some Features of the Language of Noam Chomsky. In Hunston, Susan / Thompson, Geoff (eds) *Evaluation in Text. Authorial Stance and the Construction of Discourse*. Oxford: Oxford University Press, 28-37.
Huckin, Thomas N. 1987. Surprise Value in Scientific Discourse. Unpublished paper presented at the Conference on College Composition and Communication, Atlanta, GA, 19-21 March 1987.
Huckin, Thomas N. 1996. Cultural Aspects of Genre Knowledge. *AILA Review* 12, 68-78.
Hunston, Susan 1993a. Professional Conflict. Disagreement in Academic Discourse. In Baker, Mona / Francis, Gill / Tognini-Bonelli, Elena (eds) *Text and Technology: In Honour of John Sinclair*. Amsterdam: John Benjamins, 115-134.
Hunston, Susan 1993b. Evaluation and Ideology in Scientific Writing. In Ghadessy, Mohsen (ed.) *Register Analysis. Theory and Practice*. London: Pinter, 57-73.
Hunston, Susan 1994. Evaluation and Organization in a Sample of Written Academic Discourse. In Coulthard, Malcolm (ed.) *Advances in Written Text Analysis*. London: Routledge, 191-218.
Hunston, Susan 2000. Evaluation and the Planes of Discourse: Status and Value in Persuasive Texts. In Hunston, Susan / Thompson, Geoff (eds) *Evaluation in Text. Authorial Stance and the Construction of Discourse*. Oxford: Oxford University Press, 176-207.
Hunston, Susan 2004a. Counting the Uncountable: Problems of Identifying Evaluation in a Text and in a Corpus. In Partington,

Alan / Morley, John / Haarman, Louann (eds) *Corpora and Discourse*. Bern: Peter Lang, 157-188.

Hunston, Susan 2004b. 'It Has Rightly Been Pointed Out...': Attribution, Consensus and Conflict in Academic Discourse. In Bondi, Marina / Gavioli, Laura / Silver, Marc (eds) *Academic Discourse, Genre and Small Corpora*. Rome: Officina Edizioni, 15-33.

Hunston, Susan / Thompson, Geoff (eds) 2000. *Evaluation in Text. Authorial Stance and the Construction of Discourse*. Oxford: Oxford University Press.

Hwang, Kumju 2005. The Inferior Science and the Dominant Use of English in Knowledge Oroduction. A Case Study of Korean Science and Technology. *Science Communication* 26/4, 390-427.

Hyland, Ken 1997. Scientific Claims and Community Values: Articulating an Academic Culture. *Language and Communication* 17/1, 19-31.

Hyland, Ken 1998. *Hedging in Scientific Research Articles*. Amsterdam: John Benjamins.

Hyland, Ken 1998a. Persuasion and Context: the Pragmatics of Academic Metadiscourse. *Journal of Pragmatics* 30/4, 437-455.

Hyland, Ken 1999. Academic Attribution: Citation and the Construction of Disciplinary Knowledge. *Applied Linguistics* 20/3, 341-367.

Hyland, Ken 2000. *Disciplinary Discourses. Social Interactions in Academic Writing*. Harlow: Pearson Education.

Hyland, Ken 2001. Humble Servants of the Discipline? Self-Mention in Research Articles. *English for Specific Purposes* 20/3, 207-226.

Hyland, Ken 2002. What Do They Mean? Questions in Academic Writing. *Text* 22/4, 529-557.

Hyland, Ken 2004. Engagement and Disciplinarity: The Other Side of Evaluation. In Del Lungo Camiciotti, Gabriella / Tognini Bonelli, Elena (eds) *Academic Discourse – New Insights into Evaluation*. Bern: Peter Lang, 13-30.

Hyland, Ken 2006a. *Metadiscourse. Exploring Interaction in Writing*. London: Continuum.

Hyland, Ken 2006b. Disciplinary Differences: Language Variation in Academic Discourses. In Hyland, Ken / Bondi, Marina (eds) *Academic Discourse Across Disciplines*. Bern: Peter Lang, 17-45.
Hyland, Ken 2008. 'Small Bits of Textual Material': A Discourse Analysis of Swales' Writing. *English for Specific Purposes* 27/2, 143-160.
Hyland, Ken 2009. Constraint vs Creativity: Identity and Disciplinarity in Academic Writing. In Gotti, Maurizio (ed.) *Commonality and Individuality in Academic Discourse*. Bern: Peter Lang, 25-52.
Hyland, Ken / Tse, Polly 2004a. Metadiscourse in Academic Writing: A Reappraisal. *Applied Linguistics* 25/2, 156-177.
Hyland, Ken / Tse, Polly 2004b. "I Would Like to Thank My Supervisor". Acknowledgements in Graduate Dissertations. *International Journal of Applied Linguistics* 14/2, 259-275.
Hymes, Dell 1974. *Foundations in Sociolinguistics. An Ethnographic Approach*. Philadelphia: University of Pennsylvania Press.
ISI 2006. *ISI Web of Knowledge. Multidisciplinary Resources*. Philadelphia: Thomson Scientific. Retrieved 10 March 2008 from <http://science.thomsonreuters.com/m/pdfs/mgr/wok_ multidisc_ fs.pdf>.
Ivanič, Roz 1997. *Writing and Identity. The Discoursal Construction of Identity in Academic Writing*. Amsterdam: John Benjamins.
Jenkins, Jennifer 2005. ELF at the gate: The Position of English as a Lingua Franca. *Humanising Language Teaching* 7/2. Retrieved 10 March 2008 from <http://www.hltmag.co.uk/mar05/ idea.htm>.
Kaplan, Robert B. 1966. Cultural Thought Patterns in Inter-Cultural Education. *Language Learning* 16/1-2, 1-20.
Kaplan, Robert B. 1988. Contrastive Rhetoric and Second Language Learning: Notes toward a Theory of Contrastive Rhetoric. In Purves, Alan C. (ed.) *Writing Across Languages and Cultures. Issues in Contrastive Rhetoric*. Newbury Park: SAGE, 275-304.
Keefe, Rosanna 2000. *Theories of Vagueness*. Cambridge: Cambridge University Press.
Kertész, András 2001. Scientific Enquiry as a Dialogue Game: The Case for 'Soft Disciplines'. In Kertész, András (ed.) *Approaches*

to the Pragmatics of Scientific Discourse. Frankfurt am Main: Peter Lang, 35-46.

Ketter, Jean / Hunter, Judy 2003. Creating a Writer's Identity on the Boundaries of Two Communities of Practice. In Bazerman, Charles / Russell, David R. (eds) *Writing Selves Writing Societies. Research from Activity Perspectives*. Fort Collins, CO: WAC Clearinghouse, 307-329. E-book retrieved 10 March 2008 from <http://wac.colostate.edu/books/selves_societies>.

Killingsworth, M. Jimmie / Gilbertson, Michael K. 1992. *Signs, Genres, and Communities in Technical Communication*. Amityville, NJ: Baywood.

Knorr-Cetina, Karen D. 1981. *The Manufacture of Knowledge: An Essay on the Constructivist and Contextual Nature of Science*. Oxford: Pergamon.

Knorr-Cetina, Karen D. 1983. The Ethnographic Study of Scientific Work: Towards a Constructivist Interpretation of Science. In Knorr-Cetina, Karen D. / Mulkay, Michael (eds) *Science Observed. Perspectives on the Social Study of Science*. London: SAGE Publications, 115-140.

Knorr-Cetina, Karin / Cicourel, A.V. (eds) *Advances in Social Theory and Methodology: Toward an Integration of Micro- and Macro-Sociologies*. Boston: Routledge & Kegan Paul.

Knowles, Gerry 1996. Corpora, Databases and the Organization of Linguistic Data. In Thomas, Jenny / Short, Mick (eds) *Using Corpora for Language Research. Studies in the Honour of Geoffrey Leech*. London: Longman, 36-53.

Knowles, Gerry / Zuraidah, Mohd Don 2004. The Notion of a "Lemma": Headwords, Roots and Lexical Sets. *International Journal of Corpus Linguistics* 9/1, 69-81.

Koskela, Merja 2004. Functions of References in Philosophical Research Articles. In Ahmad, Khurshid / Rogers, Margaret (eds) *New Directions in LSP Studies. Proceedings of the 14th European Symposium on Language for Special Purposes*. Guildford: University of Surrey, 133-139.

Kuhn, Thomas S. 1962 and 1970. *The Structure of Scientific Revolutions*. Chicago: University of Chicago Press.

Lakoff, George 1973. Hedges: A Study in the Meaning Criteria and the Logic of Fuzzy Concepts. *Journal of Philosophical Logic* 2, 458-508.

Lakoff, George / Johnson, Mark 1980. *Metaphors We Live By*. Chicago: University of Chicago Press.

Latour, Bruno 1987. *Science in Action. How to Follow Scientists and Engineers through Society*. Milton Keynes: Open University Press.

Latour, Bruno / Woolgar, Steve 1979. *Laboratory Life. The Social Construction of Scientific Facts*. London: SAGE Publications.

Lauer, Janice M. 2004. *Invention in Rhetoric and Composition*. West Lafayette: Parlor Press LLS.

Lave, Jean / Wenger, Etienne 1991. *Situated Learning. Legitimate Peripheral Participation*. Cambridge: University of Cambridge Press.

LCC 2003. *Library of Congress. LC Classification Outline*. 7th ed. Washington, DC: Library of Congress Cataloging Distribution Service.

Leech, Geoffrey 1983. *Principles of Pragmatics*. London: Longman.

Lemke, Jay L. 1998. Resources for Attitudinal Meaning: Evaluative Orientations in Text Semantics. *Functions of Language* 5/1, 33-56.

Lepley, Ray (ed.) 1957. *The Language of Value*. New York: Columbia University Press.

Losee, Robert M. 1996. Text Windows and Phrases Differing by Discipline, Location in Document, and Syntactic Structure. *Information Processing & Management* 32/6, 747-767.

McArthur, Tom 2001. World English and World Englishes: Trends, Tensions, Varieties, and Standards. *Language Teaching* 34, 1-20.

McCagg, Peter 1996. If You Can Lead a Horse to Water, You Don't Have to Make It Drink: Some Comments on Reader and Writer Responsibilities. In Connor, Ulla (ed.) *Contrastive Rhetoric: Writing in Professional Settings*. Special issue of "Multilingua" 15/3, 239-256.

McCloskey, Donald N. 1983. The Rhetoric of Economics. *Journal of Economic Literature* 21/2, 481-517.

Martin, James R. 1989. *Factual Writing: Exploring and Challenging Social Reality*, Oxford: Oxford University Press.

Martin, James R. 1992. *English Text. System and Structure*. Philadelphia: John Benjamins.
Martin, James R. 2000. Beyond Exchange: Appraisal Systems in English. In Hunston, Susan / Thompson, Geoff (eds) *Evaluation in Text. Authorial Stance and the Construction of Discourse*. Oxford: Oxford University Press, 142-175.
Martin, James R. / White, Peter R.R. 2005. *The Language of Evaluation. Appraisal in English*. Basingstoke: Palgrave Macmillan.
Mauranen, Anna 1993a. *Cultural Differences in Academic Rhetoric*. Frankfurt am Main: Peter Lang.
Mauranen, Anna 1993b. Cultural Differences in Academic Discourse: Problems of a Linguistic and Cultural Minority. In Löfman, Liisa / Kurki-Suonio, Liisa / Pellinen, Silja / Lehtonen, Jari (eds) *The Competent Intercultural Communicator: AfinLA Yearbook*. Helsinki: AfinLA, 157-174.
Mauranen, Anna 2003. The Corpus of English as Lingua Franca in Academic Settings. *TESOL Quarterly* 37/3, 513-525.
Mauranen, Anna 2004. Where Next? A Summary of the Round Table Discussion. In Del Lungo Camiciotti, Gabriella / Tognini Bonelli, Elena (eds) *Academic Discourse – New Insights into Evaluation*. Bern: Peter Lang, 203-215.
Mauranen, Anna 2006a. Speaking the Discipline: Discourse and Socialisation in ELF and L1 English. In Hyland, Ken / Bondi, Marina (eds) *Academic Discourse Across Disciplines*. Bern: Peter Lang, 271-294.
Mauranen, Anna 2006b. A Rich Domain of ELF: The ELFA Corpus of Academic Discourse. *Nordic Journal of English Studies* 5/2, 145-159. Special issue on "English as a Lingua Franca".
Mautner, Gerlinde 2005. The Entrepreneurial University. A Discursive Profile of a Higher Education Buzzword. *Critical Discourse Studies* 2/2, 95-120.
Mei, Wu Siew 2006a. The Operation of Value in Undergraduate English Language Essays. *Reflections on English Language Teaching* 5/1, 123-140.
Mei, Wu Siew 2006b. Creating a Contrastive Rhetorical Stance: Investigating the Strategy of Problematization in Students' Argumentation. *Regional Language Centre Journal* 37/3, 329-353.

Melander, Björn / Swales, John M. / Fredrickson, Kirstin M. 1997. Journal Abstracts from Three Academic Fields in the United States and Sweden: National or Disciplinary Proclivities? In Duszak, Anna (ed.) *Culture and Styles of Academic Discourse*. Berlin: Walter de Gruyter, 251-272.

Mercer, David 1996. Understanding Scientific/Technical Controversy. *Science, Technology and Society Research Working Papers* [Occasional Paper Series 1]. Retrieved 10 March 2008 from <http://www.uow.edu.au/arts/selpl/science/UOW018684.html>.

Merton, Robert K. 1942. The Normative Structure of Science. Reprinted in Merton, Robert K. (ed.) 1973. *The Sociology of Science. Theoretical and Empirical Investigations.* Chicago: University of Chicago Press, 267-278.

Miceli, Maria / Castelfranchi, Cristiano 1989. A Cognitive Approach to Values. *Journal for the Theory of Social Behaviour* 19/2, 169-193.

Miller, Carolyn R. 1984. Genre as Social Action. *Quarterly Journal of Speech* 70, 151-167.

Miller, Carolyn R. 1992. Kairos in the Rhetoric of Science. In Witte, Stephen P. / Nakadate, Neil / Cherry, Roger D. (eds) *A Rhetoric of Doing: Essays on Written Discourse in Honor of James L. Kinneavy.* Carbondale: Southern Illinois University Press, 310-327.

Miller, Carolyn R. 1994. Rhetorical Community: The Cultural Basis of Genre. In Freedman, Aviva / Medway, Peter (eds) *Genre and the New Rhetoric*. Bristol, PA: Taylor & Francis, 67-78.

Milroy, Lesley ^{2}1987. *Language and Social Networks*. Oxford: Basil Blackwell.

Ministero dell'Università 2000. Elenco dei settori scientifico-disciplinari [Decree No. 249, 24/10/2000]. Retrieved 10 March 2008 from <http://www.miur.it/atti/2000/alladm001004_01.htm>.

Montgomery, Scott L. 1996. *The Scientific Voice*. New York: Guildford Press.

Morgan, Jerry L. ^{2}1993. Observations on the Pragmatics of Metaphor. In Ortony, Andrew (ed.) *Metaphor and Thought*. Cambridge: Cambridge University Press, 124-134.

Morris, Leanne 2005. Performance Appraisals in Australian Universities – Imposing a Managerialistic Framework into a Collegial Culture. Paper presented at the 19th Conference of the Association of Industrial Relations Academics of Australia and New Zealand, University of Sydney, 9-11 February 2005. Retrieved 10 March 2009 from <http://airaanz.econ.usyd.edu.au/papers/Morris.pdf>.

Mukerji, Chandra 1996. The Collective Construction of Scientific Genius. In Engeström, Yrjö / Middleton, David (eds) *Cognition and Communication at Work*. Cambridge: Cambridge University Press, 257-278.

Mulkay, Michael 1976. Norms and Ideology in Science. *Social Science Information* 15/4-5, 637-656.

Mulkay, Michael / Potter, Jonathan / Yearley, Steven 1983. Why an Analysis of Scientific Discourse is Needed. In Knorr-Cetina, Karin D. / Mulkay, Michael (eds) *Science Observed. Perspectives on the Social Study of Science*. London: SAGE Publications, 171-203.

Myers, Greg 1989. The Pragmatics of Politeness in Scientific Articles. *Applied Linguistics* 10/1, 1-35.

Myers, Greg 1990. *Writing Biology. Texts in the Social Construction of Scientific Knowledge*. Madison, WI: University of Wisconsin Press.

Myers, Greg 1997. Institutions, Writing and Talk in Environmental Discourse. In Hunston, Susan (ed.) *Language at Work. Selected Papers from the Annual Meeting of the British Association for Applied Linguistics. British Studies in Applied Linguistics* 13, 1-13.

Nelson, John S. / Megilla, Allan / McCloskey Donald N. (eds) 1987. *The Rhetoric of the Human Sciences: Language and Argument in Scholarship and Public Affairs*. Madison, WI: The University of Wisconsin Press.

Nesi, Hilary / Thompson, Paul 2006. The British Academic Spoken English Corpus Manual. Retrieved 10 March 2009 from <http://www2.warwick.ac.uk/fac/soc/celte/research/base/base_manual.pdf>.

Nida, Eugene A. 1992. Sociolinguistic Implications of Academic Writing. *Language in Society* 21/3, 477-485.

OED 2009. *Oxford English Dictionary Online*. Oxford: Oxford University Press. Draft Revision March 2009. Accessed 5 May 2009.

Oishi, Shigehiro / Hahn, Jungwon / Schimmack, Ulrich / Radhakrishan, Phanikiran / Dzokoto, Vivian / Ahadi, Stephen 2005. The Measurement of Values across Cultures: A Pairwise Comparison Approach. *Journal of Research in Personality* 39/2, 299-305.

Overington, Michael 1977. The Scientific Community as Audience: Toward a Rhetorical Analysis of Science. *Philosophy and Rhetoric* 10, 143-164.

Overington, Michael A. 2000. Sociology and Rhetoric: Some Personal Musings. *Technostyle* 16/1, 165-169.

Paltridge, Brian 2004. Academic Writing. *Language Teaching* 37/1, 87-105.

van Parijs, Philippe 2007. Tackling the Anglophones' Free Ride: Fair Linguistic Cooperation with a Global Lingua Franca. In Carli, Augusto / Ammon, Ulrich (eds) *Linguistic Inequality in Scientific Communication Today*. Amsterdam: John Benjamins. Special issue of *AILA Review* 20, 72-86.

Partington, Alan 2004. Corpora and Discourse, a Most Congruous Beast. In Partington, Alan / Morley, John / Haarman, Louann (eds) *Corpora and Discourse*. Bern: Peter Lang, 11-20.

Partington, Alan / Morley, John / Haarman, Louann (eds) 2004. *Corpora and Discourse*. Bern: Peter Lang

Porter, James E. 1986. Intertextuality and the Discourse Community. *Rhetoric Review* 5/1, 34-47.

Pritchard, Rosalind 2004. Humboldtian Values in a Changing World: Staff and Students in German Universities. *Oxford Review of Education* 30/4, 509-528.

Reed, Edward S. 1996. Selves, Values, Cultures. In Brown, Terrance / Reed, Edward S. / Turiel, Elliot (eds) *Values and Knowledge*. Mahwah, NJ: Lawrence Erlbaum, 1-16.

Roberts, Celia 2003. Applied Linguistics Applied. In Sarangi, Srikant / van Leeuwen, Theo (eds) *Applied Linguistics and Communities of Practice* [British Studies in Applied Linguistics 18]. London: Continuum & BAAL, 132-149.

Römer, Ute 2008. Identification Impossible? A Corpus Approach to Realisations of Evaluative Meaning in Academic Writing. *Functions of Language* 15/1, 115-130.

Roy, Santanu / Dhawan, Sunil K. 2004. Probing the Value Space: An Empirical Study of [the] Personal Value System of Indian Scientists. Paper presented at IAMOT 2004 Conference, Washington, DC. Retrieved 10 March 2008 from <http://www.iamot.org/conference/index.php/ocs/4/paper/view/988/408>.

Ruzaite, Jurate 2004. Academic Precision Reconsidered: A Corpus-Based Account. *SKY Journal of Linguistics* 17, 217-247.

Salager-Meyer, Françoise 1990. Metaphors in Medical English Prose: A Comparative Study with French and Spanish. *English for Specific Purposes* 9/2, 145-159.

Salager-Meyer, Françoise 1999. Contentiousness in Written Medical English Discourse: A Diachronic Study (1810-1995). *Text* 19/3, 371-398.

Salager-Meyer, Françoise 2001a. From Self-Highlightedness to Self-Effacement: A Genre-Based Study of the Socio-Pragmatic Function of Criticism in Medical Discourse. *LSP & Professional Communication* 1/2, 63-84.

Salager-Meyer, Françoise 2001b. "This Book Portrays the Worst form of Mental Terrorism": Critical Speech Acts in Medical English Book Reviews (1940-2000). In Kertész, András (ed.) *Approaches to the Pragmatics of Scientific Discourse*. Frankfurt am Main: Peter Lang, 47-72.

Salager-Meyer Françoise 2002. Market-Place, Self Confidence and Criticism in Medical Editorials. *Revista Canaria de Estudios Ingleses* 44, 65-78.

Salager-Meyer, Françoise / Alcaraz Ariza, María Ángeles 2003. Academic Criticism in Spanish Medical Discourse: A Cross-Generic Approach. *International Journal of Applied Linguistics* 13/1, 96-114.

Salager-Meyer, Françoise / Alcaraz Ariza, Maria Angeles 2004. Negative Appraisals in Academic Book Reviews. A Cross-Linguistic Approach. In Candlin, Christopher N. / Gotti, Maurizio (eds) *Intercultural Aspects of Specialized Communication*. Bern: Peter Lang, 149-172.

Salager-Meyer, Françoise / Alcaraz Ariza, María Ángeles / Zambrano, Nahirana 2003. The Scimitar, the Dagger and the Glove: Intercultural Differences in the Rhetoric of Criticism in Spanish, French and English Medical Discourse (1930-1995). *English for Specific Purposes* 22, 223-247.

Salager-Meyer, Françoise / Zambrano, Nahirana 2001a. The Bittersweet Rhetoric of Controversiality in 19th and 20th Century French and English Medical Literature. *Journal of Historical Pragmatics* 2/1, 141-173.

Salager-Meyer, Françoise / Zambrano, Nahirana 2001b. The Discourse of Competing Knowledge Claims in Academic Prose. In Mayer, Felix (ed.) *Language for Special Purposes: Perspectives for the New Millennium*. Vol 2. Tübingen: Gunter Narr, 474-479.

Sampson, Rita / Lee, David Y.W. / Leicher, Sheryl / Ädel, Annelie (eds) 2007. *The Michigan Corpus of Academic Spoken English. Version 3*. Ann Arbor, MI: The University of Michigan (English Language Institute). Retrieved 10 March 2008 from <http://legacyweb.lsa.umich.edu/eli/micase/MICASE_MANUAL.pdf>.

Schwartz, S.H. 1992. Universals in the Content and Structure of Values: Theoretical Advances and Empirical Tests. *Advances in Experimental Social Psychology* 25, 1-65.

Schwartz, S.H. 1994. Are There Universal Aspects in the Structure and Contents of Human Values? *Journal of Social Issues* 50/4, 19-45.

Scott, Mike 2006. *Oxford WordSmith Tools 4.0*. Oxford: Oxford University Press.

Seidlhofer, Barbara. 2001. Closing a Conceptual Gap: The Case for a Description of English as a Lingua Franca. *International Journal of Applied Linguistics* 11/2, 133-58.

Shaw, Philip 2003. Evaluation and Promotion across Languages. *Journal of English for Academic Purposes* 2/4, 343-357.

Shaw, Philip 2004. How Do We Recognise Implicit Evaluation in Academic Book Reviews? In Del Lungo Camiciotti, Gabriella / Tognini Bonelli, Elena (eds) *Academic Discourse - New Insights into Evaluation*. Bern: Peter Lang, 121-140.

Silver, Mark 2003. The Stance of Stance: A Critical Look at Ways Stance is Expressed and Modeled in Academic Discourse. *Journal of English for Academic Purposes* 2/4, 359-374.

Sinclair, John McH. (ed.) 1987. *Collins COBUILD English Language Dictionary*. London: Harper Collins.
Sinclair, John McH. (ed.) 1990. *Collins COBUILD English Grammar*. London: Harper Collins.
Sinclair, John McH. 1994. Trust the Text. In Coulthard, Malcolm (ed.) *Advances in Written Text Analysis*. London: Routledge, 12-25.
Sinclair, John McH. 2004. Intuition and Annotation – The Discussion Continues. In Aijmer, Karin / Altenberg, Bengt (eds) *Advances in Corpus Linguistics. Papers from the 23rd International Conference on English Language Research on Computerized Corpora* [Language and Computers 49]. Amsterdam: Rodopi, 39-59.
Sinclair, John McH. 2006. Exploring a Corpus. Doctoral workshop lecture. University of Modena, Italy, November 2006.
Smart, Graham 2003. A Central Bank's "Communications Strategy": The Interplay of Activity, Discourse Genres, and Technology in a Time of Organizational Change. In Bazerman, Charles / Russell, David R. (eds) *Writing Selves Writing Societies. Research from Activity Perspectives*. Fort Collins, CO: WAC Clearinghouse, 9-61. E-book retrieved 10 March 2008 from <http://wac.colostate.edu/books/selves_societies>.
Smokler, Howard 1983. Institutional Rationality: The Complex Norms of Science. *Synthese* 57/2, 129-138.
Soler, Viviana 2002. Analysing Adjectives in Scientific Discourse: An Exploratory Study with Educational Applications for Spanish Speakers at Advanced University Level. *English for Specific Purposes* 21/2, 145-165.
Stern, Paul C. / Dietz, Thomas / Guagnano, Gregory A. 1998. A Brief Inventory of Values. *Educational and Psychological Measurement* 58/6, 984-1001.
Stotesbury, Hilkka 2003. Evaluation in Research Article Abstracts in the Narrative and Hard Sciences. *Journal of English for Academic Purposes* 2/4, 327-341.
Stubbs, Michael 1996. *Text and Corpus Analysis. Computer Assisted Studies of Language and Culture*. Oxford: Wiley-Blackwell.
Stubbs, Michael 2001. *Words and Phrases. Corpus Studies of Lexical Semantics*. Oxford: Blackwell.

Sudman, Seymour / Bradburn, Norman M. 1982. *Asking Questions. A Practical Guide to Questionnaire Design.* San Francisco: Jossey-Bass.

Svartvik, Jan 1996. Corpora Are Becoming Mainstream. In Thomas, Jenny / Short, Mick (eds) *Using Corpora for Language Research. Studies in the Honour of Geoffrey Leech.* London: Longman, 3-13.

Swales, John M. 1981. *Aspects of Article Introductions.* Birmingham: The University of Aston.

Swales, John M. 1985. English as the International Language of Research. *RELC Journal* 16/1, 1-7.

Swales, John M. 1990. *Genre Analysis. English in Academic and Research Settings.* Cambridge: Cambridge University Press.

Swales, John M. 1993. Genre and Engagement. *Revue Belge de Philologie et d'Histoire* 71/3, 687-698.

Swales, John M. 1996. Occluded Genres in the Academy: The Case of the Submission Letter. In Ventola, Eika / Mauranen, Anna (eds) *Academic Writing. Intercultural and Textual Issues.* Amsterdam: John Benjamins, 45-58.

Swales, John M. 1997. English as Tyrannosaurus rex. *World Englishes* 16/3, 373-382.

Swales, John M. 1998a. *Other Floors Other Voices. A Textography of a Small University Building.* Mahwah, NJ: Lawrence Erlbaum.

Swales, John M. 1998b. Language, Science and Scholarship. *Asian Journal of English Language Teaching* 8, 1-18.

Swales, John M. 2000. Languages for Specific Purposes. *Annual Review of Applied Linguistics* 20, 59-76.

Swales, John M. 2003. Is the University a Community of Practice? In Sarangi, Srikant / van Leeuwen, Theo (eds) *Applied Linguistics and Communities of Practice.* London: Continuum & BAAL, 203-216.

Swales, John M. 2004a. *Research Genres. Explorations and Applications.* Cambridge: Cambridge University Press.

Swales, John M. 2004b. Evaluation in Academic Speech: First Forays. In Del Lungo Camiciotti, Gabriella / Tognini Bonelli, Elena (eds) *Academic Discourse – New Insights into Evaluation.* Bern: Peter Lang, 31-53.

Swales, John M. 2004c. Then and Now: A Reconsideration of the First Corpus of Scientific English. *Ibérica* 8, 5-21.

Swales, John M. 2006. Corpus Linguistics in English for Academic Purposes. In Arnó, Elisabeth / Soler, Antonia / Rueda, Carmen (eds) *Information Technology in Languages for Specific Purposes. Issues and Prospects.* New York: Springer, 19-33.

Swales, John M. / Burke, Amy 2003. "It's Really Fascinating Work": Differences in Evaluative Adjectives across Academic Registers. In Leistyna, Pepi / Meyer, Charles F. (eds) *Corpus Analysis. Language Structure and Language Use.* Amsterdam: Rodopi, 1-18.

Swales, John M. / Feak, Christine B. 2000. *English in Today's Research World.* Ann Arbor: University of Michigan Press.

Swales, John M. / Feak, Christine B. ^{2}2004. *Academic Writing for Graduate Students. Essential Tasks and Skills.* Ann Arbor: University of Michigan Press.

Tannen, Deborah 2000. Agonism in the Academy: Surviving Higher Learning's Argument Culture. *The Chronicle of Higher Education* 46/30 (March 31), B7-B8.

Tannen, Deborah 2002. Agonism in Academic Discourse. *Journal of Pragmatics* 34/10-11, 1651-1669.

Tardy, C. 2004. The Role of English in Scientific Communication: Lingua franca or Tyrannosaurus rex? *Journal of English for Academic Purposes* 3/3, 247-269.

Teo, Peter 2007. The Marketisation of Higher Education: A Comparative Case-Study of Two Universities in Singapore. *Critical Approaches to Discourse Analysis Across Disciplines* 1/1, 95-111.

Thetela, Puleng 1997. Evaluated Entities and Parameters of Value in Academic Research Articles. *English for Specific Purposes* 16/2, 101-118.

THES (Times Higher Education Supplement) 2007. *THES-QS World University Rankings 2007.* Online resource. Retrieved 10 March 2008 from <http://www.topuniversities.com/worlduniversity rankings/results/2007>.

Thomas, Jenny / Short, Mick (eds) 1996. *Using Corpora for Language Research. Studies in Honour of Geoffrey Leech.* London: Longman.

Thomas, Sarah / Hawes, Thomas P. 1994. Reporting Verbs in Medical Journal Articles. *English for Specific Purposes* 13/2, 129-148.

Thompson, Geoff / Hunston, Susan 2000. Evaluation: An Introduction. In Hunston, Susan / Thompson, Geoff (eds) *Evaluation in Text. Authorial Stance and the Construction of Discourse*. Oxford: Oxford University Press, 1-27.

Thompson, Geoff / Ye, Yiyun 1991. Evaluation in the Reporting Verbs Used in Academic Papers. *Applied Linguistics* 12/4, 365-382.

Thompson, Paul 2009. Shared Disciplinary Norms and Individual Traits in the Writing of British Undergraduates. In Gotti, Maurizio (ed.) *Commonality and Individuality in Academic Discourse*. Bern: Peter Lang, 53-82.

Tognini Bonelli, Elena 2001. *Corpus Linguistics at Work*. Amsterdam: John Benjamins.

Tse, Polly / Ken Hyland 2006. Gender and Discipline: Exploring Metadiscourse Variation in Academic Book Reviews. In Hyland, Ken / Bondi, Marina (eds) *Academic Discourse Across Disciplines*. Bern: Peter Lang, 177-202.

Tucker, Paul 2003. Evaluation in the Art-Historical Research Article. *Journal of English for Academic Purposes* 2/4, 291-312.

Valette-Florence, Pierre / Ferrandi, Jean-Marc / Odin, Nathalie / Odin, Yorick / Usunier, Jean-Claude 1999. Personal Value Systems and Time-Style Orientations: A Cross-Cultural Comparison. In Smith, Scott M. (ed.) *Proceedings of Seventh Cross-Cultural Consumer and Business Studies Research Conference*. Association for Consumer Research & American Psychological Association. Retrieved 10 March 2008 from <http://marketing.byu.edu/htmlpages/ccrs/proceedings99/valette.htm>.

Ventola, Eija 1987. *The Structure of Social Interaction. A Systemic Approach to the Semiotics of Service Encounters*. London: Pinter.

Ventola, Eija 1998a. Textlinguistics and Academic Writing. In Evangelisti Allori, Paola (ed.) *Academic Discourse in Europe. Thought Processes and Linguistic Realisations*. Rome: Bulzoni Editore, 65-77.

Ventola, Eija 1998b. Meaningful Choices in Academic Communities – Ideological Issues. In Schulze, Rainer (ed.) *Making*

Meaningful Choices in English. On Dimensions, Perspectives, Methodology and Evidence. Tübingen: Gunter Narr, 277-294.
Ventola, Eija / Mauranen, Anna (eds) 1996 *Academic Writing. Intercultural and Textual Issues*. Amsterdam: John Benjamins.
Wagner, David L. (ed.) 1983. *The Seven Liberal Arts in the Middle Ages*. Bloomington, IN: Indiana University Press.
Watts, Richard J. / Ide, Sachiko / Ehlich, Konrad (eds) 1992. *Politeness in Language. Studies in its History, Theory and Practice*. Berlin: Mouton de Gruyter.
Webber, Pauline 2004. Negation in Linguistics Papers. In Del Lungo Camiciotti, Gabriella / Tognini Bonelli, Elena (eds) *Academic Discourse – New Insights into Evaluation*. Bern: Peter Lang, 181-202.
Wenger, Etienne 1998. *Communities of Practice. Learning Meaning and Identity*. Cambridge: Cambridge University Press.
Whitley, Richard 1985. Knowledge Producers and Knowledge Acquirers: Popularisation as a Relation between Scientific Fields and Their Publics. In Shinn, Terry / Whitley, Richard (eds) *Expository Science: Forms and Functions of Popularisation*. Dordrecht: D. Reidel, 3-28.
Willis, Gordon B. 2005. *Cognitive Interviewing. A Tool for Improving Questionnaire Design*. Thousand Oaks, CA: Sage.
Whorf, Benjamin Lee 1956. *Language, Thought and Reality: Selected Writings*. Edited by John B. Carroll. New York: John Wiley.
Widdowson, H.G. 1979. *Explorations in Applied Linguistics*. Oxford: Oxford University Press.
Yakhontova, Tatyana 2006. Cultural and Disciplinary Variation in Academic Discourse: The Issue of Influencing Factors. *Journal of English for Academic Purposes* 5/2, 153-167.
Ziman, John 2000. *Real Science. What It Is, and What It Means*. Cambridge: Cambridge University Press.

Appendix 1. Corpus texts

Anthropology

Auerbach, Benjamin M. / Raxter, Michelle H. 2008. Patterns of clavicular bilateral asymmetry in relation to the humerus: variation among humans. *Journal of Human Evolution* 54, 663-674.

Balzeau, Antoine / Radovcic, Jakov 2008. Variation and modalities of growth and development of the temporal bone pneumatization in Neandertals. *Journal of Human Evolution* 54, 546-567.

Barrickman, Nancy L. / Bastian, Meredith L. / Isler, Karin / van Schaik, Carel P. 2008. Life history costs and benefits of encephalization: a comparative test using data from long-term studies of primates in the wild. *Journal of Human Evolution* 54, 568-590.

Cardini, Andrea / Elton, Sarah 2008. Variation in guenon skulls (I): species divergence, ecological and genetic differences. *Journal of Human Evolution* 54, 615-637.

Chauhan, Parth R. 2008. Soanian lithic occurrences and raw material exploitation in the Siwalik Frontal Zone, northern India: a geoarchaeological perspective. *Journal of Human Evolution* 54, 591-614.

Dean, M. Christopher 2007. A radiographic and histological study of modern human lower first permanent molar root growth during the supraosseous eruptive phase. *Journal of Human Evolution* 53, 635-646.

Hardy, Bruce L. / Bolus, Michael / Conard, Nicholas J. 2008. Hammer or crescent wrench? Stone-tool form and function in the Aurignacian of southwest Germany. *Journal of Human Evolution* 54, 648-662.

López-Polín, Lucía / Ollé, Andreu / Cáceres, Isabel / Carbonell, Eudald / Bermúdez de Castro, José María 2008. Pleistocene human remains and conservation treatments: the case of a mandible from Atapuerca (Spain). *Journal of Human Evolution* 54, 539-545.

Smith, Heather F. / Grine, Frederick E. 2008. Cladistic analysis of early *Homo* crania from Swartkrans and Sterkfontein, South Africa. *Journal of Human Evolution* 54, 684-704.

Watson, J.C. / Payne, R.C. / Chamberlain, A.T. / Jones, R.K. / Sellers, W.I. 2008. The energetic costs of load-carrying and the evolution of bipedalism. *Journal of Human Evolution* 54, 675-683.

Biology

Ango, Fabrice / Wu, Caizhi / Van der Want, Johannes J. / Wu, Priscilla / Schachner, Melitta / Huang, Josh 2008. Bergmann glia and the recognition molecule CHL1 organize GABAergic axons and direct innervation of Purkinje cell dendrites. *PLOS Biology 6*, 739-756.

Dunne, Jennifer A. / Williams, Richard J. / Martinez, Neo D. / Wood, Rachel A. / Erwin, Douglas H. 2008. Compilation and network analyses of Cambrian food webs. *PLOS Biology* 6, 693-708.

Grant, Andrew J. / Restif, Olivier / McKinley, Trevelyan J. / Sheppard, Mark / Maskell, Duncan J. / Mastroeni, Pietro 2008. Modelling within-host spatiotemporal dynamics of invasive bacterial disease. *PLOS Biology* 6, 757-770.

Green, Jessica J. / McDonald, John J. 2008. Electrical neuroimaging reveals timing of attentional control activity in human brain. *PLOS Biology* 6, 730-738.

Hatzold, Julia / Conradt, Barbara 2008. Control of apoptosis by asymmetric cell division. *PLOS Biology* 6, 771-784.

Hughes, Julian R. / Meireles, Ana M. / Fisher, Katherine H. / Garcia, Angel / Antrobus, Philip R. / Wainman, Alan / Zitzmann, Nicole / Deane, Charlotte / Ohkura, Hiroyuki / Wakefield, James G. 2008. A microtubule interactome: complexes with roles in cell cycle and mitosis. *PLOS Biology* 6, 785-795.

Nogués-Bravo, David / Rodríguez, Jesús / Hortal, Joaquín / Batra, Persaram / Araújo, Miguel B. 2008. Climate change, humans, and the extinction of the woolly mammoth. *PLOS Biology* 6, 685-692.

Pinkas, Daniel M. / Strop, Pavel / Brunger, Axel T. / Khosla, Chaitan 2007. Transglutaminase 2 undergoes a large conformational change upon activation. *PLOS Biology* 5, 2788-2796.

Potrzebowski, Lukasz / Vinckenbosch, Nicolas / Marques, Ana Claudia / Chalmel, Frédéric / Jégou, Bernard / Kaessmann, Henrik 2008. Chromosomal gene movements reflect the recent origin and biology of therian sex chromosomes. *PLOS Biology 6*, 709-716.

Wesson, Daniel W. / Carey, Ryan M. / Verhagen, Justus V. / Wachowiak, Matt 2008. Rapid encoding and perception of novel odors in the rat. *PLOS Biology* 6, 717-729.

Computer science

Begole, James "Bo" / Tang, John C. 2007. Incorporating human and machine interpretation of unavailability and rhythm awareness into the design of collaborative applications. *Human-Computer Interaction* 22, 7-45.

Cheverst, Keith / Dix, Alan / Fitton, Daniel / Rouncefield, Mark / Graham, Connor 2007. Exploring awareness related messaging through two situated-display-based systems. *Human-Computer Interaction* 22, 173-220.

DiMicco, Joan Morris / Hollenbach, Katherine J. / Pandolfo, Anna / Bender, Walter 2007. The impact of increased awareness while face-to-face. *Human-Computer Interaction* 22, 47-96.
Dourish, Paul / Anderson, Ken 2006. Collective information practice: exploring privacy and security as social and cultural phenomena. *Human-Computer Interaction* 21, 319-342.
Lyons, Kent / Starner, Thad / Gane, Brian 2006. Experimental evaluations of the twiddler one-handed chording mobile keyboard. *Human-Computer Interaction* 21, 343-392.
Matthews, Tara / Rattenbury, Tye / Carter, Scott 2007. Defining, designing, and evaluating peripheral displays: an analysis using activity theory. *Human-Computer Interaction* 22, 221-261.
Oulasvirta, Antti / Petit, Renaud / Raento, Mika / Tiitta, Sauli 2007. Interpreting and acting on mobile awareness cues. *Human-Computer Interaction* 22, 97-135.
Rittenbruch, Markus / Viller, Stephen / Mansfield, Tim 2007. Announcing activity: design and evaluation of an intentionally enriched awareness service. *Human-Computer Interaction* 22, 137-171.
Wegge, Jürgen 2006. Communication via videoconference: emotional and cognitive consequences of affective personality dispositions, seeing one's own picture, and disturbing events. *Human-Computer Interaction* 21, 273-318.
Ziefle, Martina / Bay, Susanne 2006. How to overcome disorientation in mobile phone menus: a comparison of two different types of navigation aids. *Human-Computer Interaction* 21, 393-433.

Economics

Bloom, Nicholas / Van Reenen, John 2007. Measuring and explaining management practices across firms and countries. *The Quarterly Journal of Economics* 122, 1351-1408.
Caplin, Andrew / Dean, Mark 2008. Dopamine, reward prediction error, and economics. *The Quarterly Journal of Economics* 123, 663-701.
Currie, Janet / MacLeod, W. Bentley 2008. First do no harm? Tort reform and birth outcomes. *The Quarterly Journal of Economics* 123, 795-830.
Doepke, Matthias / Zilibotti Fabrizio 2008. Occupational choice and the spirit of capitalism. *The Quarterly Journal of Economics* 123, 747-793.
Ferraz, Claudio / Finan, Frederico 2008. Exposing corrupt politicians: the effects of Brazil's publicly released audits on electoral outcomes. *The Quarterly Journal of Economics* 123, 703-745.
Gopinath Gita / Rigobon, Roberto 2008. Sticky borders. *The Quarterly Journal of Economics* 123, 531-575.

Helpman, Elhanan / Melitz, Marc / Rubinstein, Yona 2008. Estimating trade flows: trading partners and trading volumes. *The Quarterly Journal of Economics* 123, 441-487.
Kircher, Philipp / Postlewaite, Andrew 2008. Strategic firms and endogenous consumer emulation. *The Quarterly Journal of Economics* 123, 621-661.
Mullainathan, Sendhil / Schwartzstein, Joshua / Shleifer, Andrei 2008. Coarse thinking and persuasion. *The Quarterly Journal of Economics* 123, 577-619.
Verhoogen, Eric A. 2008. Trade, quality upgrading, and wage inequality in the Mexican manufacturing sector. *The Quarterly Journal of Economics* 123, 489-530.

Engineering

Adamowski, Jan F. 2008. Development of a short-term river flood forecasting method for snowmelt driven floods based on wavelet and cross-wavelet analysis,. *Journal of Hydrology* 353, 247-266.
Carrera-Hernández, J.J. / Gaskin, S.J. 2008. Spatio-temporal analysis of potential aquifer recharge: application to the Basin of Mexico. *Journal of Hydrology* 353, 228-246.
Cloutier, Vincent / Lefebvre, René / Therrien, René / Savard, Martine M. 2008. Multivariate statistical analysis of geochemical data as indicative of the hydrogeochemical evolution of groundwater in a sedimentary rock aquifer system. *Journal of Hydrology* 353, 294-313.
El Bakouri, Hicham / Morillo, José / Usero, José / Ouassini, Abdelhamid 2008. Potential use of organic waste substances as an ecological technique to reduce pesticide ground water contamination. *Journal of Hydrology* 353, 335-342.
Liu, Yuhong / Fan, Ningjiang / An, Shuqing / Bai, Xiaohua / Liu, Fude / Xu, Zhen / Wang, Zhongsheng / Liu, Shirong 2008. Characteristics of water isotopes and hydrograph separation during the wet season in the Heishui River, China. *Journal of Hydrology* 353, 314-321.
Mathon, Bree R. / Ozbek, Metin M. / Pinder, George F. 2008. Transmissivity and storage coefficient estimation by coupling the Cooper-Jacob method and modified fuzzy least-squares regression. *Journal of Hydrology* 353, 267-274.
Montzka, Carsten / Canty, Morton / Kunkel, Ralf / Menz, Gunter / Vereecken, Harry / Wendland, Frank 2008. Modelling the water balance of a mesoscale catchment basin using remotely sensed land cover data. *Journal of Hydrology* 353, 322-334.
Santos, Isaac R. / Niencheski, Felipe / Burnett, William / Peterson, Richard / Chanton, Jeffrey / Andrade, Carlos F.F. / Milani, Idel B. / Schmidt, Axel / Knoeller, Kay 2008. Tracing anthropogenically driven groundwater discharge into a coastal lagoon from southern Brazil. *Journal of Hydrology* 353, 275-293.
Tatard, L. / Planchon, O. / Wainwright, J. / Nord, G. / Favis-Mortlock, D. / Silvera, N. / Ribolzi, O. / Esteves, M. / Huang, Chi Hua 2008. Measurement and

modelling of high-resolution flow-velocity data under simulated rainfall on a low-slope sandy soil. *Journal of Hydrology* 353, 1-12.
Zhang, Qiang / Xu, Chong-Yu / Zhang, Zengxin / Chen, Yongqin David / Liu, Chun-ling / Lin, Hui 2008. Spatial and temporal variability of precipitation maxima during 1960-2005 in the Yangtze River basin and possible association with large-scale circulation. *Journal of Hydrology* 353, 215-227.

History

Boxer, Marilyn J. 2007. Rethinking the socialist construction and international career of the concept "bourgeois feminism". *American Historical Review* 112, 131-158.
Delay, Brian 2007. Independent Indians and the U.S.-Mexican war. *American Historical Review* 112, 35-68.
Eltis, David / Morgan, Philip / Richardson, David 2007. Agency and diaspora in Atlantic history: reassessing the African contribution to rice cultivation in the Americas. *American Historical Review* 112, 1329-1357.
Grehan, James 2006. Smoking and "early modern" sociability: the great tobacco debate in the Ottoman Middle East (seventeenth to eighteenth centuries). *American Historical Review* 111, 1352-1377.
Konishi, Sho 2007. Reopening the "opening of Japan": a Russian-Japanese revolutionary encounter and the vision of anarchist progress. *American Historical Review* 112, 101-130.
Levy, Jonathan Ira 2006. Contemplating delivery: futures trading and the problem of commodity exchange in the United States, 1875-1905. *American Historical Review* 111, 307-335.
Manela, Erez 2006. Imagining Woodrow Wilson in Asia: dreams of East-West harmony and the revolt against Empire in 1919. *American Historical Review* 111, 1327-1351.
Schoenbrun, David L. 2006. Conjuring the modern in Africa: durability and rupture in histories of public healing between the Great Lakes of East Africa. *American Historical Review* 111, 1403-1439.
Williams, Louise Blakeney 2007. Overcoming the "contagion of mimicry": the cosmopolitan nationalism and modernist history of Rabindranath Tagore and W.B. Yeats. *American Historical Review* 112, 69-100.
Zahra, Tara 2006. "Each nation only cares for its own": empire, nation, and child welfare activism in the Bohemian lands, 1900-1918. *American Historical Review* 111, 1378-1402.

Mathematics

Aschbacher, Michael 2008. On intervals in subgroup lattices of finite groups. *Journal of the American Mathematical Society* 21, 809-830.

Avila, Artur / Lyubich, Mikhail 2008. Hausdorff dimension and conformal measures of Feigenbaum Julia Sets. *Journal of the American Mathematical Society* 21, 305-363.

Bernard, Patrick 2008. The dynamics of pseudographs in convex Hamiltonian systems. *Journal of the American Mathematical Society* 21, 615-669.

Burq, Nicolas / Lebeau, Gilles / Planchon, Fabrice 2008. Global existence for energy critical waves in 3-D domains. *Journal of the American Mathematical Society* 21, 831-845.

Caffarelli, L.A. / Lin, Fang-Hua 2008. Singularly perturbed elliptic systems and multi-valued harmonic functions with free boundaries. *Journal of the American Mathematical Society* 21, 847-862.

Giordano, Thierry / Matui, Hiroki / Putnam, Ian F. / Skau, Christian F. 2008. Orbit equivalence for Cantor minimal Z2-systems. *Journal of the American Mathematical Society* 21, 863-892.

Guralnick, R.M. / Kantor, W.M. / Kassabov, M. / Lubotzky, A. 2008. Presentations of finite simple groups: a quantitative approach. *Journal of the American Mathematical Society* 21, 711-774.

Klainerman, Sergiu / Rodnianski, Igor 2008. On the radius of injectivity of null hypersurfaces. *Journal of the American Mathematical Society* 21, 775-795.

Kumar, Shrawan 2008. On the Cachazo-Douglas-Seiberg-Witten conjecture for simple lie algebras. *Journal of the American Mathematical Society* 21, 797-808.

Ozsváth, Peter / Szabó, Zoltán 2008. Link Floer homology and the Thurston norm. *Journal of the American Mathematical Society* 21, 671-709.

Medicine

Calis, Job C.J. / Phiri, Kamija S. / Faragher, E. Brian / Brabin, Bernard J. / Bates, Imelda / Cuevas, Luis E. / de Haan, Rob J. / Phiri, Ajib I. / Malange, Pelani / Khoka, Mirriam / Hulshof, Paul J.M. / van Lieshout, Lisette / Beld, Marcel G.H.M. / Teo, Yik Y. / Rockett, Kirk A. / Richardson, Anna / Kwiatkowski, Dominic P. / Molyneux, Malcolm E. / Boele van Hensbroek, Michaël 2008. Severe anemia in Malawian children. *The New England Journal of Medicine* 358, 888-899.

Gurm, Hitinder S. / Yadav, Jay S. / Fayad, Pierre / Katzen, Barry T. / Mishkel, Gregory J. / Tanvir K. Bajwa / Ansel, Gary / Strickman, Neil E. / Wang, Hong / Cohen, Sidney A. / Massaro, Joseph M. / Cutlip, Donald E. 2008. Long-term results of carotid stenting versus endarterectomy in high-risk patients. *The New England Journal of Medicine* 358, 1572-1579.

Hoge, Charles W. / McGurk, Dennis / Thomas, Jeffrey L. / Cox, Anthony L. / Engel, Charles C. / Castro, Carl A. 2008. Mild traumatic brain injury in U.S. soldiers returning from Iraq. *The New England Journal of Medicine* 358, 453-463.

Kastelein, John J.P. / Akdim, Fatima / Stroes, Erik S.G. / Zwinderman, Aeilko H. / Bots, Michiel L. / Stalenhoef, Anton F.H. / Visseren, Frank L.J. / Sijbrands, Eric J.G. / Trip, Mieke D. / Stein, Evan A. / Gaudet, Daniel / Duivenvoorden, Raphael / Veltri, Enrico P. / Marais, A. David / de Groot, Eric 2008. Simvastatin with or without ezetimibe in familial hypercholesterolemia. *The New England Journal of Medicine* 358, 1431-1443.

Mai, Nguyen Thi Hoang / Chau, Tran Thi Hong / Thwaites, Guy / Chuong, Ly Van / Sinh, Dinh Xuan / Nghia, Ho Dang Trung / Tuan, Phung Quoc / Phong, Nguyen Duy / Phu, Nguyen Hoan / Diep, To Song / Chau, Nguyen van Vinh / Duong, Nguyen Minh / Campbell, James / Schultsz, Constance / Parry, Chris / Torok, M. Estee / White, Nicholas / Chinh, Nguyen Tran / Hien, Tran Tinh / Stepniewska, Kasia / Farrar, Jeremy J. 2007. Dexamethasone in Vietnamese adolescents and adults with bacterial meningitis. *The New England Journal of Medicine* 357, 2431-2440.

Pelliccia, Antonio / Di Paolo, Fernando M. / Quattrini, Filippo M. / Basso, Cristina / Culasso, Franco / Popoli, Gloria / De Luca, Rosanna / Spataro, Antonio / Biffi, Alessandro / Thiene, Gaetano / Maron, Barry J. 2008. Outcomes in athletes with marked ECG repolarization abnormalities. *The New England Journal of Medicine* 358, 152-161.

Svilaas, Tone / Vlaar, Pieter J. / van der Horst, Iwan C. / Diercks, Gilles F.H. / de Smet, Bart J.G.L. / van den Heuvel, Ad F.M. / Anthonio, Rutger L. / Jessurun, Gillian A. / Tan, Eng-Shiong / Suurmeijer, Albert J.H. / Zijlstra, Felix 2008. Thrombus aspiration during primary percutaneous coronary intervention. *The New England Journal of Medicine* 358, 557-567.

Tyson, Jon E. / Parikh, Nehal A. / Langer, John / Green, Charles / Higgins, Rosemary D. 2008. Intensive care for extreme prematurity – moving beyond gestational. *The New England Journal of Medicine* 358, 1672-1681.

Victor, John C. / Monto, Arnold S. / Surdina, Tatiyana Y. / Suleimenova, Saida Z. / Vaughan, Gilberto / Nainan, Omana V. / Favorov, Michael O. / Margolis, Harold S. / Bell, Beth P. 2007. Hepatitis A vaccine versus immune globulin for postexposure prophylaxis. *The New England Journal of Medicine* 357, 1685-1694.

Watson-Jones, Deborah / Weiss, Helen A. / Rusizoka, Mary / Changalucha, John / Baisley, Kathy / Mugeye, Kokugonza / Tanton, Clare / Ross, David / Everett, Dean / Clayton, Tim / Balira, Rebecca / Knight, Louise / Hambleton, Ian / Le Goff, Jerome / Belec, Laurent / Hayes, Richard 2008. Effect of herpes simplex suppression on incidence of HIV among women in Tanzania. *The New England Journal of Medicine* 358, 1560-1571.

Physics

Appleby, Stephen A. / Battye Richard A. Aspects of cosmological expansion in F(R) gravity models 2008. *Journal of Cosmology and Astroparticle Physics* 5, 28 pp.

Barvinsky, A.O. / Deffayet, C. / Kamenshchik, A. Yu 2008. Anomaly driven cosmology: big boost scenario and AdS/CFT correspondence. *Journal of Cosmology and Astroparticle Physics* 5, 17 pp.

Bjælde, Ole Eggers / Brookfield, Anthony W. / van de Bruck, Carsten / Hannestad, Steen / Mota, David F. / Schrempp, Lily / Tocchini-Valentini, Domenico 2008. Neutrino dark energy – revisiting the stability issue. *Journal of Cosmology and Astroparticle Physics* 1, 24 pp.

Gannouji, Radouane / Polarski, David 2008. The growth of matter perturbations in some scalar-tensor DE models. *Journal of Cosmology and Astroparticle Physics* 5, 14 pp.

Huber, Stephan J. / Konstandin, Thomas 2008. Production of gravitational waves in the nMSSM. *Journal of Cosmology and Astroparticle Physics* 5, 22 pp.

Huston, Ian / Lidsey, James E. / Thomas, Steven / Ward, John 2008. Gravitational wave constraints on multi-brane inflation. *Journal of Cosmology and Astroparticle Physics* 5, 20 pp.

Li, Miao / Lin, Chunshan / Wang, Yi 2008. Some issues concerning holographic dark energy. *Journal of Cosmology and Astroparticle Physics* 5, 15 pp.

Matsuda, Tomohiro 2008. Modulated inflation from the kinetic term. *Journal of Cosmology and Astroparticle Physics* 5, 12 pp.

Podolsky, Dmitry / Majumder, Jaydeep / Jokela, Niko 2008. Disorder on the landscape. *Journal of Cosmology and Astroparticle Physics* 5, 35 pp.

Wang, Yun 2008. Differentiating dark energy and modified gravity with galaxy redshift surveys. *Journal of Cosmology and Astroparticle Physics* 5, 10 pp.

Sociology

Inclán, María de la Luz 2008. From the ¡Ya Basta! to the Caracoles: Zapatista mobilization under transitional conditions. *American Journal of Sociology* 113, 1316-1350.

Keister, Lisa A. 2008. Conservative Protestants and wealth: how religion perpetuates asset poverty. *American Journal of Sociology* 113, 1237-1271.

King, Ryan D. 2008. Conservatism, institutionalism, and the social control of intergroup conflict. *American Journal of Sociology* 113, 1351-1393.

Koçak, Özgecan / Carroll, Glenn R. 2008. Growing church organizations in diverse U.S. communities, 1890-1926. *American Journal of Sociology* 113, 1272-1315.

Luders, Joseph 2006. The economics of movement success: business responses to civil rights mobilization. *American Journal of Sociology* 111, 963-998.

Martin, Andrew W. 2008. The institutional logic of union organizing and the effectiveness of social movement repertoires. *American Journal of Sociology* 113, 1067-1103.

McCammon, Holly J. / Chaudhuri, Soma / Hewitt, Lyndi / Muse, Courtney Sanders / Newman, Harmony D. / Smith, Carrie Lee / Terrell, Teresa M. 2008. Becoming full citizens: the U.S. women's jury rights campaigns, the pace of reform, and strategic adaptation. *American Journal of Sociology* 113, 1104-1147.

Sharkey, Patrick 2008. The intergenerational transmission of context. *American Journal of Sociology* 113, 931-969.

Shiao, Jiannbin Lee / Tuan, Mia H. 2008. Korean adoptees and the social context of ethnic exploration. *American Journal of Sociology* 113, 1023-1066.

Wimmer, Andreas 2008. The making and unmaking of ethnic boundaries: a multilevel process theory. *American Journal of Sociology* 113, 970-1022.

Appendix 2. Corpus outline

ANTH											*All*
Tokens	3,411	6,088	5,712	5,779	6,590	12,138	12,943	9,979	13,725	9,593	85,958
Types	988	951	1,204	1,127	1,510	1,840	2,179	1,579	1,306	1,256	7,004
TTR	29.84	16.89	22.04	20.21	24.06	15.89	17.56	16.52	10.20	14.042	8.59
STTR	42.30	29.72	37.70	35.82	41.18	38.00	42.71	36.72	29.71	32.55	36.42
Sentence l.	19.47	24.06	25.41	26.43	22.74	22.18	27.64	23.26	19.33	28.21	23.52

BIO											*All*
Tokens	5,134	11,583	4,323	9,818	6,316	11,745	8,276	9,712	7,436	5,548	79,891
Types	993	1,613	896	1,465	1,089	1,631	1,522	1,200	1,499	1,305	6,495
TTR	21.19	14.77	22.22	15.80	18.00	15.03	19.59	13.90	21.71	25.65	8.75
STTR	34.25	34.52	36.05	36.52	35.42	35.61	38.04	28.30	38.70	40.48	35.52
Sentence l.	27.56	29.35	26.36	25.82	28.40	24.38	28.55	29.37	23.01	22.82	26.49

CS											*All*
Tokens	13,326	15,420	13,162	11,516	16,890	15,135	14,561	14,008	8,662	15,358	138,038
Types	1,974	2,009	2,298	1,991	2,435	2,082	1,773	1,774	1,843	1,734	8,244
TTR	15.26	13.52	18.17	17.50	14.72	13.99	13.00	13.17	21.59	11.94	6.18
STTR	38.51	34.88	40.29	39.58	39.07	36.88	33.32	36.91	42.50	32.95	37.20
Sentence l.	22.86	26.83	23.86	20.32	30.74	22.44	25.55	22.60	27.53	19.70	23.87

ECO											*All*
Tokens	10,694	9,447	11,547	10,710	8,998	8,581	10,960	14,064	9,499	11,870	106,370
Types	1,359	1,543	1,707	1,353	1,483	1,631	1,531	2,344	1,514	1,884	7,220
TTR	12.98	16.61	15.36	13.08	17.29	19.59	14.37	17.15	16.19	16.24	6.98
STTR	33.83	35.99	34.76	33.34	36.71	38.05	36.62	40.03	36.65	39.46	36.63
Sentence l.	26.31	23.75	22.32	21.65	29.57	23.25	26.37	24.94	24.61	22.57	24.28

ENG											*All*
Tokens	5,120	9,167	11,427	4,225	9,409	8,624	3,759	6,348	4,702	7,104	69,885
Types	826	1,481	1,189	777	1,699	1,348	705	1,252	1,024	1,381	5,765
TTR	17.33	17.04	11.14	19.33	19.34	16.78	19.90	20.71	23.31	20.43	8.77
STTR	28.07	36.61	26.43	32.55	39.92	34.34	30.83	38.38	35.62	38.65	34.28
Sentence l.	20.72	38.63	29.98	27.91	26.14	22.95	29.27	23.99	24.81	22.99	26.44

HIST											*All*
Tokens	11,179	10,829	11,888	9,287	9,398	10,104	10,144	11,098	10,413	12,053	106,393
Types	2,881	2,211	2,571	2,409	2,218	2,893	2,182	2,610	2,334	2,410	11,757
TTR	26.02	20.56	21.71	26.25	23.80	28.79	21.75	23.62	22.75	20.34	11.15
STTR	49.52	42.45	44.64	48.15	45.94	50.57	43.81	46.56	44.67	43.18	45.93
Sentence l.	21.25	27.57	26.31	26.99	31.38	22.43	31.15	26.56	20.27	27.24	25.55

MATH											*All*
Tokens	30,724	16,647	36,958	10,691	4,638	14,359	3,912	7,967	18,897	27,079	171,872
Types	1,455	1,333	1,866	977	633	822	608	865	1,082	1,687	4,925
TTR	5.07	8.77	5.81	9.99	14.94	6.48	17.96	12.34	6.26	6.73	3.17
STTR	22.62	28.47	25.39	25.64	27.55	19.71	28.67	26.94	21.93	26.34	24.71
Sentence l.	22.69	22.25	21.47	23.91	18.59	15.76	20.27	22.91	20.78	7.37	16.21

MED											*All*
Tokens	3,786	4,423	3,473	4,631	4,096	4,110	4,531	3,078	3,850	3,995	39,973
Types	711	947	733	890	893	845	951	697	721	856	3,837
TTR	20.24	23.07	22.58	20.73	24.49	22.38	22.66	24.67	20.72	22.72	10.41
STTR	32.10	34.82	33.00	32.07	35.07	33.20	33.67	33.80	30.73	34.37	33.29
Sentence l.	35.13	30.18	28.23	33.02	23.83	29.72	32.79	32.85	28.52	30.38	30.18

PHY											*All*
Tokens	4,642	9,512	9,327	6,842	3,259	3,289	6,829	4,655	6,044	8,633	63,032
Types	677	1,303	866	1,140	593	578	1,088	700	1,046	1,116	3,646
TTR	15.62	14.46	9.91	17.70	19.99	18.20	16.59	16.38	18.44	13.69	6.15
STTR	27.65	33.27	26.79	35.45	30.05	28.10	35.17	30.17	34.88	32.50	31.77
Sentence l.	21.45	27.98	26.65	30.97	29.38	24.62	22.61	26.55	27.94	29.97	26.77

SOC											*All*
Tokens	10,023	12,560	9,695	12,562	11,694	15,432	17,338	8,810	14,366	12,293	124,773
Types	1,572	1,836	1,684	2,240	1,722	2,919	2,739	1,722	2,099	2,597	9,513
TTR	16.21	15.18	18.11	18.35	15.14	19.32	16.11	20.23	15.01	21.57	7.84
STTR	37.77	36.28	39.43	42.61	37.01	46.35	41.85	42.64	39.30	46.85	41.26
Sentence l.	25.38	25.04	28.79	25.80	35.55	31.74	23.12	32.36	26.79	27.81	27.51

Appendix 3. Candidate value-marking items

Item	*Rank Position*	*Occurrences*
well	125	754
new	126	753
large	146	615
values	150	604
small	164	539
important	170	527
value	185	476
general	211	420
early	230	401
positive	270	357
modern	278	346
right	339	291
simple	348	283
significant	372	268
larger	386	261
good	409	250
greater	416	247
central	429	242
negative	440	237
problem	458	229
major	488	217
strong	496	215
peripheral	513	207
error	515	206
consistent	519	204
best	545	198
better	552	197
complex	553	197
problems	558	195
full	581	188
recent	582	188
little	594	184
useful	609	179
simply	613	177
effective	618	175
impact	620	175
clear	635	172

key	636	172
late	643	171
smaller	671	165
great	695	160
specific	705	159
earlier	711	157
already	738	152
success	745	152
compact	746	151
free	751	150
limited	753	150
determined	759	149
effort	760	149
interest	763	148
certain	772	145
typically	787	144
interests	828	138
importance	854	134
personal	856	134
privacy	857	134
equal	867	132
relevant	878	131
older	900	128
organized	901	128
poor	909	127
significantly	914	126
enough	924	124
empirical	931	123
complete	930	123
organization	939	123
understand	944	123
novel	952	122
normal	978	119
old	987	118
interesting	1,021	114
appropriate	1,050	110
entire	1,067	109
whole	1,080	109
easy	1,104	106
easily	1,113	105
largely	1,133	103

depth	1,145	102
substantial	1,156	102
original	1,161	101
precisely	1,162	101
true	1,172	100

Index

Linguistic Insights

Studies in Language and Communication

This series aims to promote specialist language studies in the fields of linguistic theory and applied linguistics, by publishing volumes that focus on specific aspects of language use in one or several languages and provide valuable insights into language and communication research. A cross-disciplinary approach is favoured and most European languages are accepted.

The series includes two types of books:

- **Monographs** – featuring in-depth studies on special aspects of language theory, language analysis or language teaching.
- **Collected papers** – assembling papers from workshops, conferences or symposia.

Each volume of the series is subjected to a double peer-reviewing process.

Vol. 1 Maurizio Gotti & Marina Dossena (eds)
Modality in Specialized Texts. Selected Papers of the 1st CERLIS Conference.
421 pages. 2001. ISBN 3-906767-10-8. US-ISBN 0-8204-5340-4

Vol. 2 Giuseppina Cortese & Philip Riley (eds)
Domain-specific English. Textual Practices across Communities and Classrooms.
420 pages. 2002. ISBN 3-906768-98-8. US-ISBN 0-8204-5884-8

Vol. 3 Maurizio Gotti, Dorothee Heller & Marina Dossena (eds)
Conflict and Negotiation in Specialized Texts. Selected Papers of the 2nd CERLIS Conference.
470 pages. 2002. ISBN 3-906769-12-7. US-ISBN 0-8204-5887-2

Editorial address:

Prof. Maurizio Gotti Università di Bergamo, Facoltà di Lingue e Letterature Straniere,
Via Salvecchio 19, 24129 Bergamo, Italy
Fax: 0039 035 2052789, E-Mail: m.gotti@unibg.it

Vol. 4 Maurizio Gotti, Marina Dossena, Richard Dury, Roberta Facchinetti & Maria Lima
Variation in Central Modals. A Repertoire of Forms and Types of Usage in Middle English and Early Modern English.
364 pages. 2002. ISBN 3-906769-84-4. US-ISBN 0-8204-5898-8

Vol. 5 Stefania Nuccorini (ed.)
Phrases and Phraseology. Data and Descriptions.
187 pages. 2002. ISBN 3-906770-08-7. US-ISBN 0-8204-5933-X

Vol. 6 Vijay Bhatia, Christopher N. Candlin & Maurizio Gotti (eds)
Legal Discourse in Multilingual and Multicultural Contexts. Arbitration Texts in Europe.
385 pages. 2003. ISBN 3-906770-85-0. US-ISBN 0-8204-6254-3

Vol. 7 Marina Dossena & Charles Jones (eds)
Insights into Late Modern English. 2nd edition.
378 pages. 2003, 2007.
ISBN 978-3-03911-257-9. US-ISBN 978-0-8204-8927-8

Vol. 8 Maurizio Gotti
Specialized Discourse. Linguistic Features and Changing Conventions.
351 pages. 2003, 2005.
ISBN 3-03910-606-6. US-ISBN 0-8204-7000-7

Vol. 9 Alan Partington, John Morley & Louann Haarman (eds)
Corpora and Discourse.
420 pages. 2004. ISBN 3-03910-026-2. US-ISBN 0-8204-6262-4

Vol. 10 Martina Möllering
The Acquisition of German Modal Particles. A Corpus-Based Approach.
290 pages. 2004. ISBN 3-03910-043-2. US-ISBN 0-8204-6273-X

Vol. 11 David Hart (ed.)
English Modality in Context. Diachronic Perspectives.
261 pages. 2003. ISBN 3-03910-046-7. US-ISBN 0-8204-6852-5

Vol. 12 Wendy Swanson
Modes of Co-reference as an Indicator of Genre.
430 pages. 2003. ISBN 3-03910-052-1. US-ISBN 0-8204-6855-X

Vol. 13 Gina Poncini
Discursive Strategies in Multicultural Business Meetings.
2nd edition. 338 pages. 2004, 2007.
ISBN 978-3-03911-296-8. US-ISBN 978-0-8204-8937-7

Vol. 14 Christopher N. Candlin & Maurizio Gotti (eds)
Intercultural Aspects of Specialized Communication.
2nd edition. 369 pages. 2004, 2007.
ISBN 978-3-03911-258-6. US-ISBN 978-0-8204-8926-1

Vol. 15 Gabriella Del Lungo Camiciotti & Elena Tognini Bonelli (eds)
Academic Discourse. New Insights into Evaluation.
234 pages. 2004. ISBN 3-03910-353-9. US-ISBN 0-8204-7016-3

Vol. 16 Marina Dossena & Roger Lass (eds)
Methods and Data in English Historical Dialectology.
405 pages. 2004. ISBN 3-03910-362-8. US-ISBN 0-8204-7018-X

Vol. 17 Judy Noguchi
The Science Review Article. An Opportune Genre in the Construction of Science.
274 pages. 2006. ISBN 3-03910-426-8. US-ISBN 0-8204-7034-1

Vol. 18 Giuseppina Cortese & Anna Duszak (eds)
Identity, Community, Discourse. English in Intercultural Settings.
495 pages. 2005. ISBN 3-03910-632-5. US-ISBN 0-8204-7163-1

Vol. 19 Anna Trosborg & Poul Erik Flyvholm Jørgensen (eds)
Business Discourse. Texts and Contexts.
250 pages. 2005. ISBN 3-03910-606-6. US-ISBN 0-8204-7000-7

Vol. 20 Christopher Williams
Tradition and Change in Legal English. Verbal Constructions in Prescriptive Texts.
2nd revised edition. 216 pages. 2005, 2007. ISBN 978-3-03911-444-3.

Vol. 21 Katarzyna Dziubalska-Kolaczyk & Joanna Przedlacka (eds)
English Pronunciation Models: A Changing Scene.
2nd edition. 476 pages. 2005, 2008. ISBN 978-3-03911-682-9.

Vol. 22 Christián Abello-Contesse, Rubén Chacón-Beltrán, M. Dolores López-Jiménez & M. Mar Torreblanca-López (eds)
Age in L2 Acquisition and Teaching.
214 pages. 2006. ISBN 3-03910-668-6. US-ISBN 0-8204-7174-7

Vol. 23 Vijay K. Bhatia, Maurizio Gotti, Jan Engberg & Dorothee Heller (eds)
Vagueness in Normative Texts.
474 pages. 2005. ISBN 3-03910-653-8. US-ISBN 0-8204-7169-0

Vol. 24 Paul Gillaerts & Maurizio Gotti (eds)
Genre Variation in Business Letters. 2nd printing.
407 pages. 2008. ISBN 978-3-03911-681-2.

Vol. 25 Ana María Hornero, María José Luzón & Silvia Murillo (eds)
Corpus Linguistics. Applications for the Study of English.
2nd printing. 526 pages. 2006, 2008. ISBN 978-3-03911-726-0

Vol. 26 J. Lachlan Mackenzie & María de los Ángeles Gómez-González (eds)
Studies in Functional Discourse Grammar.
259 pages. 2005. ISBN 3-03910-696-1 / US-ISBN 0-8204-7558-0

Vol. 27 Debbie G. E. Ho
Classroom Talk. Exploring the Sociocultural Structure of Formal ESL Learning.
2nd edition. 254 pages. 2006, 2007. ISBN 978-3-03911-434-4

Vol. 28 Javier Pérez-Guerra, Dolores González-Álvarez, Jorge L. Bueno-Alonso & Esperanza Rama-Martínez (eds)
'Of Varying Language and Opposing Creed': New Insights into Late Modern English.
455 pages. 2007. ISBN 978-3-03910-788-9

Vol. 29 Francesca Bargiela-Chiappini & Maurizio Gotti (eds)
Asian Business Discourse(s).
350 pages. 2005. ISBN 3-03910-804-2 / US-ISBN 0-8204-7574-2

Vol. 30 Nicholas Brownlees (ed.)
News Discourse in Early Modern Britain. Selected Papers of CHINED 2004.
300 pages. 2006. ISBN 3-03910-805-0 / US-ISBN 0-8204-8025-8

Vol. 31 Roberta Facchinetti & Matti Rissanen (eds)
Corpus-based Studies of Diachronic English.
300 pages. 2006. ISBN 3-03910-851-4 / US-ISBN 0-8204-8040-1

Vol. 32 Marina Dossena & Susan M. Fitzmaurice (eds)
Business and Official Correspondence: Historical Investigations.
209 pages. 2006. ISBN 3-03910-880-8 / US-ISBN 0-8204-8352-4

Vol. 33 Giuliana Garzone & Srikant Sarangi (eds)
Discourse, Ideology and Specialized Communication.
494 pages. 2007. ISBN 978-3-03910-888-6

Vol. 34 Giuliana Garzone & Cornelia Ilie (eds)
The Use of English in Institutional and Business Settings.
An Intercultural Perspective.
372 pages. 2007. ISBN 978-3-03910-889-3

Vol. 35 Vijay K. Bhatia & Maurizio Gotti (eds)
Explorations in Specialized Genres.
316 pages. 2006. ISBN 3-03910-995-2 / US-ISBN 0-8204-8372-9

Vol. 36 Heribert Picht (ed.)
Modern Approaches to Terminological Theories and Applications.
432 pages. 2006. ISBN 3-03911-156-6 / US-ISBN 0-8204-8380-X

Vol. 37 Anne Wagner & Sophie Cacciaguidi-Fahy (eds)
Legal Language and the Search for Clarity / Le langage juridique et la quête de clarté.
Practice and Tools / Pratiques et instruments.
487 pages. 2006. ISBN 3-03911-169-8 / US-ISBN 0-8388-5

Vol. 38 Juan Carlos Palmer-Silveira, Miguel F. Ruiz-Garrido &
Inmaculada Fortanet-Gómez (eds)
Intercultural and International Business Communication:
Theory, Research and Teaching.
2nd edition. 343 pages. 2006, 2008. ISBN 978-3-03911-680-5

Vol. 39 Christiane Dalton-Puffer, Dieter Kastovsky, Nikolaus Ritt &
Herbert Schendl (eds)
Syntax, Style and Grammatical Norms: English from 1500–2000.
250 pages. 2006. ISBN 3-03911-181-7 / US-ISBN 0-8204-8394-X

Vol. 40 Marina Dossena & Irma Taavitsainen (eds)
Diachronic Perspectives on Domain-Specific English.
280 pages. 2006. ISBN 3-03910-176-0 / US-ISBN 0-8204-8391-5

Vol. 41 John Flowerdew & Maurizio Gotti (eds)
Studies in Specialized Discourse.
293 pages. 2006. ISBN 3-03911-178-7

Vol. 42 Ken Hyland & Marina Bondi (eds)
Academic Discourse Across Disciplines.
320 pages. 2006. ISBN 3-03911-183-3 / US-ISBN 0-8204-8396-6

Vol. 43 Paul Gillaerts & Philip Shaw (eds)
The Map and the Landscape: Norms and Practices in Genre.
256 pages. 2006. ISBN 3-03911-182-5 / US-ISBN 0-8204-8395-4

Vol. 44 Maurizio Gotti & Davide Giannoni (eds)
New Trends in Specialized Discourse Analysis.
301 pages. 2006. ISBN 3-03911-184-1 / US-ISBN 0-8204-8381-8

Vol. 45 Maurizio Gotti & Françoise Salager-Meyer (eds)
Advances in Medical Discourse Analysis: Oral and Written Contexts.
492 pages. 2006. ISBN 3-03911-185-X / US-ISBN 0-8204-8382-6

Vol. 46 Maurizio Gotti & Susan Šarcević (eds)
Insights into Specialized Translation.
396 pages. 2006. ISBN 3-03911-186-8 / US-ISBN 0-8204-8383-4

Vol. 47 Khurshid Ahmad & Margaret Rogers (eds)
Evidence-based LSP: Translation, Text and Terminology.
584 pages. 2007. ISBN 978-3-03911-187-9

Vol. 48 Hao Sun & Dániel Z. Kádár (eds)
It's the Dragon's Turn: Chinese Institutional Discourses.
262 pages. 2008. ISBN 978-3-03911-175-6

Vol. 49 Cristina Suárez-Gómez
Relativization in Early English (950-1250): the Position of Relative Clauses.
149 pages. 2006. ISBN 3-03911-203-1 / US-ISBN 0-8204-8904-2

Vol. 50 Maria Vittoria Calvi & Luisa Chierichetti (eds)
Nuevas tendencias en el discurso de especialidad.
319 pages. 2006. ISBN 978-3-03911-261-6

Vol. 51 Mari Carmen Campoy & María José Luzón (eds)
Spoken Corpora in Applied Linguistics.
274 pages. 2008. ISBN 978-3-03911-275-3

Vol. 52 Konrad Ehlich & Dorothee Heller (Hrsg.)
Die Wissenschaft und ihre Sprachen.
323 pages. 2006. ISBN 978-3-03911-272-2

Vol. 53 Jingyu Zhang
The Semantic Salience Hierarchy Model: The L2 Acquisition of Psych Predicates
273 pages. 2007. ISBN 978-3-03911-300-2

Vol. 54 Norman Fairclough, Giuseppina Cortese & Patrizia Ardizzone (eds)
Discourse and Contemporary Social Change.
555 pages. 2007. ISBN 978-3-03911-276-0

Vol. 55 Jan Engberg, Marianne Grove Ditlevsen, Peter Kastberg & Martin Stegu (eds)
New Directions in LSP Teaching.
331 pages. 2007. ISBN 978-3-03911-433-7

Vol. 56 Dorothee Heller & Konrad Ehlich (Hrsg.)
Studien zur Rechtskommunikation.
322 pages. 2007. ISBN 978-3-03911-436-8

Vol. 57 Forthcoming.

Vol. 58 Carmen Frehner
Email – SMS – MMS
294 pages. 2008. ISBN 978-3-03911-451-1

Vol. 59 Isabel Balteiro
The Directionality of Conversion in English: A Dia-Synchronic Study.
276 pages. 2007. ISBN 978-3-03911-241-8

Vol. 60 Maria Milagros Del Saz Rubio
English Discourse Markers of Reformulation.
237 pages. 2007. ISBN 978-3-03911-196-1

Vol. 61 Sally Burgess & Pedro Martín-Martín (eds)
English as an Additional Language in Research Publication and Communication.
259 pages. 2008. ISBN 978-3-03911-462-7

Vol. 62 Sandrine Onillon
Pratiques et représentations de l'écrit.
458 pages. 2008. ISBN 978-3-03911-464-1

Vol. 63 Hugo Bowles & Paul Seedhouse (eds)
Conversation Analysis and Language for Specific Purposes.
2nd edition. 337 pages. 2007, 2009. ISBN 978-3-0343-0045-2

Vol. 64 Vijay K. Bhatia, Christopher N. Candlin & Paola Evangelisti Allori (eds)
Language, Culture and the Law.
The Formulation of Legal Concepts across Systems and Cultures.
342 pages. 2008. ISBN 978-3-03911-470-2

Vol. 65 Jonathan Culpeper & Dániel Z. Kádár (eds)
Historical (Im)politeness.
300 pages. 2010. ISBN 978-3-03911-496-2

Vol. 66 Linda Lombardo (ed.)
Using Corpora to Learn about Language and Discourse.
237 pages. 2009. ISBN 978-3-03911-522-8

Vol. 67 Natsumi Wakamoto
Extroversion/Introversion in Foreign Language Learning.
Interactions with Learner Strategy Use.
159 pages. 2009. ISBN 978-3-03911-596-9

Vol. 68 Eva Alcón-Soler (ed.)
Learning How to Request in an Instructed Language Learning Context.
260 pages. 2008. ISBN 978-3-03911-601-0

Vol. 69 Domenico Pezzini
The Translation of Religious Texts in the Middle Ages.
428 pages. 2008. ISBN 978-3-03911-600-3

Vol. 70 Tomoko Tode
Effects of Frequency in Classroom Second Language Learning.
Quasi-experiment and stimulated-recall analysis.
195 pages. 2008. ISBN 978-3-03911-602-7

Vol. 71 Egor Tsedryk
Fusion symétrique et alternances ditransitives.
211 pages. 2009. ISBN 978-3-03911-609-6

Vol. 72 Cynthia J. Kellett Bidoli & Elana Ochse (eds)
English in International Deaf Communication.
444 pages. 2008. ISBN 978-3-03911-610-2

Vol. 73 Joan C. Beal, Carmela Nocera & Massimo Sturiale (eds)
Perspectives on Prescriptivism.
269 pages. 2008. ISBN 978-3-03911-632-4

Vol. 74 Carol Taylor Torsello, Katherine Ackerley & Erik Castello (eds)
Corpora for University Language Teachers.
308 pages. 2008. ISBN 978-3-03911-639-3

Vol. 75 María Luisa Pérez Cañado (ed.)
English Language Teaching in the European Credit Transfer System:
Facing the Challenge.
251 pages. 2009. ISBN 978-3-03911-654-6

Vol. 76 Marina Dossena & Ingrid Tieken-Boon van Ostade (eds)
Studies in Late Modern English Correspondence. Methodology and Data.
291 pages. 2008. ISBN 978-3-03911-658-4

Vol. 77 Ingrid Tieken-Boon van Ostade & Wim van der Wurff (eds)
Current Issues in Late Modern English.
436 pages. 2009. ISBN 978-3-03911-660-7

Vol. 78 Marta Navarro Coy (ed.)
Practical Approaches to Foreign Language Teaching and Learning.
297 pages. 2009. ISBN 978-3-03911-661-4

Vol. 79 Qing Ma
Second Language Vocabulary Acquisition.
333 pages. 2009. ISBN 978-3-03911-666-9

Vol. 80 Martin Solly, Michelangelo Conoscenti & Sandra Campagna (eds)
Verbal/Visual Narrative Texts in Higher Education.
384 pages. 2008. ISBN 978-3-03911-672-0

Vol. 81 Meiko Matsumoto
From Simple Verbs to Periphrastic Expressions:
The Historical Development of Composite Predicates, Phrasal Verbs,
and Related Constructions in English.
235 pages. 2008. ISBN 978-3-03911-675-1

Vol. 82 Melinda Dooly
Doing Diversity. Teachers' Construction of Their Classroom Reality.
180 pages. 2009. ISBN 978-3-03911-687-4

Vol. 83 Victoria Guillén-Nieto, Carmen Marimón-Llorca & Chelo Vargas-Sierra (eds)
Intercultural Business Communication and
Simulation and Gaming Methodology.
392 pages. 2009. ISBN 978-3-03911-688-1

Vol. 84 Maria Grazia Guido
English as a Lingua Franca in Cross-cultural Immigration Domains.
285 pages. 2008. ISBN 978-3-03911-689-8

Vol. 85 Erik Castello
Text Complexity and Reading Comprehension Tests.
352 pages. 2008. ISBN 978-3-03911-717-8

Vol. 86 Maria-Lluisa Gea-Valor, Isabel García-Izquierdo & Maria-José Esteve (eds)
Linguistic and Translation Studies in Scientific Communication.
317 pages. 2010. ISBN 978-3-0343-0069-8

Vol. 87 Carmen Navarro, Rosa Mª Rodríguez Abella, Francesca Dalle Pezze
& Renzo Miotti (eds)
La comunicación especializada.
355 pages. 2008. ISBN 978-3-03911-733-8

Vol. 88 Kiriko Sato
The Development from Case-Forms to Prepositional Constructions
in Old English Prose.
231 pages. 2009. ISBN 978-3-03911-763-5

Vol. 89 Dorothee Heller (Hrsg.)
Formulierungsmuster in deutscher und italienischer Fachkommunikation.
Intra- und interlinguale Perspektiven.
315 pages. 2008. ISBN 978-3-03911-778-9

Vol. 90 Henning Bergenholtz, Sandro Nielsen & Sven Tarp (eds)
Lexicography at a Crossroads. Dictionaries and Encyclopedias Today,
Lexicographical Tools Tomorrow.
372 pages. 2009. ISBN 978-3-03911-799-4

Vol. 91 Manouchehr Moshtagh Khorasani
The Development of Controversies: From the Early Modern Period
to Online Discussion Forums.
317 pages. 2009. ISBN 978-3-3911-711-6

Vol. 92 María Luisa Carrió-Pastor (ed.)
Content and Language Integrated Learning: Cultural Diversity.
178 pages. 2009. ISBN 978-3-3911-818-2

Vol. 93-94 Forthcoming.

Vol. 95 Facchinetti Roberta, Crystal David, Seidlhofer Barbara (eds)
From International to Local English – And Back Again.
268 pages. 2010. ISBN 978-3-0343-0011-7

Vol. 96 Cesare Gagliardi & Alan Maley (eds)
EIL, ELF, Global English: Teaching and Learning Issues
376 pages. 2010. ISBN 978-3-0343-0010-0

Vol. 97 Sylvie Hancil (ed.)
The Role of Prosody in Affective Speech.
403 pages. 2009. ISBN 978-3-03911-696-6

Vol. 98 Marina Dossena & Roger Lass (eds)
Studies in English and European Historical Dialectology.
257 pages. 2009. ISBN 978-3-0343-0024-7

Vol. 99 Christine Béal
Les interactions quotidiennes en français et en anglais.
De l'approche comparative à l'analyse des situations interculturelles.
424 pages. 2010. ISBN 978-3-0343-0027-8

Vol. 100 Maurizio Gotti (ed.)
Commonality and Individuality in Academic Discourse.
398 pages. 2009. ISBN 978-3-0343-0023-0

Vol. 101 Javier E. Díaz Vera & Rosario Caballero (eds)
Textual Healing: Studies in Medieval English Medical,
Scientific and Technical Texts.
213 pages. 2009. ISBN 978-3-03911-822-9

Vol. 102 Nuria Edo Marzá
The Specialised Lexicographical Approach: A Step further in Dictionary-making.
316 pages. 2009. ISBN 978-3-0343-0043-8

Vol. 103 Carlos Prado-Alonso, Lidia Gómez-García, Iria Pastor-Gómez &
David Tizón-Couto (eds)
New Trends and Methodologies in Applied English Language Research.
Diachronic, Diatopic and Contrastive Studies.
348 pages. 2009. ISBN 978-3-0343-0046-9

Vol. 104-108 Forthcoming.

Vol. 109 Ángeles Linde López & Rosalía Crespo Jiménez (eds)
Professional English in the European context: The EHEA challenge.
374 pages. 2010. ISBN 978-3-0343-0088-9

Vol. 110 Rosalía Rodríguez-Vázquez
The Rhythm of Speech, Verse and Vocal Music: A New Theory.
394 pages. 2010. ISBN 978-3-0343-0309-5

Vol. 111 Anastasios Tsangalidis & Roberta Facchinetti (eds)
Studies on English Modality. In Honour of Frank Palmer.
392 pages. 2009. ISBN 978-3-0343-0310-1

Vol. 115 Giuliana Garzone & Paola Catenaccio (eds)
Identities across Media and Modes: Discursive Perspectives.
379 pages. 2009. ISBN 978-3-0343-0386-6

Vol. 116 Elena Landone
Los marcadores del discurso y cortesía verbal en español.
390 pages. 2010. ISBN 978-3-0343-0413-9

Vol. 117 Maurizio Gotti & Christopher Williams (eds)
Legal Discourse across Languages and Cultures.
339 pages. 2010. ISBN 978-3-0343-0425-2

Vol. 118 David Hirsh
Academic Vocabulary in Context.
217 pages. 2010. ISBN 978-3-0343-0426-9

Vol. 119-120 Forthcoming.

Vol. 121 Davide Simone Giannoni & Celina Frade (eds)
Researching Language and the Law. Textual Features and Translation Issues.
278 pages. 2010. ISBN 978-3-0343-0443-6

Vol. 122 Forthcoming.

Vol. 123 Vijay K. Bhatia, Christopher N. Candlin & Maurizio Gotti (eds)
The Discourses of Dispute Resolution.
290 pages. 2010. ISBN 978-3-0343-0476-4

Vol. 124 Davide Simone Giannoni
Mapping Academic Values in the Disciplines. A Corpus-Based Approach.
288 pages. 2010. ISBN 978-3-0343-0488-7

FSC
www.fsc.org
MIX
Papier | Fördert gute Waldnutzung
FSC® C083411

Kolibri 360 GmbH
Ferdinand-Jühlke-Straße 7
99095 Erfurt, Deutschland
produktsicherheit@kolibri360.de